ENVIRONMENTAL POLLUTION
SOCIETAL IMPACTS AND EARTH MATTERS

ENVIRONMENTAL POLLUTION SOCIETAL IMPACTS AND EARTH MATTERS

By

K.C. Sahu

Earth Scientist

M.Tech (IIT-Kharagpur)

Ph.D. (University of Sheffield, UK)

DPH

DISCOVERY PUBLISHING HOUSE PVT. LTD.

INDIA

Published by:
Namit Wasan
DISCOVERY PUBLISHING HOUSE PVT. LTD.
4383/4B, Ansari Road, Darya Ganj
New Delhi-110 002 (India)
Phone : +91-11-23279245, 43596064-65
Fax : +91-11-23253475
E-mail : discoverypublishinghouse@gmail.com
namitwasan9@gmail.com
sales@discoverypublishinggroup.com
web : www.discoverypublishinggroup.com

***First Edition:* 2018**

ISBN: 978-93-5056-897-2

Environmental Pollution, Societal Impacts and Earth Matters

Printed at:
Infinity Imaging Systems
Delhi

This Book is Dedicated

To

Dr. Anil Agarwal

Founder Director

Center for Science and Environment, New Delhi

Message

I would like to congratulate Prof. K.C. Sahu for this essential publication. His contribution to building a scientific literate and environmentally aware policy is immense. Prof Sahu's association with the Centre for Science and Environment (CSE) goes back many decades. This book, with this coverage of key environmental issues and deep knowledge and insight on the matters of heavy metal contamination, will go a long way in fulfilling our common dream of a healthy and sustainable Planet.

Sunita Narain

Center for Science and Environment

New Delhi

Preface

The compilation of 38 articles in this book have been presented in two groups, A and B. Group A deals mostly on Pollution and its impact on Society and Group B on Earth matters, especially critical review of annual events like World Environment Day, Earth Day, Wet Land Day etc. Some of the articles of Group A have been presented in Conferences and Seminars and printed in Proceedings and Bulletins. Many of the articles of Group B were published in Media (Planet Powai). Figures and pictures reproduced from text books, News Reports and Net (Google) have enriched the quality of the articles and are acknowledged in respective places.

The purpose of this book is to arouse deep understanding and insight into various environmental issues at micro-, macro- and global levels and is meant for people of all strata, Students, Scholars, Social Activists and public in general.

I am deeply indebted to Shri S.K.Saksena, a former Director of Siemens Ltd. and Ex-Director of Indo-German Training center, Mumbai, who has edited the script and made valuable modifications.

K.C. Sahu

sahukc_kc@yahoo.com

Contents

Group - B: Earth Matters

Group - A
Environmental Pollution and Societal Impacts

1

Heavy Metal Pollution of Air, Water and Soil

A Review

Life Originated with Metals

The core of the earth is more than 99 per cent metal and of iron nickel alloy only. The crust of the earth is one quarter metals and seven are metallic among the most ten abundant elements. In the Periodic Table, 83 elements are classified as metals, that is, 79% of the atomic building blocks are metallic. Life has evolved amidst these lithophile elements and represents nothing but a structured architecture of these primary chemicals. It is therefore natural that a coherence exists between the elemental composition of life and lithosphere except perhaps for carbon which overtakes silicon in the biospheric shell, because of the higher solubility of its oxide in water. While many of the abundant metals play great role in life and environment that is in biosphere, trace metals, though present in levels of part per million (ppm) or less in earth's crust, are not less significant.

Characteristics of Heavy Metals

The metals with a density greater than 5 g/cm^3 are termed Heavy Metals. An exception is As, which though lighter and non-metallic, is clubbed with the heavy metal group because its chemico-ecological effects resemble those of the heavy metals. All heavy metals have relatively smaller cationic size because of the heavier nucleus and increasingly compressed electrons. The "electron thirst" makes many of them to hanker after the loosely held outer shell electrons of sulphur thus forming sulphides as in Pb, Zn, Cu and Hg or prevents them to yield to electron hungry elements like oxygen (by oxidation) and preserve their "nobleness" as in Au, Pt, Ag etc. It is this fundamental chalcophile character of the heavy metal that threatens the sulphur atoms either in the sulphydryl group or disulphide bridge between the giant protein molecules in the living system. For instance mercaptants or "Mercury capture" known as *Minamata* disease is due to entry of Hg into this group (Fig. 1.1). The ecologically more significant heavy metals Pb, Zn, Cu, Cd, As, Hg and Ni play similar disruptive role when they enter body system in higher than the required amounts.

Role of Heavy Metals in Life

Many metals are useful to life (Table 1.1), for examples, Fe as oxygen carrier in hemoglobin, Ca and P in bone building and Mg in chlorophyll.

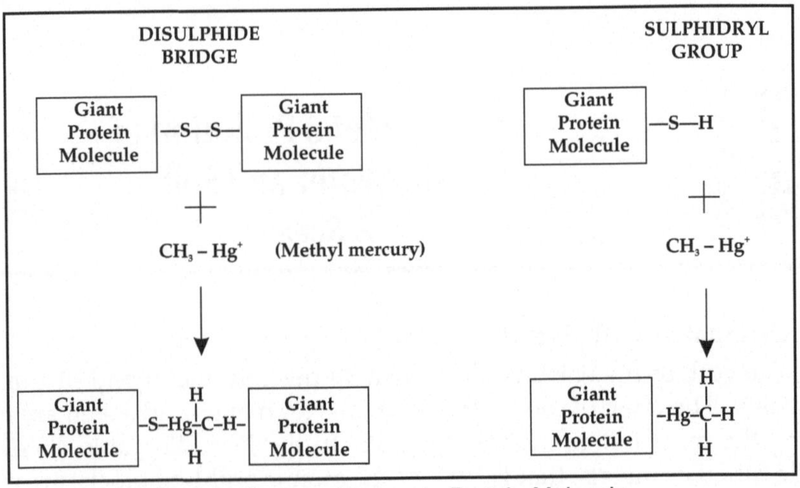

Fig. 1.1: Mercury Capture in Protein Molecule

Table 1.1: Probable role of chemical elements in life processes (Horne, 1978)

Elements necessary for life H, B, C, N, C, O, F, Na, Mg, Si, P, S, Si, K, Ca, Mn, Fe, Co, Ni, Cu, Zn, Br, I
Elements probably necessary for life Al, Ti, As, Sn, Pb.
Elements probably not necessary for life. He, Li, Be, La, Ar, Se, Cr, Ga, Ge, Sc, Kr, Pb, Sr, Y, Zr, Nb, Te, Ru, Rh, Pd, Ag, Cd, In, Sb, Te, Xe, Cs, Ba, La, REE, Hf, Ta, W. Re, Os, Ir, Pt, Au, Hg, Tl, Bl, Po, At, Rn, Fr, Ac, Th, Pa, U.

Some heavy metals, notably Cu, Zn, Co, Cr are essential to life when present in traces, therefore are essential trace metals. They are vital in the molecular architecture of various proteins, enzymes and vitamins. However, with their increasing concentration in the environment they produce toxicity (Table 1.2), retard growth and result in ultimate destruction (death) of the living organism (Fig. 1.2). Some heavy metals have no metabolic role in living cells but are found to enter (sneak into) the living organism because of their availability in the environment. Not uncommonly the functions of trace metals are intrinsically linked with one another in either synergistic or even antagonistic manner. Thus a Cu deficient diet produces anemia while Zn and Mo can interfere with utilization of Cu. Controlled doses of Se can be an antidote to Hg poisoning since both the metals maintain an optimum ratio of "Se-Hg compartment" in living cells. While Mn in excess can cause "manganism" it can mobilize (solublize) the inert carbon particles which are known to be seeds or nuclei of carcinogenic sites on body tissue. Thus the incidence of cancer associated with manganese deficient soils in Finland may probably be accountable. Even more elaborate relationship that can be derived (and is exploited) is powerful toxicity or 'poisoning' effect of an unnecessary element like Hg in strong fungicides. The dilemma however is, removal of the 'pollutant' from environment or 'fungus' from the food and water for human consumption (Horne, 1978).

Table 1.2: Threshold limit values (TLV) and toxicity of some heavy metals

Elements	TLV (air) mg/m^3	TLV (water) µg/l	Toxicity
Cu	0.2	<1	Wilson disease, liver problem
Pb	0.15 in 8 hours	0.05	Nephritis (Kidney disease) convulsion, insomnia, headache, muscle pain, encephalopathy.
Zn	Chloride1 Zn fume5 stearate10	5	Fever, Tremor.
Cd	0.1 to 0.05	0.01	Kidney damage, High BP, Cd-ring teeth, *'itai-itai'*, Skeletal deformation, impairment of bone marrow, aging, Carcinogenic.
Hg	0.005	0.005	Neurological and Kidney damage *Minamata* disease (crippling)
Mo	5 to 10	<0.005	Pulmonary disorders
As	0.002 to 0.25	<.03	Dermatitis Cancer, conjunctivitis, hearing loss, Black foot disease, Hyperkeratosis.
Ni	Carbonyl 0.007, Metal	<0.0051.0	Carcinogenic (skin), Carbonyl poisoning
Cr	0.1 to 0.5	<0.05	Dermatitis, Skin Cancer, Perforation of nasal septum
Mn	0.3 to 10	<0.05	Parkinson disease, Manganism, Respiratory disorder, Pneumoconiosis
V	Dust 0.05	<0.1	Respiratory irritation, Cardiovascular disease, may be carcinogenic
Sn	Organic 0.1 SnO_2 10 inorganic 2	–	Pneumoconiosis Stannosis, Neurological damage

Thus limited presence of many heavy metals at low concentration can be beneficial to humans because of their germicidal property. For examples, the "sacredness" of Ganges water is evidently due to presence of traces of copper cation derived from dispersed copper sulphide deposits in Himalayas and the traditional habit in Maharashtra to drink water, the first thing in the morning from an overnight stored copper Jug has the same meaning. Similarly, the commercial application of silver anode pencil to purify a glass of water, when dipped for a few seconds, vis a vis protection of easily decomposable cheese products like "*Burfis & Rasgollas*" with a silver foil are mere antibacterial measures, so commonly used without being aware of it.

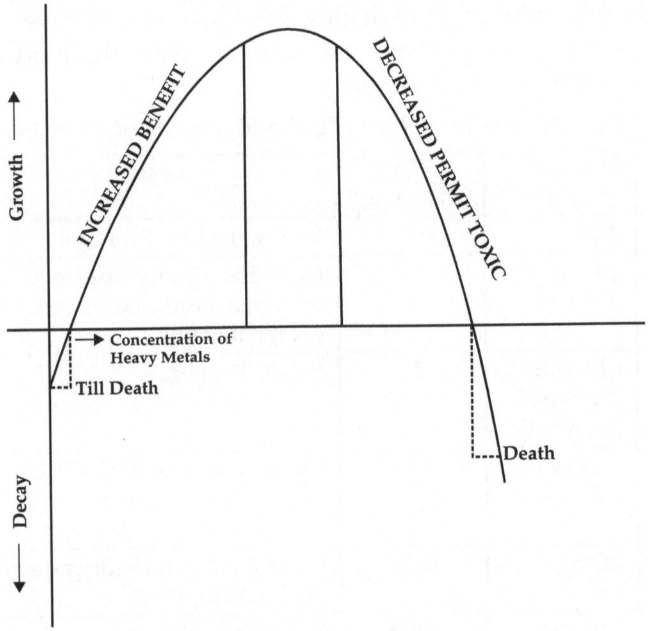

Fig. 1.2: Heavy Metal Impact in Life (Baccini *et.al.*,1976)

Speciation and Bioavailability

The mobility or phytoavailability/bioavailability and toxicity of a metal is very much dependent on its valence state and speciation. Chemical speciation of many metals have been extensively studied and so also techniques of their determination. Copper may be present in several species. Fe^{+2} is more mobile than Fe^{+3} and hexavalent chromium is hundred to thousand times more toxic than the trivalent chromium. While organic mercury is easily bioavailable and more toxic than inorganic mercury, when it comes to arsenic the reverse is true. Some metals are more harmful in volatile forms such as those of vanadium and nickel.

The relationship between toxicity and chemical speciation is best understood by the ionic size difference between Cr^{+3} and Cr^{+6}. The former is about 0.65 A and the later, having stripped off its three more outer electrons, attains an effective cationic size of about 0.52 A. It so happens that the pores (passage) of the cell-wall being of intermediate size (>0.52 but <0.65 A), the relatively smaller cation Cr^{+6} can easily slip into the cell but not the larger Cr^{+3}. On entry, the Cr^{+6} is easily reduced to trivalent state in an anoxic cell fluid, making the exit of the resultant Cr^{+3} impossible. The chromium in the cell thus becomes carcinogenic. The carcinogenicity, producing an inert cell, is again best understood by the tanning action of chromium where the raw hide or skin becomes an inert (durable) piece of leather.

As against the dissolved metal species, described above, the concept of solid speciation attempts to classify the presence of the metal in five different geochemical pools such as, exchangeable phase, carbonate phase, reducible phase, organic/sulphidic phase and lithogenic (structural or lattice) phase in order of immobility. It also represents the ease of transfer of the metals from solid to dissolved state. Like the techniques of determination of the chemical species, the solid species of a metal can be analyzed by sequential extraction but with a certain amount of overlap between each stage of extraction.

Many national and international authorities have attempted to assign acceptable limits for the presence of various heavy metals in food and potable water. The limits (values) stipulated can be accepted only as guiding figures and are not absolute. For example, an urban child receives lead doses from piped water, automobile fumes, whereas a rural child has limited sources of lead intake. Therefore the drinking water standard of Pb for an urban child ought to be much lower than a rural child. Besides the stipulation of an acceptable value is based on analysis of a water sample filtered thorough a Millipore filter paper (only dissolved species), but no water supply can attend the removal of sub micron particles which are normally store house of adsorbed heavy metals. On the analytical front too the value of a standard is very much dependent on the limit of detection and allied factors. For example, in 1964 the normal acceptable concentration of chromium in human blood was 1000 ng/L but in 1971 the value dropped to 0.1 ng/L and the present day acceptable value is quoted as 0.1 to 1 ng/L.

The problems of heavy metal pollution is that, unlike other chemical parameters like pH, alkalinity, hardness, BOD, COD etc. which can be estimated in a simple laboratory, determination of heavy metals need sophisticated equipment's like Atomic Absorption Spectrophotometer (AAS), XRF, ICPS, INA etc., and the pollutants are present in ppm or ppb levels. Therefore, the problem is less highlighted, in spite of the fact that a chronic low level dose of heavy metal is more harmful than an occasional high dose.

Sources of Heavy Metal Pollution

Our biochemistry reflects the composition of the uncontaminated primeval biosphere, is attuned to the composition and dependent on it. Soil, a product of chemical weathering of crustal rocks in geological time scale, envisages an equilibrium state of most heavy metals at least within a person's lifetime. The crust of the earth has low Clarke of most of the toxic heavy metals, immobilized in mineral constituents and their lithogenic release to the environment is therefore low. However of late man has turned out to be a stronger geological agent, at least locally and has brought about enormous changes in mass movements and chemical alteration in some segments of the earth's crust with consequent changes and adjustment in internal biochemistry through food chains. Mammals, unlike microorganisms, plants and insects do not adopt to marked changes in normal trace element distributions pattern and we run the risk of creating serious biochemical disturbances if we continue to allow the soil to be contaminated in the long term, with toxic trace elements which can pass into plants and then into food chain.

Large scale mass movement of materials by man either in the form of resources use or waste disposals and significant changes in the chemistry of the pedosphere which supports life including humans, are found to occur precisely in four different setups, namely:

- In exploration and mining of minerals and metals,
- In agriculture, dairy and animal husbandry,
- In industries, transport and processing units,
- Around urban settlements.

Mining, Smelting and Metal Processing

Mining exposes a large volume of mineral matters, originally in apparent equilibrium in earth's crust, to various natural processes like oxidation, hydrolysis, dissolution and leaching by way of increased surface area of reaction with natural reagents. Mineralized water percolating through pores and fissures in contact with ore minerals has long been known to carry enhanced levels of concerned metals and overlying soil and water in mining district are rich in metals and even develop flora known to be metal indicator in geobotanical prospecting.

Large dumps of mine waste and low grade minerals, so common in many mining districts are point sources of dispersion of concerned elements into the ecosystem of the mining belt. Pyrites a common mineral in many sulphide mines produce acidic mining water (sulphuric acids) as well as ferrous sulphates, the former dissolves away and activates metals from country rock and the latter mobilizes similar cations by stoichiometric reaction with their oxides leaving iron oxides as the immobile residue.

FeS *Pyrite*	+	H_2O *Water*	+	O_2 *Atmospheric Oxygen*	→	$FeSO_4$ *Ferrous Sulphate*	+	H_2SO_4 *Sulphuric Acid*
M^{++} *Metal Oxide*		*Oxide* *Ferrus Sulphate*	+	$FeSO_4$ *Metal Sulphate*	→	$MESO_4$	+	$Fe(OH)_3$ *Hydrated Iron Oxide*

Waste water and tailings of beneficiation plants (Fig. 1.3), fall out from smelting and refining stacks (Fig. 1.4) as well as solid waste disposal in the downstream metallurgical process contaminate the environment with heavy metals. Cadmium contamination of various eco-compartments along Jintsu river of Japan and consequent *itai itai* disease, the "Red rivers" draining out of some of the iron ore belts of N. Orissa, Madhya Pradesh and Bihar, base metal contamination of rivers flowing through or out skirting lead zinc and copper belts of Rajasthan and Bihar, pollution of lake Ontario or most of the water courses of Derbyshire in U.K. are well known examples of heavy metal contamination by mining and smelting.

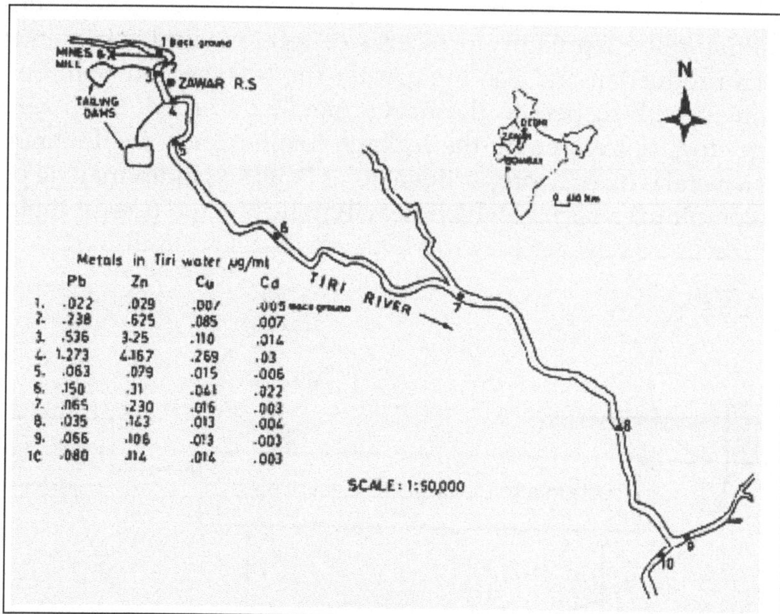

Fig. 1.3: Metal Contamination from Mines and Millings at Zawar, Rajasthan

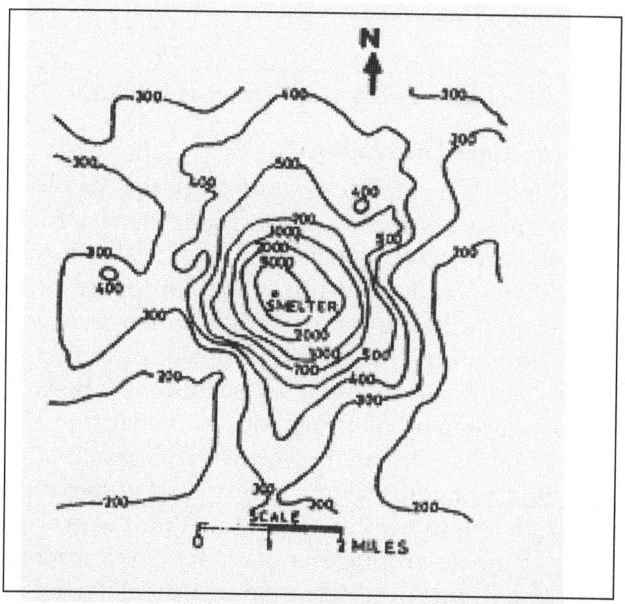

Fig. 1.4: Distribution of Pb in mg/g in Soil around New Lead Belt smelter in Missouri, USA (Jennett *et al.*, 1975)

Along the long track of utility cycle of most metals, that is from mining, beneficiation, smelting, production of finished goods, use in society to recycling of scraps, there are always points of leakage (spillage) of the metal into environment (Fig. 1.5). Even if the degree of leakage is kept constant or at its minimum by regulatory pressures or technological achievements, the larger the production and use the greater the leakage and pollution of the environment with respect to the heavy metal concerned. Even zero waste discharge does not eliminate the leakage totally. Thus the Technophyllity Index of a metal is directly proportional to its Pollution Index making pollution a fait accompli for a society which heavily relies on the uses of metals.

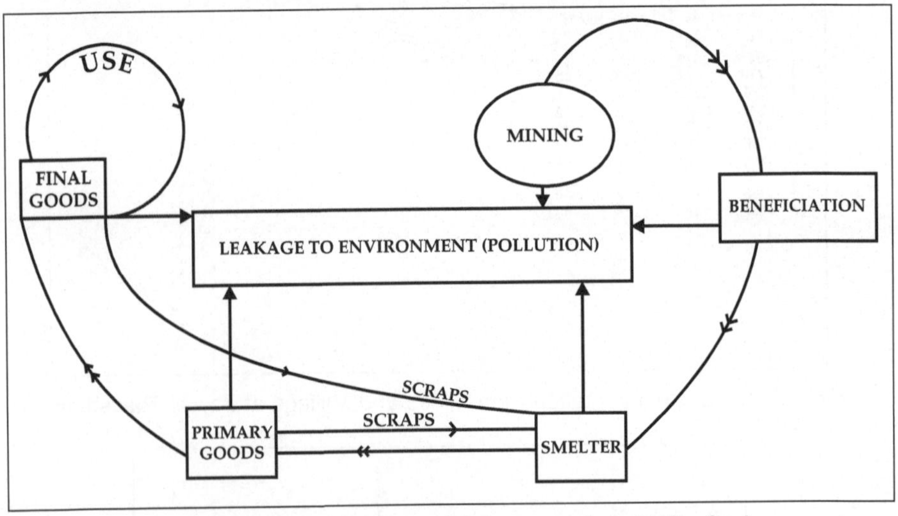

Fig. 1.5: Pollution: Leakage of Resources from Utility Cycle

Heavy Metals from Coal Utilization

A geological insight to coal formation in basins of plant accumulation indicates that the coal seams and associated sedimentary rocks like shale are repositories of many toxic trace metals. Mining of coal brings out these metals to the surface which spread from the mine dumps by percolating water. Most coals, having deposited in anoxic environment are rich in sulphur or iron pyrites and these on oxidation on the surface produce sulphuric acids and whose metal mobilization capacity has already been discussed. It is estimated that coal mining alone brings out to the surface about 20,000 tons of uranium, 7% of worlds estimated resources (Barney, 1980), which spreads around the biosphere and whose effect is very little understood. Conspicuous consumption of coal, rich in heavy metals, in a thermal power plant can load various eco-compartments around the plant with a considerable amount of heavy metals, the magnitude of which can only be realized by detailed analysis of mass balances of all the chemical constituents. The result appears stupendous and frightening (Fig. 1.6). Investigations show that most of the toxic metals of the feed coal, after combustion are sited within 300 Angstroms surface layer of the ash particles (Natusch *et al.* 1979) and therefore are vulnerable to release to the environment around thermal plants which generate millions of tonnes of ahs per year. Although no confirmed toxicological damage has yet been reported around coal burning thermal plants, except the case of arsenic poisoning in Czechoslovakia (Bencko *et al.* 1977), scientific surveillance needs to be maintained around such ecologically fragile sites. The toxicological effect of such impacts being chronic, unlike atmospheric pollution around thermal plants, the damage function goes unnoticed and completely camouflaged by what is sociopolitically known as 'regional development' and increased energy production.

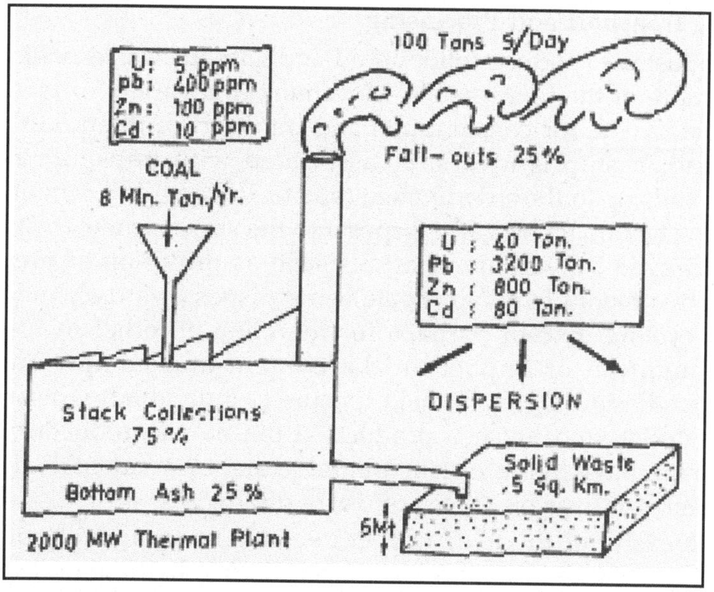

Fig. 1.6: Trace Metal Balance: Coal Ash to Environment

Agriculture, Animal Husbandry and Diary

Agricultural practices generate the largest amount of soil movement by way of disturbances of the top layer of the pedosphere and produce conspicuous particle and water interaction. The compost and the organic acids tend to dissolve many trace metals and either pump them (make phyto-available) into the plants or mobilize them into the percolating water in the form of soluble metallo-organic complexes.

Application of fertilizers such as rock phosphates, saltpeter, guano and slags, carrying large doses of trace metal like U, Cd, V, Ni, Se, As etc. and herbicide and insecticide add many a toxic metals into the soil. There is no denial that Green Revolution, primed by application of chemical fertilizers and pesticides has considerably increased heavy metals in soil, water and food products, but has prevented mass hunger and starvation. That is people in less developed countries have accepted death due to poisonous food rather that death due to starvation. Inorganic fertilizers may replace many important trace elements, and even "shot-gun mixtures" for essential trace element replacements are commercially available. However, such applications lead to soil toxicity with respect to other constituents and total dependence on such "vitamins" without which the soil becomes sterile. Disposals from animal feedlots, piggeries, dairies and breweries, molasses from sugar factory etc., besides introducing metal contaminants, increase the BOD and COD levels of the surrounding aquatic regime. The anoxic condition created encourages aquatic mobilization of many metals in the environment.

Industries, Transport and Processing

All industries produce solid, liquid and gaseous wastes which are rich in one or more of the toxic metals. Movement of a variety of raw materials into the factory site for consumption and transport of the processed goods by rail, road or ship is invariably associated with transport loss which ultimately ends up in the environment (opcite: leakage) and cannot be totally eliminated. The impact of waste disposal to the surrounding environment is today minimized by various measures such as provision of precipitators, scrubbers, treatment plants, surrogate waste disposal yards/ponds, dilution or even recycling. Except perhaps for recycling all other measures have variable quantum of impact on the content and composition of the environment. Besides occupational exposure to individuals who are close to the raw materials and finished products at the site of production, the toxic substances reach the living system around, either by accidental release or by enhancement from various types of waste discharges.

The intensity of the toxic impact depends upon mobility of the toxic constituent, meteorological and terrain conditions, hydrological features as well as the scale of operation.

The modern transport system based either on burning of liquid hydrocarbon gasoline or diesel or on electrical energy derived from burning of fossil fuels, diesel, even nuclear reaction, has no less contribution to heavy metal enhancement or carcinogenic substances. The tetraethyl lead from gasoline, the benzopyrene from diesel engine or the radon from nuclear waste, not to speak of the controversial discharge of active hydroxyl ions and NO_x into the stratosphere by high altitude aviation threatening the ozone layer, are equally harmful to the life system in this planet. However, the pace of industrialization continues unabated because the progress of civilization cannot be reversed, even slowing down is considered stupid. After all, all of us argue that industrialization is the only panacea to meet the various demands and needs of the growing population.

Urban Settlement

Population growth and industrialization has led to uncontrolled urbanization and large scale settlements. Congregation of people results not only in gravitation of variety of consumer goods but also in generation of waste and sewerage which are normally the toxic rejects not accepted by the metabolic systems. In the absence of suitable isolation network for these "societal" discharges which normally pervade the water and soil in most cities of developing countries, the urban habitants live on the same toxic discardants in one form or other. The sprawling municipal waste dumps in and around the metropolis, the sewerage or sludge applicated garden vegetables and the atmosphere laden with automobile fumes, industrial stack emissions, domestic smokes and carcinogenic suspended particulates, all have enhanced levels of toxic metals. Even the garden soil receiving atmospheric fallouts has been found to be contaminated with sufficient Pb so that the kitchen garden products may also be considered harmful in a home. Thus not only the "natural" food baskets of urban home has always a higher content of heavy metals, the "cocktail air" they breathe in has higher Pb and carcinogens and the tinned food stuffs that overwhelmingly supplement their daily requirements have larger doses of heavy metals and continuously change the biochemistry of the urban population. Transplacental transfer of Pb, Hg and Cd has been noted in human fetus. Since the migrants to urban settlements are normally in their prime reproductive stage, the largest section of the earth's population (the future urbanites) run the risk of toxic metal exposure in the most sensitive stage of life, that is in the foetal state, when the teratogenic impact is maximum, permanent and beyond any recuperative mechanism of physiologic or metabolic correction. Added to this the societal habits like the lead wine vats which perhaps resulted in the extinction of the Roman civilization, we have in India, colorful *"jilebbies"* and silver/aluminum foil coated *"Barfis"*, chromium colored green peas not to speak of "vermilion beauty spots" " plumbic eyelids" or various metallic or metal coated utensils which play equal role in pumping heavy metals into our metabolic structure.

Epilogue

Man has become a major geological agent and armed with latest technological tools and vast sources of energy, is bent to change the face of the earth to his convenience. The amount of lithogenic flux developed by man, excluding that in agricultural practices is in order of 10^{16} to 10^{17} grams and surpasses any natural agents like erosion and crust mantle transformation. So also in global mobilization of metals (Table 1.3). The future pattern of metal emission is likely to increase and exposure to population as well. The exhaustion of known ore deposits will lead to exploitation of either new mineralized belts or lower grade ores, which mean increased metal pollution per kg. of products. Deforestation on a large scales and draining of major marsh will reduce the number of sinks available for mobilized toxic metals. Silting of water ways and agricultural soil can markedly affect the mobility. Chemical fertilizer and compost may likewise introduce unwanted metals into the soil or greatly affect the metals in soil. Increased urbanization will put more people at a risk of increased exposure to pollutants and increased consumption of processed, not-traditional food. Enrichment factor of many elements such as Pb, Fe, Cd, Zn, Cu, Sb, As, Se in urban air has been confirmed over many cities of the world. Even deep ocean and polar ice is no longer excluded from the anthropogenic inputs of metals form atmosphere (Nriagu *et al.* 1988).

Table 1.3: Industrial and natural mobilizations of trace metals in the Biosphere thousand tonnes per year (Nriagu, 1988)

Elements	Production from Mines	Total Industrial Discharges	Weathering Mobilization
Antimony	55	41	15
Arsenic	45	105	90
Cadmium	19	24	4.5
Chromium	6800	1010	810
Cobalt	36		120
Copper	8114	1048	375
Lead	3077	565	180
Manganese	16000	1894	4800
Mercury	6.8	11	0.9
Molybdenum	98	98	15
Nickel	778	356	255
Selenium	1.6	76	4.5
Vanadium	34	75	855
Zinc	6040	1424	540

Although considerable disagreement exists regarding pathways of exposure to metals in a multimedia context, an urgent need has been felt to recognize the short and long term effects ultimately on humans. However, it has been proved beyond doubt that body burden of many "Civilization metals" in selective metabolic organs has shown a clear increase in humans exposed to such high levels of metals all over the world.

Presently neither extensive nor any confirmatory data on metal toxicity are available in scientific literature except for a few isolated episodes like Minamata tragedy. The impact of metal toxicity rampant in developing and underdeveloped countries is camouflaged by malnutrition, poor hygienic conditions as well as effect of various other diseases and even sincere epidemiological study fails to single out a factor for the symptoms. It is also a stupendous task to determine the normal exposure synonymous to "no effect" exposure, biological sign of subclinical poisoning to severe clinical disease and death due to metal toxicity. The 'threshold health effect' casually neglected by many health officials is perhaps most dangerous since it is the low chronic dose which has disastrous teratogenic impact and goes unnoticed till it appear in a larger societal damage. Experimental verification of long term effect of low level exposure to toxic metals is a difficult proposition since human subjects are rarely candidate for study and there are still many unresolved uncertainties in extrapolating the data from animal model to human beings. Full understanding of ecotoxicology or pathological implication which can be approached in a highly abstracted laboratory setting where life processes have been severely curtailed, cannot be translated to natural real life phenomena. Interpretation of epidemiological data can also be "stylized" by scientists in process language in interjurisdictional investigation and negotiations, and conventional scientists can be severely biased.

REFERENCES

Baccini, P. & Roberts, P.V. (1976.) Die belastung der gewasser durch metalle. Bile Forsch.Tech. Neus. zucher. 2.,18, pp. 57-58.

Barney, G.R. (1980). The Global 2000 Report to President. Govt. Printing Office, Washington DC.

Benco, V. Symon, K., Chladek, V.,Phirt, J. (1977). Health Aspects of Burning Coal with a High Arsenic Content. Env. Research. 13, pp. 386-395.

Horne, R.A. 1978. The Chemistry of our Environment. NY,Wiley. 869 p.

Jennett, Charles & James, L. Foil. (1979). Trace Metal Transport from Mining, Milling and Smelting Watershed. Water Polln. Control Federation Jrnl. v. 51, No. 2, pp. 378-402.

Natusch, D.F.S., Wallace, J.R. & Evans, C.A. (1974). Toxic Trace Elements: Preferential Concentration on Respirable Particles. Sc. 183, pp. 203-204.

Nriagu, J.O. & J. Pacyna. (1988). Quantitave Assessment of World Wide Contamination of Air, Water and Soil by Trace Metals. Nature. 333 pp 134-139.

2 Arsenic Pollution in Gangetic Delta

An Anthropogenic Model or Backlash of Technological Progress

Large scale arsenic pollution in parts of West Bengal and Bangladesh has been reported. Creditable works to mitigate the disaster has been taken up by delineation of arsenic prone aquifers and by provision of simple indigenous purification set-ups for dearsenification of drinking water in the target areas. Mitigation at the "end of the pipe" has brought immediate relief, but for a long term solution and prevention of reoccurrence elsewhere, the issue must be examined at the "beginning of the pipe line" of contamination.

Sediments are fossilized records of ancient environment. Similarly near shore and deltaic deposits give significant information on "what is cooking" onshore or in the hinterland, that is, anthropogenic activities upstream. Of late, anthropogenic transfer of materials on earth surface has assumed geological proportion, equivalent to that of erosion or crust mantle transformation. When it comes to heavy metals, especially toxic ones like Cu, Pb, Zn, Cd, Hg and As, anthropogenic mobilization and dispersion exceeds lithogenic mobilization and dispersion. "We are leaving our foot prints in the recent sediments".

The facts that are known about arsenic pollution in Gangetic delta are as follows:

- The problem is a recent one; no historical records exist on its past occurrence. The problem arose when an oversea agency made several deep bore holes to supply drinking water in the region.
- Surface water and dug-well water at shallow depth, used earlier, are not contaminated; so also very deep aquifers. The intermediate depth aquifers around 50 to 80 ft. below are considered to be the vulnerable zone.
- Arsenic in this vulnerable zone is found in the limonitic coating over detrital grains. Obviously, the coating is secondary (epigenetic) and post-dates the deposition of the sediment.
- Demographic survey indicates arsenic toxicity dominates along and around courses of Ganga and Padma rivers, that is, the said rivers have something to do with the spread of the contaminant.

The present thinking on the source of arsenic is:

Himalayan source: The element leached from arsenic rich ore bodies in Himalayas reached the deltaic sediment and precipitated over detrital grains of the aquifer. But no large arsenic ore bodies are found in Himalayas.

Volcanic source: Volcanic rocks are rich in arsenic. The adjacent Dalma Trap in Bihar and Dhanjori volcanics at delta head of Ganga could supply the element by leaching and weathering. If this is so, arsenic pollution ought to have occurred also in historic past. The absence of arsenic contamination around the vast area of Deccan Trap, an equivalent volcanic rock, does not support the theory of volcanic source. Besides, no primary arsenic minerals have been reported from the Dalma Trap or Dhanjori volcanic, or any skeletal semi-weathered equivalents in the contaminated sediment of the aquifer.

Deep seated ore bodies as the source: The Precambrian shield below the thick deltaic sediment may have arsenic rich ore bodies and ascending water from these could bring the element up into the contaminated aquifer. No such ore bodies have been encountered in any earlier deep holes made in the Bengal basin.

All these above arguments attempt to suggest that the source of arsenic is lithogenic or natural, arsenic pollution is fait accompli, and avoid anthropogenic responsibility. Since none of the arguments hold strong ground, the alternative view of the arsenic source is proposed to be anthropogenic and arises from:

- Reckless use of artificial fertilizers, pesticides, fungicides and insecticides in Ganga - Brahmaputra basin which heralded the Green Revolution and the "ill-famed" Indigo cultivation, practiced during early British rule. While rock phosphates carry as much as 10 to 20 ppm (gms. per ton) of arsenic and manufacture of urea needs arsenic catalyst (Zuary Agrochemicals factory in Goa has earlier caused fish death by arsenic poisoning), some of the pesticides are pure arsenic compounds.
- Smelting, foundry and metallurgical industries as well as artifacts of metals and alloys commonly found in the Indogangetic plains of north India.
- Chemicals, Pharmaceutical, Refineries, Petrochemicals, dyes, detergents, leather and textiles and wood preservative practices.
- Fossil fuel burning in power plants and related practices: Arsenopyrites (FeAsS) is a common mineral in coal, and coal is reported to carry between 56 to 156 mg/kg of arsenic. The Czech. coal has 1500 mg/kg and its burning has caused extensive arsenic dispersion. The leachable arsenic even in pond ash of Indraprastha Power Plant in Delhi is in the order of 25 mg/kg, when most of the element ought to have been lost to atmosphere during coal combustion and major fraction from ash is lost to supernatant pond water. The two power plants at Indraprastha

and Rajghat combined are estimated to contribute annually about 5 to 6 tons of arsenic to Yamuna water from ash leaching alone.

A crude conservative estimate of annual anthropogenic arsenic inputs over the catchments of Ganga and Brahmaputra is significantly high.

Arsenic and arsenic compounds are relatively more volatile; therefore move into the atmosphere with ease and transported long distance. All the coal and lignite fed power plants in India, the complex jargon of Green and Industrial Revolutions, presently the country is going through and a bizarre of cultural events cracking fire-works in every single celebrations, add a large amount of the element to the atmospheric aerosol over India. Arsenic content of the recently reported Asian Brown Haze is yet to be confirmed but is likely to be significant in view of its possible sources of origin. The winter fog (smog) over the Indo-Gangetic plains supplements the anthropogenic inputs. The configuration of the Himalayan range and the meteorological circulation over the Indian subcontinent presupposes penultimate transfer of the entire atmospheric arsenic generated by modern developmental practices, to the foot hills of Himalayas, where from it migrates down to plains through the net work of aquatic channels.

Arsenic being a non degradable substance, ultimately stock and barrel, migrates to the discharge region of the water channel; in this case to the Gangetic delta either in dissolved species or adsorbed ions on particulates. The concentration of the element builds up from infinite dilution in the remotest part of the water channel to appreciable concentration at the delta region by mere cumulative addition, where upon, the relatively Arseniferous water trickles down the coarse deltaic sediments and precipitates the element when dissolved oxygen depletes at intermediate depth or on encounter of organic material in the sediment. The precipitation of the element at intermediate depth prevents contamination of the deeper aquifer. However, the mechanism of precipitation is likely to spread both upward and downward as the middle aquifer gets saturated. Subsequently, pumping of water remobilizes the arsenic from the surface coating of the grains giving the lethal level of the element to drinking water.

The question therefore is, can arsenic pollution in Gangetic delta be a consequence of the combination of green and black (coal combustion) Revolutions and related cultural development in the Ganga-Bramhaputra watershed in particular and the subcontinent of India in general?

Assignment of an anthropogenic source for the fatal element presents a dilemma:

- To deny the model of anthropogenic source will be a blatant disregard to logics and will be a conceit of conscience.
- To accept the model means to decry the very basis of modern development and accept responsibility of the tragedy that presently affects millions of people.

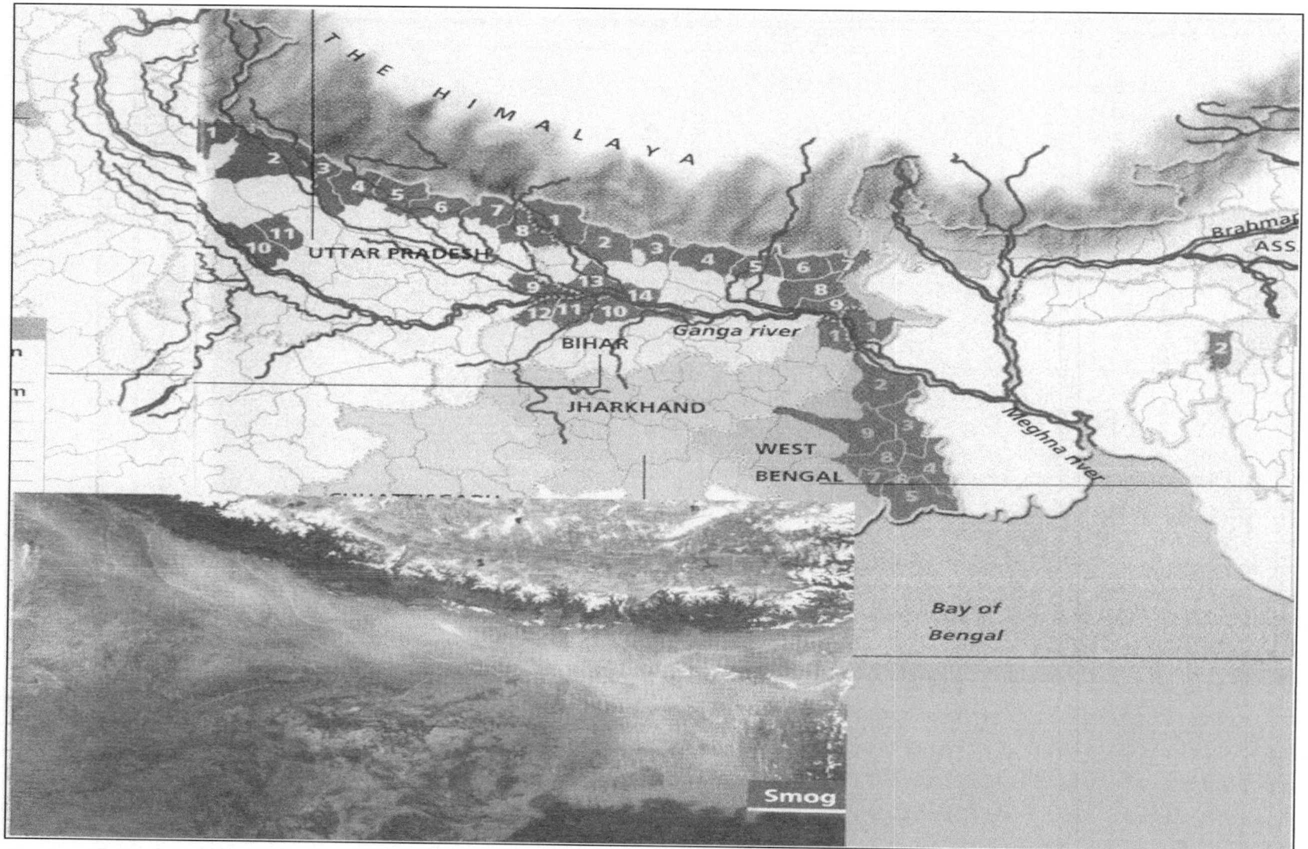

Fig. 2.1: Upper part of the figure – Map of India showing Arsenic enrichment areas along Himalayan slope, along Ganga course and Arsenic-endemic zone in Gangetic Delta (Down To Earth). Lower figure. :Satellite picture of atmospheric haze in North India

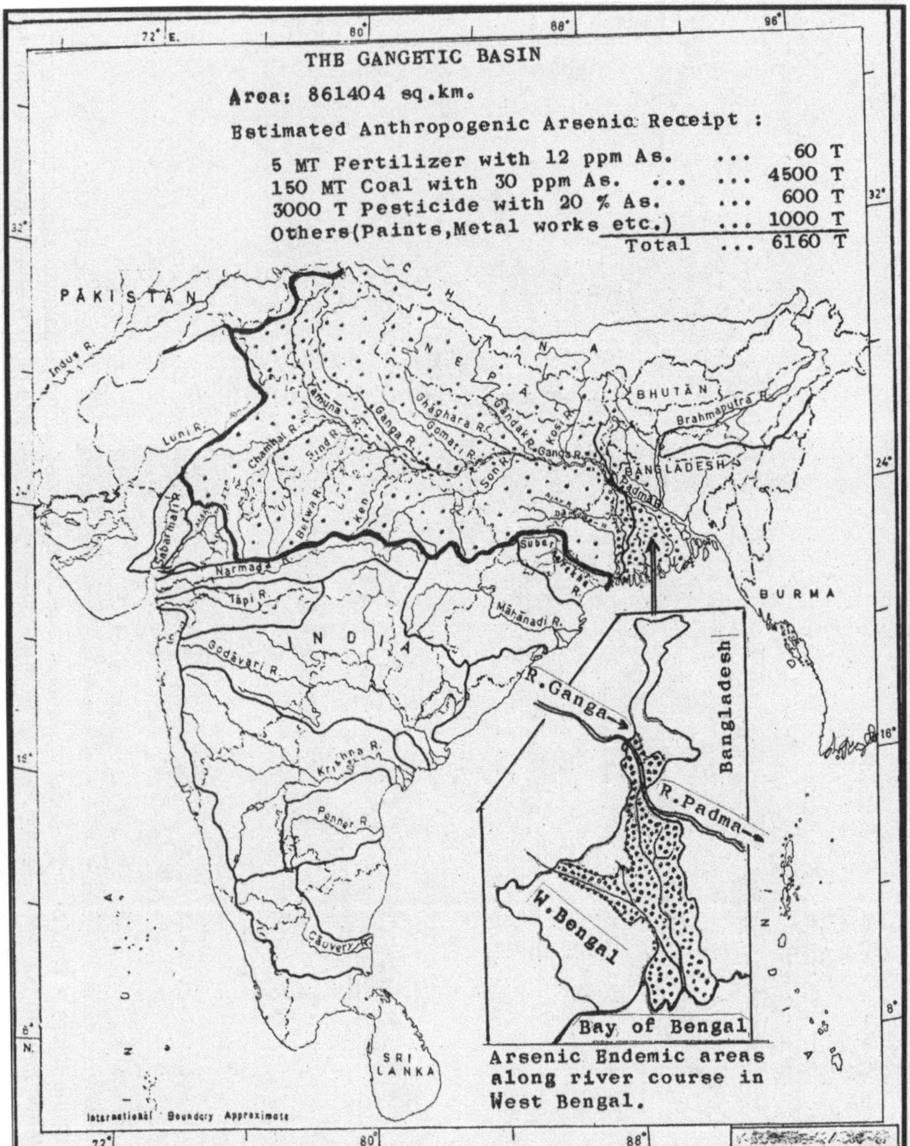

Fig. 2.2: Map of India showing the Endemic Arsenic Delta andestimated Arsenic inputs in Gangetic watershed

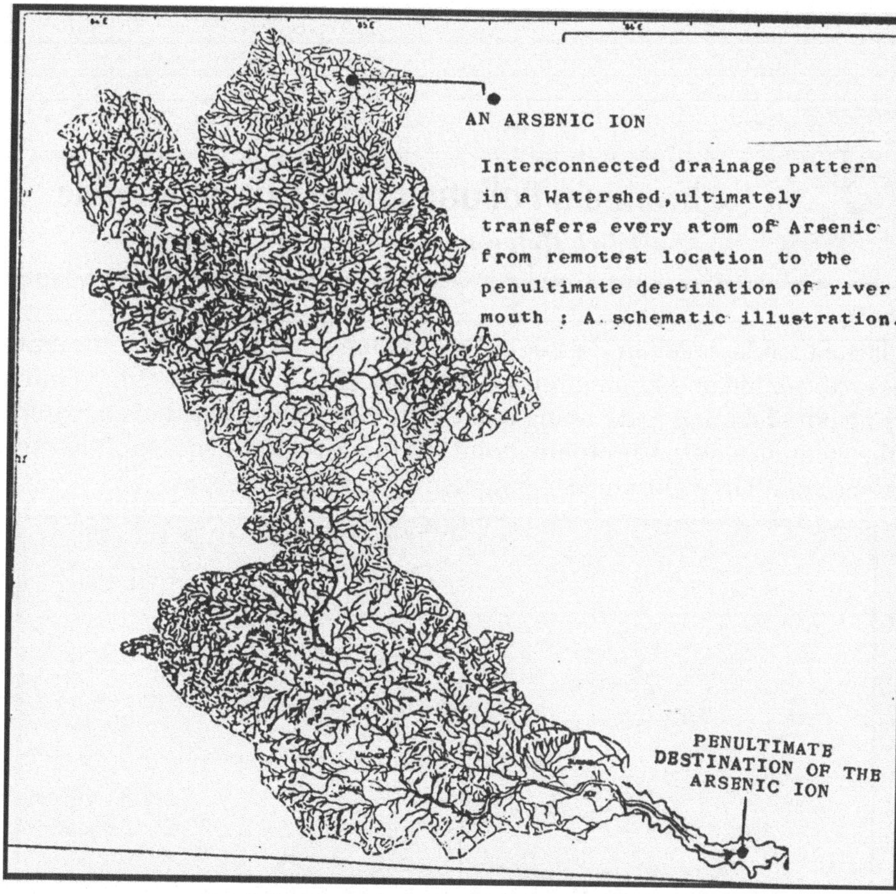

Fig. 2.3: Fate of Arsenic dispersion in Watershed

But the episode confirms the basic principles that:

(a) Pollution does not obey national boundaries (Transmigration of pollutants across national borders).

(b) As much as Global Warming in planetary scale is "An Inconvenient Truth" to world citizens, arsenic pollution is "An Unkind Truth" in local scale to Indian citizens.

It seems, modern man walked over the earth and left foot prints of disaster such as ones in Germany and Hiroshima in World War 2, in Minamata (Japan), Bhopal (India) and Iraq, to mention a few. The nature of arsenic tragedy in Gangetic delta is another such episode awaiting recognition.

3 Chromium Pollution from Chromite Mine

With Reference to Sukinda in Odissa

Of late, Sukinda valley in Orissa, India, is in limelight for its large chromites resource, mining and mining related activities (Fig. 3.1). No doubt, pollution arising out of mining and mining related activities has reached to an extreme in the Sukinda valley. Chromium pollution in the region, because of the mere presence of a large chromites resource, is a matter of debate.

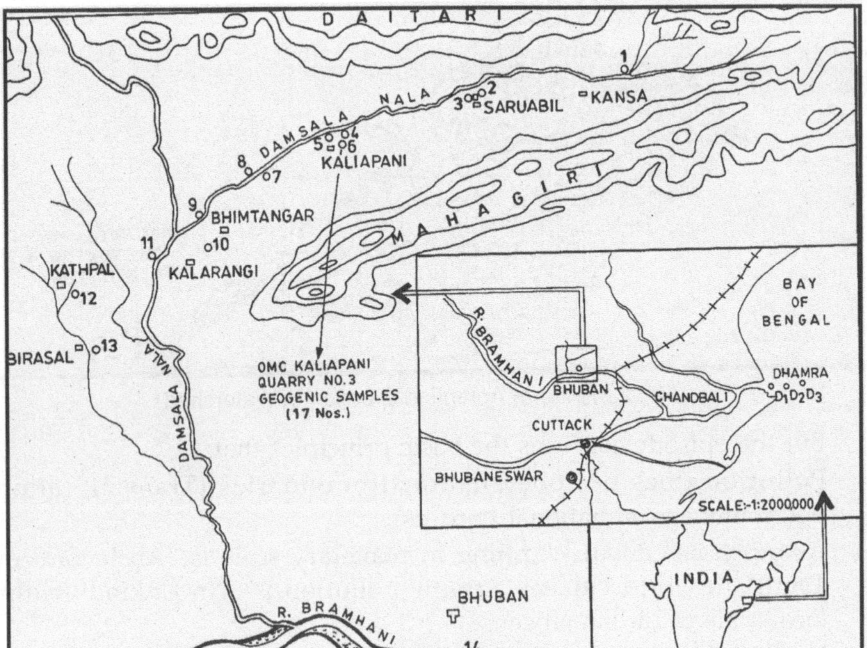

Fig. 3.1: Map showing Chromite Mines in Sukinda Valley

Colored quarry water, polarized scientific investigations and media-hyped epidemiographic survey, have blown up the issue out of proportion. Consistent and reliable analysis of Cr in ppb (parts per billion) level needs a dedicated laboratory and conventional Scientists are known to be bias. The observed colour of the quarry water may likely to be due to dissolved Fe and Mg chemicals which mimicry the yellowish tinge of Cr chemicals dissolved in natural alkaline medium. Nasal septum perforation, typical sign of Cr-Toxicity is not reported from the region. Other indicators like skin cancer can arise from entirely different routes. Nobody has reported siderosis or manganosis from the nearby Iron and Manganese Belts of Orissa.

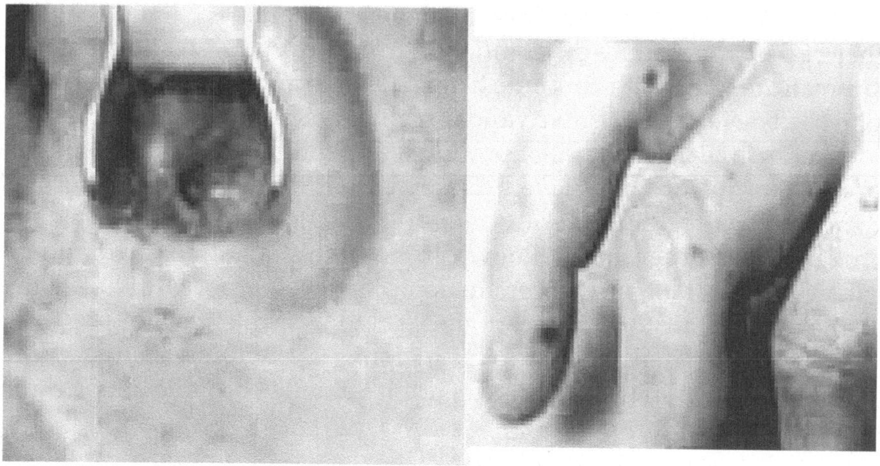

Fig. 3.2: Perforation of Nasal Septum and Skin Cancer are symptoms of Cr-Toxicity

"It is but normal that when Swine flu is in the corner every sneeze is looked upon as a likely infection of the disease and with GHG shooting in atmosphere every hot summer, missing winter or a cyclone is considered to be an indicator of Global Warming". The media hype of Cr-Toxicity is not an exception.

Cr - Toxicity arises by mobilization of Cr into human environment, by its bioavailability and injestion into human metabolic system.

Cr in a chromite deposit is not only not bioavailable but also locked in immobile state in a close packed inverted Spinel structure. Every Chemist who analyses Chromites knows that even the strongest acid cannot dissolve the mineral. The only way to break the mineral structure is by severe alkali fusion at high temperature which converts the Trivalent Cr to Hexavalent state as done in chrome chemical manufacture. Cr can also be mobilized into aqueous environment in strong chromic acids used in Tannery and electroplating baths and to some extent pumped into flue gas emission of coal based power plants. Obviously no such extreme conditions of high temperature and acidity can be expected in a chromites deposit or in chromites mining. In other words, mobilization of Cr into environment can take place only on industrial processing of chromites and not by mere digging or mining of the mineral. No doubt convention Geoscientists emphatically deny Cr pollution around chromite mines. This of course, is only partially true.

When one looks in to the stability fields of various Cr Species in Eh-pH diagram, Cr-6 has a small overlap on the regime of Natural water. It means it is possible to have a restricted amount of Cr-6 in natural environment at higher Eh-Ph conditions even in normal temperature and pressure. As a matter of fact, leaching experiments carried out on chromite samples of Sukinda showed maximum leaching of Cr at alkaline pH, intermediate at acidic pH and minimum leaching at near normal environment.

There are two types of chromite deposits, the Layered and the Alpine, either of them formed by differentiation from a dry ultra-mafic magma. Dry ultra-mafic magma with chromite bands when intrude into soft sediments of mobile belt develops a positive vapor pressure gradient towards the intruding body, sucks in water vapor that produces serpentinization and synkinamatic deformations in chromites layers. Observed under microscope, deformation extends well into the mineral grains (Fig. 3.3). Abrasion pH of olivine, pyroxene and serpentine is known to be highly alkaline. Oxidation and deuteric alteration of such chromite deposits develop pore fluid of high Eh-pH, that could transform a part of the Cr-3 to hexavalent state. That means, Alpine chromites deposit in tropical region is likely to pose environmental pollution during mining. The state of art in Sukinda chromite deposits ought to be examined in this context.

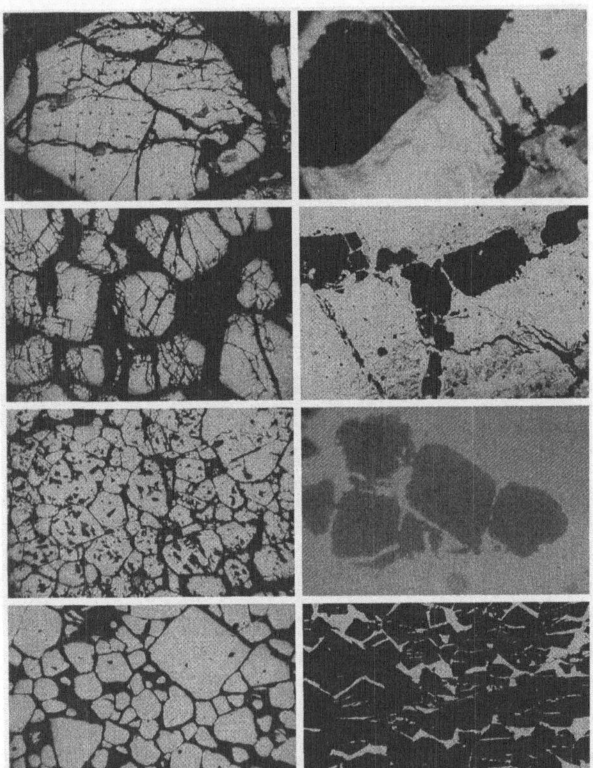

Fig. 3.3: Deformation Fractures in Chromite Grains seen under Microscope under Reflected (Left) and Transmitted (Right) Lights

It is not just mobility and bioavailability, the chromium must find a way into the human tissue to produce toxicity. Chromium is known to have 7 valence states, two of which Cr-3 and Cr-6 are common in Nature. The most common and least mobile one with 3 of the outer electrons stripped out, has a cationic dia. Of about 0.65 Angstrom. With further removal of 3 more outer electrons it attains a size of 0.5 Angstrom in Cr-6. The average pore diameter of cell walls being of the order of 0.52 Angstrom, only Cr-6 can penetrate the cell and rest even though ingested are easily expelled through urine or cuticular exudation. The reducing cellular fluid prevents the fugitive Cr-6 from further entry into nucleus by reverting it to larger Cr-3, failing which the Cr-6 enter the nucleus, produce DNA aberration and genotoxicity. The entrapped Cr-3 inside the cell or nucleus cannot be expelled out. Thus it is the entrapped Cr-3 that is responsible for all the Cr-related disease and not Cr-6 which is widely believed to be the toxic ion just because of its mobility and reduced size (Fig. 3.4).

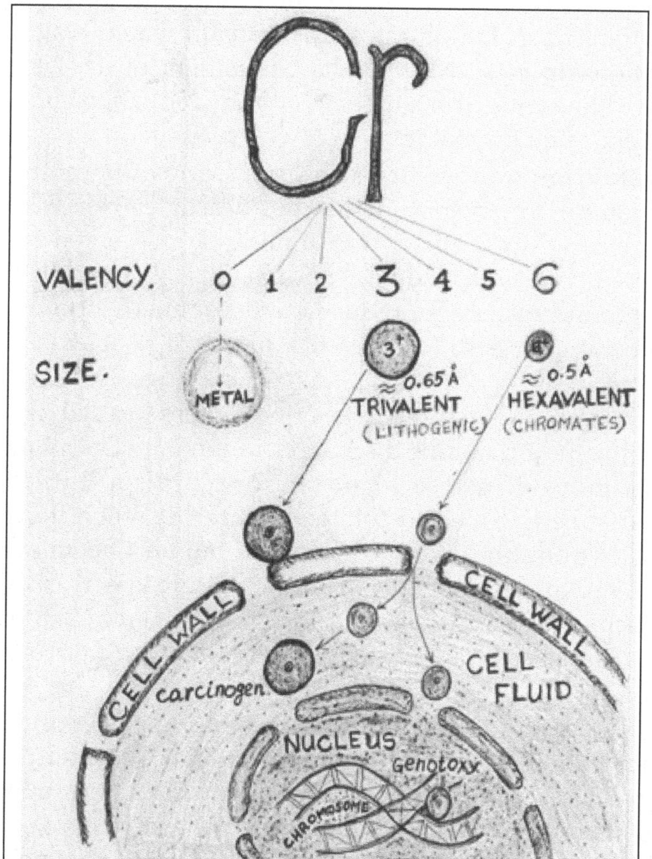

Fig. 3.4: Entry of Chromium ion into Cell – A Conceptual Model

The fact that chromite deposits with immobile Cr-3, under tropical Alpine environment can generate and release mobile Cr-6, led to a study of the Sukinda deposit for possible pollution.

To begin with, chromites samples from Sukinda when subjected to leaching studies, the amount of Cr leached was found to be maximum at pH 8, intermediate at pH 3 and minimum at pH 5.

Water samples from mine floors showed large Cr-6 concentration, as high as 1000 ppb (parts per billion), but samples along Damsala stream draining the mine area showed erratic values but at lower concentration due to (a) dilution of the quarry discharges along its course and (b) reduction conversion by organic materials, as the stream passes through dense vegetation. Almost ND (non-detectable) level of Cr in some of the village wells is due to percolation of ground-water through laterite whose principal constituent goethite is a sponge or scavenger for Cr ions.

Surface incrustation over detrital grains collected along Damsala stream was leached and analyzed for Cr, Al, Fe, and Mn. The incrustation is presumed to have precipitated as hydolyzates from stream water, was confirmed by positive relationship of Cr-Mn-Al. The Cr. content of the leachate, 0 to 12 ppm, ought to have come from stream water by reduction conversion of Cr-6 received from mine discharge.

The overall importance of leaching experiments on mine samples, analyses of natural waters and incrustation leachates clearly show that Cr, even if it is released from the chromite mines is prevented to travel far in dissolved state because: (a) the near normal or slightly acidic nature of the surface and ground waters; (b) reducing environment encountered in some sections of the stream and; (c). presence of strongly absorbent goethite in the region.

Detection of high level of Cr in mine waters has led to some sort of chemical treatment of the mine discharges to mitigate Cr-pollution. Effluent treatment is more effective in point source of pollution where the contaminated stuff is collected for treatment. But when it comes to non-point source of pollution like the sprawling mines and mineral deposits, remediation by effluent treatment is a technological hype, marketing gimmick of process technology or "a placebo for environmental activists". On the other hand it may lead to unwanted addition of chemicals to the discharge water.

In the background of possible Cr pollution in Sukinda region the dechromification of mine water by chemical treatment ought to be supplemented by a wider approach to cover the entire mining belt for mitigation of a non-point source of pollution. A research project undertaken at IIT-Bombay to monitor Cr in the effluent discharge channel of a chrome chemical factory which uses Sukinda chromites, discovered that when the open effluent channel passes through cattle sheds and slum areas, the channel water is extensively dechromified because of reduction precipitation of the dissolved chromate ions. It is felt that, development of cattle sheds (Dairy practices), animal husbandry (Hatchery, Piggery) and allied organic trades (Fruiticulture, Floricultures, food canning etc) around the quarries and dumps undertaken by mine workers as supplementary vocation or by corporate sectors in commercial scales, will not only mitigate the basic problem of Cr-pollution but also usher a parallel socio-economic development in Sukinda valley. An integrated approach of mineral excavation, organic practices stated above for a balanced socio-economic development would counteract the negative impact of monotrack mineral excavation which has led to the specter of Cr pollution and social upheaval in the Sukinda valley.

4 Heavy Metal Dispersion from Coal Combustion in Thermal Power Plant

ABSTRACT

The basic geochemical principle of coal formation indicates that coal deposits are sinks of a variety of toxic heavy metals. Burning of a large amount of high ash coal in a thermal power plant produces a considerable amount of solid waste in the form of ash. Coal ash has been found to have enriched concentration of many of the toxic metals as adsorbed species which on contact with rain water easily leach out of the matrix only to disperse into various compartments of the ecosystem around the thermal plant. It is suggested that while recognizing the deleterious environmental impact of use of large amount of high ash coal in thermal plants, precautionary measures should be taken to prevent the entry of the metals into the ecosystem. The ash should be carefully utilized for various developmental purposes.

Introduction

The need and demand for energy in a developing country like India cannot be underestimated. With a restricted source of liquid fuel, non-dependability of hydro-power and lack of technology for tapping of nonconventional energy like wind, solar, tidal and geothermal sources, it is but natural to go for large scale use of the available coal resources in the country. This may also help in prevention of deforestation of the countryside. It is also easier to transmit electrical energy to far off places than to transfer equal amount of coal by any method. Therefore, the Working Group of energy Policy of Government of India has rightly emphasized establishment of a chain of thermal and super thermal power stations in and around various Indian coal fields to meet the growing energy demand.

Establishment of coal based thermal plants consuming large amounts of high ash coal leads to a chain of processes disturbing ecological balance and consequent environmental degradation.

Genesis of Toxic Heavy Metals in Coal

The Indian coal deposits are known to have been formed by plant debris deposited in ancient lakes, bounded by trough faults. Gondowana time is also considered by geologists to have had a hot humid climate. Under such a climatic condition, extensive chemical weathering, intensive mobilization and movement of various metals from the ancient shield to depositional basins is most likely. The Precambrian shield of India which provided this lithogenic flux, both in solution and particulate, is made up of granites and gneisses, mafics and ultramafics, alkaline complexes, metasediments and hybrid rocks, all rich in metal content to varying degrees. This large scale mass movement by solution and particulate ultimately contributes to the mineral matter in coal and associated shales. The reducing environment created by partial decomposition of plants debris in lake bottom adds further to the coagulation and precipitation of the dissolved heavy metals as organo-metallic complexes. Carbon filtration (Fyfe, 1981) and retention of certain heavy metals by plants in nutrient cycle add to the stock. Besides these syngenetic detrial and solution precipitates and the bio-filtered metal found in coal, inorganic mineral matter may also be introduced into the coal strata by epigenetic solution-percolation, precipitation and by various mechanisms of solution particulate interaction. Thus, the coal ash representing the inherited and adventitious (both syngenetic and epigenetic) mineral matter is considerably enriched in toxic metals like As, Cd, Co, Cu, Hg, Mo, Ni, Pb, Sb, Th, U, V etc. The anaerobic process of coal genesis is also ideal for accumulation and retention of a considerable amount of sulphur in native, sulphide and sulphate forms. A host of heavy elements, which were imbibed and otherwise remained relatively immobile within the coal deposit in the subsurface environment, become mobile on the earth surface with the exploitation of coal. It is estimated that coal mining moves to the surface and into the atmosphere not less than 20,000 tons of uranium per year (Barney, 1980).

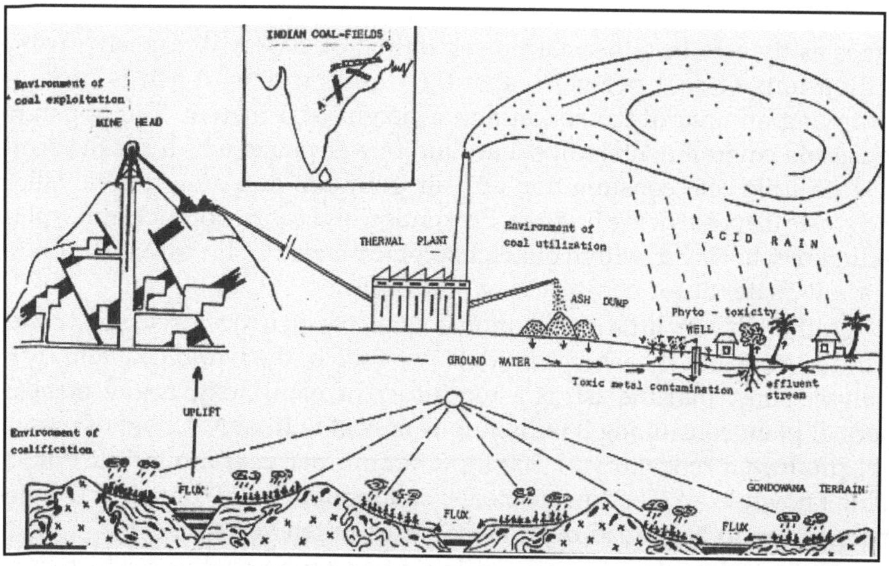

Fig. 4.1: A Schematic Representation of Environmental impacts of Coal Utilization

Environmental Impact

Environmental degradations as a result of exploitation of coal at the mine head are: land-waste, mine excavation and to some extent, atmospheric and groundwater contamination by volatiles, dust and spontaneous oxidation and leaching of coal dumps. Underground gasification of unextractable coal seams, may lead to considerable amount of atmospheric and groundwater contamination by organic and inorganic volatiles derived from both coal macerals and inertinites.

Considerable work has been done on environmental and climatic impact of coal based thermal power plant with emphasis on aerosol emission and formation and atmospheric pollution. Trace element emission during coal combustion (Lim, 1979 of NCB) and toxic metal contamination due to power plant effluent discharges (Singh, 1979; Van Hook, 1977) have been reviewed and discussed for environmental impact assessment. Analytical aspects of coal and coal products with special reference to fly ash have been described in detail by Karr (1978) and problems related to coal preparation and uses have been presented in the proceedings of 9th International Coal Preparation Congress (Rao, 1982).

Presently, 65 percent of the coal produced in India is consumed by thermal power stations and this coal carries as much as 30 to 40% of ash. By 2000 with the coming up of a series of superthermal power stations, consumptions will get doubled and coal of 45 per cent ash may come to be utilized. In a pulverized mass of coal, designed to feed the power plants, 5 to 15 percent of the ash escapes into the atmosphere through chimneys as fines, 15 to 25 percent falls as bottom ash and rest is collected in various stages as fly ash. In a thermal power station of 2000 MW capacity, using 8 million tons of coal per year, about 2.4 million tons of ash is produced occupying an area of 0.5 sq.km and a height of 5 meters. The apparently noticeable environmental impact around power plants which are the centers of large scale coal consumption are, air pollution and atmospheric fallouts and waste disposal of the fine ash. Prevention and control of such atmospheric pollution is, however, within our technological capacity. Fly ash can be utilized as a raw material for constructional purposes.

Although very little information is available on toxic heavy metal content of Indian coal and fly ash, recent data on some of the world coal and fly ash analyses show that the ash is a repository of many toxic heavy metals. A thermal plant consuming 8 million tons of coal with only 1 ppm of uranium will produce a repository of 800 kg. uranium per year around it. With the value known from Gondowana coals, an amount of 800 tonnes of the metal are expected to be spread over a small area in ten years time.

The metal content in coal can be of two types: (a) those which can be volatilized at the temperature of burning of the furnace such as Hg, As, Sb and to some extent Pb, Zn, Cd and U; and (b) those which are non-volatile and remain in the ash forming oxides and silicates. A major portion of the trace metals does not enter into the lattice structure of the refractory alumino-silicate minerals in the ash but are distributed in finer fractions as a surface labile layer (Fisher and Natusch, 1979). The brunt product, which is partly glassy, is in an energized condition and is more susceptible to leaching. The large specific surface area created by spongy and porous morphology and finer size of the ash particulates increases the leachability of the adsorbed metal cations.

A noteworthy character of the particulate matter is the increased concentration of toxic elements in the finer fraction vis a vis their retention and interaction with the human organs during inhalation. For example, ash particulates of 10 to 1μm (which predominate in ash) are caught up in the nasal mucous during inhalation. 75% of these are swallowed and enter the stomach where the toxic metals are extracted by the gastric acid and enter the body system. Particulates measuring about 1 μm diameter are retained inside the lungs resulting in the transfer of toxic cations into the blood plasma across cell membranes.

A 2000 MW thermal power station releases to the atmosphere about a hundred tonnes of sulphur per day as oxide. Acid rain characteristics of the power plant atmosphere because of sulphrous, nitrous and phosphatic as well as various hydrocarbonic gases from the burning coal increases the solution activity in the ash dumps and encourages leaching of the mobile metallic elements. The particulate fallouts enriched in more volatile metals return to the earth surface and join the leachates from the ash dumps. Leaching of the metal leads to:

1. dispersion in top soil and sediments by various processes like adsorption, exchange and formation of organometallic complexes;
2. contamination of surface and ground water;
3. accumulation in flora, fauna and habitats in small doses and remain unnoticed till phyto-toxicity are attained and appear in human species. The process is cumulative and irreversible.

The entire process from deposition of coal in carboniferous strata to the problems of environmental degradation consequent to coal exploitation is illustrated in figure 4.1.

Future Work Proposed

The easiest approach to combat pollution is to dilute the pollutant to below threshold limit and release it. Such an act is shortsighted and unscientific because:

(a) the threshold limit is relative and is only a socio-economic-political agreement in space and time;

(b) dilution by dispersion puts the pollutant in a regime which can go out of control; and

(c) the pollutant is lost for ever.

With a view to prevent and combat pollution and to utilize thermal plant wastes – gaseous and solids, the following measures are suggested:

Recognition of the types and levels of toxic metals distributed in Indian coal.

1. Develop methods to either recover or remove the deleterious constituents by physiochemical methods before feeding the coal to thermal plants.
2. Recover or entrap of sulphur and valuable volatile elements from the flue gas.
3. Install effective dust precipitators to reduce fallouts.
4. Design scientific disposal systems for solid wastes including their use as stoping materials in coal mine excavations.
5. Utilize coal ash for various purposes

REFERENCES

Barney, G.R. (1980) The Global 2000 Report to the President. Govt. Printing Office, Washington, D.C.

Karr, C. Jr. (1978). Analytical methods of Coal and Coal Products. Acad. Press, 580 p.

Rao, S.S.R. (1982). Procd. Ninth Intrnl. Coal Preparation Congress. (Ed), N.Delhi, Oxford, IBH, 245 p.

Singh, J.J. & Deepak, Adarsh. (1979). Environmental and Climatic Impacts of Coal Utilization procd. of Sympsium. Acad. Press. 655 p.

Vaan Hook, (1977). Environmental Studies on Trace Element Measurement and the Coal Fired Stram Plant, Compiled by W.S.Lyon, CRC Press.

5 Environmental Impact of Fly Ash Disposal, Management and use

Introduction

Sixty five percent of the electrical energy in India is produced by some eighty and odd coal fired thermal power plants. Indian coals are rich in ash. Machine mining, ushered to supply large requirements of coal in power plants further increases the ash content in the feed coal. Reduction of ash in coal has many limitations and the statutory requirement of less than 30% ash in feed coal is rarely complied. Coal reaching Indian power plants may carry 40 to 50 percent ash materials and the combustion residue (Ash) produced piles up at the backyard of the plant. A power station of 2000 MW capacity using 8 million tons of coal per year will produce 2.5 million tons of ash which will occupy 0.5 sq.km. area and pile up to a height of 5 mt. In India about 100 million tons of ash is estimated to be generated annually from various coal fired furnaces. Barely 10% of the production is profitably utilized. The nature of ash itself brings great concern and constraint for their disposal because of possible adverse impact to the environment.

Nature of Ash

The inorganic matter in coal, known as inertinite, may be inherent or attritus and genetically, primary or secondary. On combustion, they form the solid residue and collected as furnace slag or Bottom Ash below the combustion chamber. A major fraction blown out of the chamber with flue gas, are trapped at various collectors as Fly Ash and a minor amount escapes to the atmosphere through stack. Approximate proportions of ashes generated are 25% Bottom Ash and 75% Fly Ash, of which Fall-outs vary considerably depending upon the battery of electrostatic precipitators and presence or absence of scrubber at end.

Chemically the matrix composition of the ash is silica rich alumino - silicates. But the nature of the inorganic constituents in the pulverized feed coal, mechanism of combustion and temperature inside the furnace, greatly influence the physical and chemical properties of the ash at various places of collection along the passage. For examples:

(a) The Bottom Ash is relatively coarse, saccharoidal, crystalline, and denser, devoid of characteristic spherical grains and may contain large proportion of unburnt carbon.

(b) The Fly Ash (more appropriately, precipitator ash) are finer, lighter and carry conspicuous amount of spherical grains or fragments of broken spheres. Large surface tension of silicate melt on carbon surface produces ash globules inside the furnace while the out gassing volatiles generate ash bubbles of cenospheres and plerospheres. The Fly Ash is also richer in toxic trace elements that have volatilized at the furnace and condensed on cooling ash surface while ascending along the chute. Increased concentration of toxic trace metals have been demonstrated by many workers with the help of sophisticated surface analyses as well by time controlled leaching tests. While the ash may not show any size dependence for major matrix elements like Fe, Al, Si, Na, etc, finer particles may be enormously enriched with nonmatrix toxic trace elements.

(c) The Fall-Outs (which are literarily fly ash) are the lightest and finest fraction that escapes entrapment at bag-filters, electrostatic precipitators or even the scrubber.

Under normal circumstances, grains of 100 microns dominate the Bottom Ash or more, Fly Ash has a wider range of 100 micron to sub micron size and the stack emission carries less than 0.5-micron particles. Many workers have reported bimodal size distribution for the thermal plant aerosol.

Besides the size factors and chemical composition, the most crucial parameters of the ash are its mineral morphology and degree of diaphaneity, which greatly influence its use. The balloon shaped cenospheres and plerospheres make up a major proportion in fly ash, which constitutes more than 75% of the ash generated in the plant and impart a surface area, ten thousand times the equivalent size of the normal granular and saccharoidal grains (Natush, *et al*, 1979). This increases the physical and chemical reactivity of the ash manifold. Mineral-morphological characters of Ash are easily brought out by observation under various microscopes. Ash being 80% glassy and 20% cryptocrystalline, X-Ray diffraction provides an ideal technique.

Heavy metals are known to be present only in negligible amounts in ash and therefore are not considered to be a threat to environment. But because they are not lodged in lattice sites of any ash minerals, they are extremely labile and mobile. Quartz, a dominant ash mineral and with close packed structure too, has no lattice site for any heavy metals. The large specific surface of ash grains and diaphaneity, combined, greatly increase the mobility of the heavy metals, making fly ash a potential source of metal contamination by aquatic leaching. Considering the magnitude of ash generation, the total toxic release from fly ash into environment is alarming. Calculation by Rubin *et al* (1999) and revelation of EPA (1998) show that the "electrical utility" release of toxic elements to the environment substantially exceeds either of the two top polluting industries, namely, Chemical and Metallurgical, and could be as large as the two combined.

The Indian scenario of toxic release from coal-based power plants is least known. Sahu (1995) has emphasized that a super thermal power plant, using 8 million tons of coal, having 5 ppm of U, 40 ppm of Pb, 100 ppm of Zn and 10 ppm of Cd, will pump into its surrounding, 40 tons of U, 320 tons of Pb, 800 tons of Zn and 80 tons of Cd annually, the fate of which is never realized. No wonder, of late, Fly Ash is listed by EPA as a "Hazardous Waste" based on Total Toxic Release Inventory (TRI) from the electrical utility services.

Like any carbonaceous sedimentary rocks, coal is a repository of Uranium. Coal mining and coal combustion annually brings out and disperse into biosphere, about 5000 tons of U, 13,000 tons of Th and many other daughter nuclides such as radium, pollonium, bismuth, lead and K-40. Chakravarty (1991) reported uranium concentration in Indian coal in the range of 1.1-3.6 ppm (uniform component) and 33-46 ppm (nonuniform component), where as in Fly Ash it varies from 8-11 ppm (uniform) to 55-71 ppm (nonuniform). Since the radio nuclides accumulate year after year, a century of coal combustion would elevate the global anthropogenic radiation to a level of " Subdued Nuclear Evening" without going into large scale nuclear warfare. According to an ORNL Report the amount of U-235 alone dispersed by coal combustion is equivalent of a dozen nuclear reactor fuel loadings. No wonder, a coal based thermal power plant is considered more vulnerable than a regulated nuclear power plant when it comes to hidden fall outs.

Ash Disposal

Ash generated at various points of collection in a thermal plant is made into a slurry, hydraulically transported and deposited in an Ash Pond. About an acre of land is required for ash disposal for every MW installed capacity. Although the storing capacity of the pond can be marginally increased by suitable design of Ash Dykes around the pond, the physical properties of the ash, mostly size, density and morphology exert great restriction in its piling and storage. In a decade or so the storing capacity of the pond is reached and new site for ash disposal is looked for.

Ignorance of toxic release capacity of fly ash, as well as the extensive and expensive nature of treatment needed for developing a leak proof ash pond has prevented most power plants in India, to provide an environmentally benign pond, thereby threatening the surrounding aquatic regime. Various geotechnical measures are available for ash pond treatment and the modern generation of power plants is seized with the issue.

To limit land requirement and to avoid leaching problems, a new technology of Dry Disposal has been initiated. Dry disposal forms an ash mound, segregates various types of ash to be required for different uses in future and unlike the Wet Disposal method, preserves the pozolanic property of the stored material. Here too, stability of the slope and height of the ash mound, decided by water-holding capacity and other physical properties of the ash itself, control the capacity of the disposal site. A Garland Canal around the mound takes care of the toxic leachate.

Ash Utilization

The best way of disposal and management of ash is its guided utilization. A Mission mode approach of ash utilization has been undertaken by the Govt. of India to face the fly ash problem. Since the order of generation of ash in India is in the order of 100 million tons, the solution lies only in venues, which can utilize large bulk of the material.

Ash can find use in many civil engineering practices such as, cement, brick and tile manufacture, construction of embankment, reclamation and filling of fallow lands, mine stowing and for soil conditioning in agriculture. Even its use as herbicide or pesticide carrier, is considered possible. Production of zeolites, recovery of magnetic and refractory cenosphere and manufacture of special lightweight structural materials are also some of the venues of ash utilization.

Ash-Water Interaction

Fly ash in contact with water or moisture slowly develops an incrustation of polysialate or zeolite on grain surface in due course of time. Polysialatization of ash has great significance when long-term use of ash either in soil conditioning or brick manufactures is concerned.

Polysialate or zeolite are 3D-network of Si/Al-O tetrahedral having exchangeable sites of multiple co-ordination. A six fold co-ordinated site with a lattice space of 0.6 Angstrom ideally accommodates heavy metals, many of which are known to be micronutrient for plants, whereas the twelve fold co-ordinated site with a larger lattice space of 1.0 Angstrom is suitable to house larger cations or anionic radicals like Ca, K, Phosphates etc. Adsorption exchange of cations and anions being pH dependent, these sites can be selectively activated by control of pH of the soil media. An ash grain in soil, with even a monomolecular rind of zeolite formed by ash-water interaction, will therefore act as a molecular pump for micro- and macro nutrients (Sahu, 1999).

The phenomenon of polysialatization of ash in long run appears to be a set back to ash brick manufacture. Moisture or water in contact with ash particles in an originally standard ash brick, when develops an incrustation of zeolite around ash grains, will obviously reduce the brick strength endangering stability of the structure built with fly ash brick, albeit after a lapse of several years (Sahu, 1999). Therefore more thoughts may be given for selective use of fly ash bricks in construction industry.

Epilogue

The need of energy for survival, sustenance and progress is inevitable and the solid fossil fuel, though considered dirtier, reasonably fulfils this basic need.

Coal combustion, however apparently leads to various environmental problems such as air pollution by toxic emissions and land and water pollution by solid waste disposal. Indian coals are low in sulphur, thereby SOx emission is reduced, but the high content of ash in coal generates a large amount of fly ash, disposal of which is riddled with various problems. It is no exaggeration that " The limit of power generation from thermal plants in India will be decided by limits of our capacity of fly ash utilization", and this has given a strong drive to Indian scientists and technologists to transfer as much fly ash as possible to the utility cycles such as, brick manufacture, land applications etc. The ash producers (Thermal plant authorities) too, provide every incentive to off-load the growing dump in their backyard.

Apparently, fly ash is a pollutant in the ash pond or ash mound (A resource out of place) and can be transformed into utility products; but its long term impacts and acceptability in the transformed environment must be fully understood. For examples, question has been raised on the consistency of the strength of ash bricks, discordant properties of ash and soil when it comes to agriculture, and finally the heavy metal release into the environment when a large amount of ash is used as land fillings. In our enthusiasm to solve the problem of ash accumulation, it may not be prudential to take hasty step to pump the generated ash into any environment in bulk quantity because retrieval is not possible. Our Scientists must look into long-term impacts of the environmental equation, which they are initiating in ash disposal through different utilization processes.

The questions that must be asked and problems looked for are:

1. What types of life disrupting trace compounds could be synthesized in the combustor and along the exhaust chute of the power plant, keeping in mind the nature of the macerals and minerals in our coal.
2. What types of trace emissions including organics and halogenated compounds leave the stack along with the fly ash and their fate in atmosphere or when they reach terrestrial ecosystems?
3. What are the long-term impacts of increased toxic pollution on the three basic life supporting systems, namely, air, water and soil around a thermal power plant? Are the impacts compensated by the "Bread and Circus" game we are provided in the name of progress and regional development?
4. A regional Inventory of Toxic Release (TRI) from thermal plants has come to due.

5. Will the soil, so important to an agrarian country like India accept the ash for a sustainable agricultural yield. Reported positive results of larger yield in ash amended soil and heavy metals brought into the food chain through the process must be carefully examined.

There are many such issues Indian Scientists must ask before going for a large-scale utilization of fly ash.

REFERENCES

EPA. *Toxic Release Inventory, Public Data Release*. US – EPA, Washington, 1998. EPA-745-R-98-005.

Natush, D.F.S. and Fisher, G.L. *Analytical methods for Coal and Coal Products*. Ch.4. Ed. C. Karr, Jr. Acad. Press. 1979.

Sahu, K.C. 1999. *Mineralogy of Coal and Fly Ash*. Ind.Jr.Geol, 71(1 & 2), pp. 93-103.

Sahu, K.C. *Fly Ash for Agricultural use*. Procd. Fly Ash Characterization and its Geotechnical Applications. IISc. Bangalore, 1999. pp. 1748-1753.

6

Vision of Green Minerals

ABSTRACT

Importance of mining and mineral industries has been emphasized and adverse impacts of mineral exploitation are recognized. Two examples of alternative process of exploitation and use of minerals have been conceived to heal and repair environmental damage imbibed by usual process of mining and mineral exploitation in the modern society. These are:

(a) Encapsulation of synthetic fertilizer grains with natural Bentonite; and
(b) utilization of Fly Ash for agricultural practices after suitable alteration.

Introduction

Since Stone Age, minerals have been in use to keep the human civilization in progress. A host of metallic minerals like that of Fe, Mn, Cr, Cu, Ni etc., nonmetallic minerals such as Limestone, Dolomite, Clays etc. run all the basic industries; Coal, Petroleum, Natural Gas and Nuclear minerals provide energy at homes, factories and streets; Limestone, Marble, Granites and Rip-raps support the building industries and road-rail networks; fertilizer minerals like Phosphates, Nitrates and Gypsum have increased agricultural productivity and banished world hunger; precious metals like Gold and Platinum keep country's fiscal economy healthy and along with precious stones like Diamond, Ruby and Emerald hold human vanity high.

But the problems with mining and mineral industries are:

1. Most nonmetallic minerals and fuels like Limestone, Dolomites, Coal and Oil occur in sedimentary rocks, the argillaceous components of which develop thick fertile residual soil and sustain dense vegetation and forest over the mineral properties. Similarly, the metallic minerals occur in pristine mountainous terrains whose ecological importance is presently held high. In either cases, mining activities, however carefully done imbibe adverse effects on environment, but cannot be stopped if progress and development of the society is to be achieved and maintained. Besides, mining activities are area specific and can not be relegated to some other "safer sites" but can only be regulated and controlled for optimum benefit.
2. By irony of fate, the mineral rich belts of the world are inhabited by natives who are poor and solely depend on the natural environment.

The benefit of the resources generated by mining, which destroys their sources of livelihood, is pumped out to distant places leaving the natives with mere "Bread and Circus". Education and awakening of the natives has brought out many socio-economic problems in mining and mineral industries.

While actual mining activities imbibe physical scars on earth's terrain, chemical pollution of the environment, decrease biodiversity and generate economic imbalance and social unrest, a visionary exploitation of certain category of minerals can heal and prevent environmental damage caused by resources use in the present tecnoholic society. Two such examples are cited below.

1. Bentonite for greening of synthetic fertilizers.
2. Fly Ash for greening of "White Deserts" and usher second Green Revolution.

BENTTONITE FOR GREENING OF SYNTHETIC FERTILIZER

Introduction

Lunch is never free in Nature. Green Revolution, riding on the shoulder of synthetic fertilizers, brought food security in India but not without a cost. Vast tracts of land got salinitised and the entire water regime of the country, surface or ground water, in wells, streams, lakes, rivers and near shore coastal strip got polluted with Phosphates, Sulphates, Nitrates and Heavy Metals (Arsenic episode of Gangetic delta not excluded). This is a national issue more wide spread than impact of mining in India.

The Issue

For every 100 kg. of synthetic fertilizer applicated to land, only 40% is taken up by the plants and the rest, as much as 60% is lost by dissolution removal from the site by runoff. Considering the total amount of synthetic fertilizer that have been applicated on land during last 50 years period, the cumulative effect on the water regimes of the country, is considered alarming. No wonder, 50 years before one could directly drink water from any well, pond, stream and river in India but dares not to do it today.

The Vision

If the synthetic fertilizer, before release to the market is encapsulated by providing a coating on the grains or granules, with a suitable material, not soluble in water but allows plant to avail the macro - and micro nutrients from the encapsulated grains, the net result will be:

- No loss of fertilizer by dissolution runoff
- No pollution of water by the fertilizer elements
- Decrease in amount of fertilizer used without affecting grain production
- Decrease in requirement (production) of fertilizer and hence reduction of emission, effluents and energy use etc.

- Lesser degree of soil degradation
- Enable the plants to avail fertilizer elements as and when required during its growth period.

The Wander Mineral for Encapsulation

Unless hydroponic, plants grow on soil and uptake their nutrients by Cation/Anion exchange through Clay minerals or organic complexes like Humic and Fulvic compounds (sketch below). Clay, more specifically clay minerals are major constituents in soil and are not soluble in water. A double layer TOT type clay mineral (T stands for Silicon-Oxygen Tetrahedra and O stands for Aluminum-Oxygen Octahedra) represented by a specie named Montmorillonite has the optimum exchangeable sites per unit cell formula and can be micronized to nano level without losing exchangeable capacity. On the other hand decrease in particle size increases its exchangeable capacity. This mineral is also flaky like mica, therefore capable of wrapping over grains and provides the thinnest possible layer over any grain size (sketch below). This is a material popularly known as "Multani Matti" and used in naturo-therapy and beauty parlors to detoxify and clean skin by absorption exchange of toxic radicals from the pores of the skin. Natural Montmorillonite known as Bentonite is widely available in Kutch Dist. of Gujarat and in many other places but does not require extensive mining.

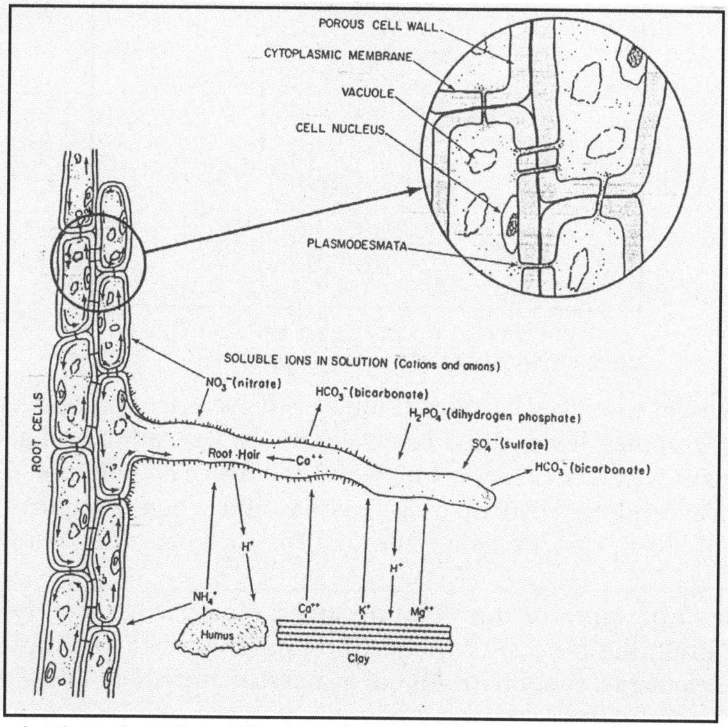

Mechanism of uptake of Nutrients by Plants by exchange through Clay

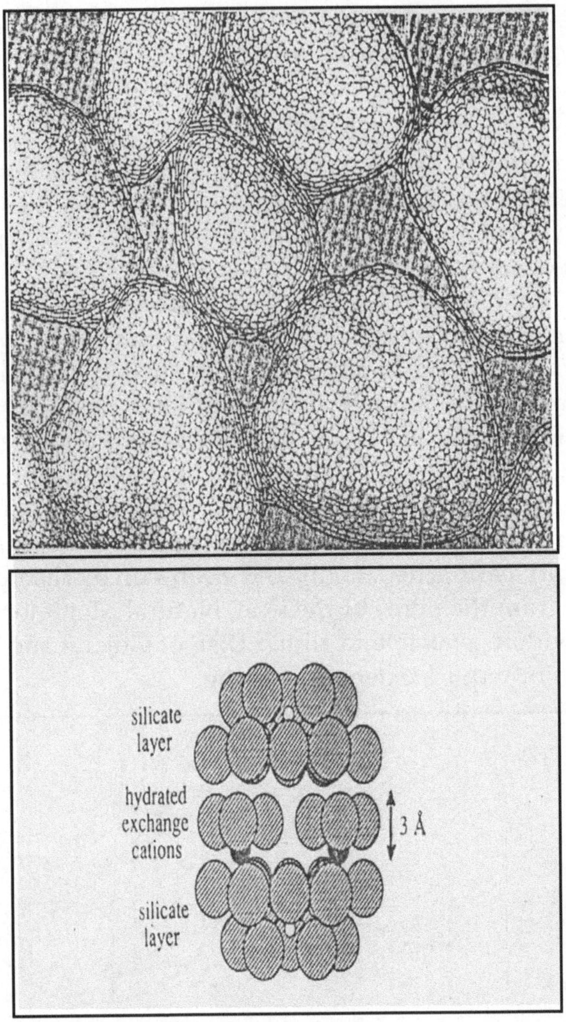

Top: Idealized Encapsulated Fertilizer Grains.
Bottom : 3 Angstrom wide Exchangeable site in Bentonite

Such a micronized clay with a suitable adhesive, if sprayed over fertilizer grains or granules, it will provide a water insoluble coating so that there will be no loss of fertilizer elements into water and hence no pollution. The plants can uptake fertilizer elements selectively as and when it requires by usual process of absorption/exchange through the exchangeable sites of the clay mineral.

The importance of this "Nature given material" is that, being a soil mineral itself, the residue of the fertilizer-capsule after total uptake of the fertilizer elements, is not harmful but is a useful ingredient to the applicated land.

Till today, waste-water treatment for pollution control and remediation of contamination has remained confined to the "curative measure" of modern technology which is very well known to ushers Checks and Balance of Nature. That is, the water is purified, but added with some other agents (less harmful contaminant?) or the pollutant isolated, dumped into some other ecosectors where it becomes a different pollutant or the residue remobilized to enter back to environment through another utility channel. The present technique of runoff water pollution control by Bentonite encapsulation of fertilizer grains is a "preventive measure" and natural, therefore has no adverse downstream effects at all. It is also a challenge and opportunity for Mineralogists to enter into an applied field dominated by Chemical Engineers and Chemists only.

FLY ASH FOR GREENING OF "WHITE DESERT" AND USHER 2nd GREEN REVOLUTION

Introduction

India produces more than 100 million tones of Fly Ash in its hundred and odd thermal power plants. Except for a small percentage of its use in construction and building industries more than 80% of the material remains dumped around the power plants in Tailing Dams and Mounds creating a bizarre of environmental problems such as pollution of land, soil, air and water. The disposal site is known as "The White Deserts". Fly Ash disposal is land intensive. Presently about 65,000 acres of land is occupied by these White Deserts in various power plants and by 2015, this occupation is estimated to be in the order of 1000 square kilometer or one Sq.Meter per person in India.

The Problem

Fly Ash is a saccharoidal material of average sand to silt size particles of spherical shape, evidently due to the mechanism of formation by "bubble bursting" in the furnace during coal combustion. The spherical particles, solid or empty, are known as cenosphere and plerosphere, possess surface area ten to hundred times the equivalent grain size and being amorphous (glassy), are highly reactive. Chemically, the ash is silica rich with some silicates of alkalis and alkaline earths and mineralogically, consists of high temperature silica polymorphs like Tridymite and minor amounts of Feldspars, Foids, Mullite and Magnetite. Because of its fine size its mineralogy is best brought out by X-Ray diffraction analysis and morphology is best observed under an electron microscope.

Fly Ash has been in use in building, construction and cement industries to a limited extent (maximum of 20%) and some research efforts have been made for its use as a soil conditioner in agricultural practices and even as a weed killer.

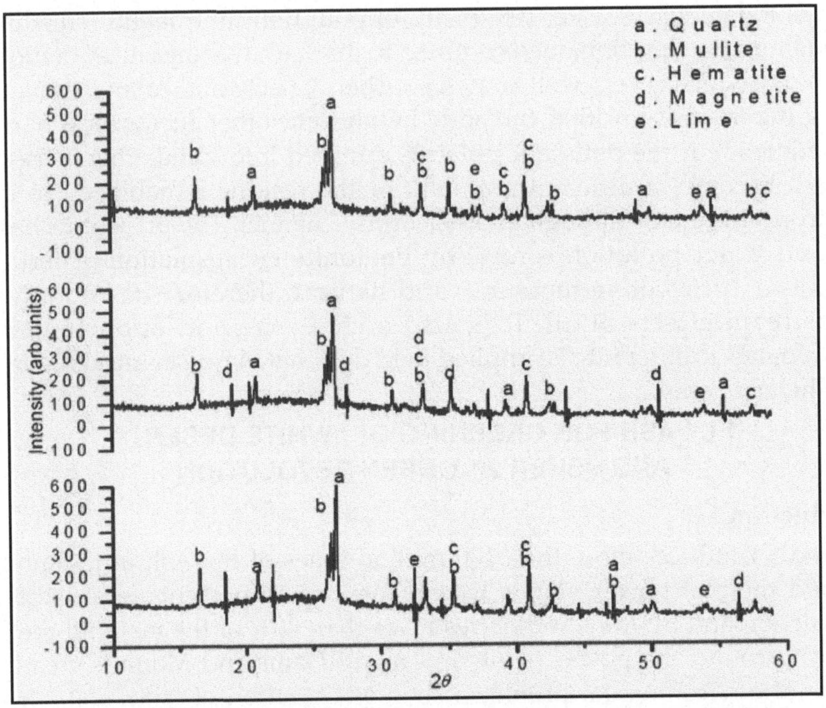

A Typical set of X-Ray Diffractograms of Fly Ash for Mineral identification

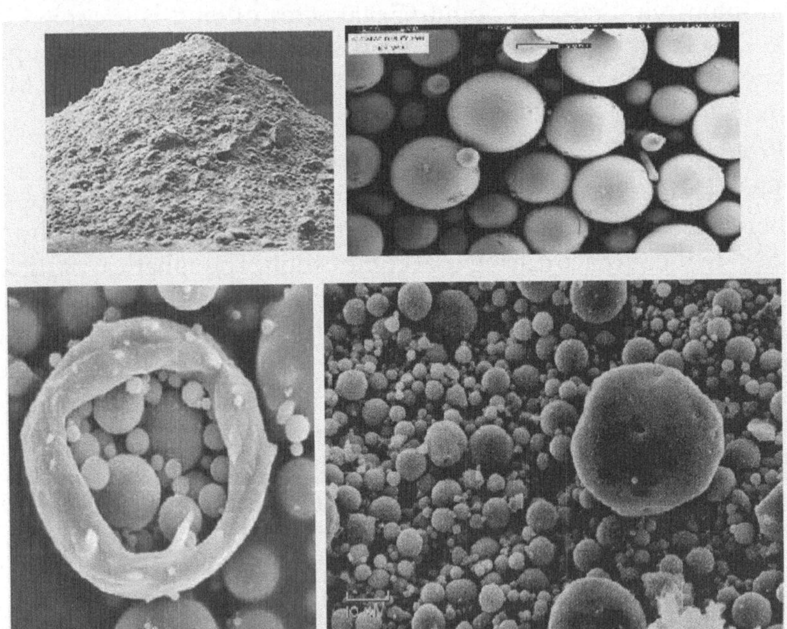

A typical set of Electron Micrographs of Fly Ash showing Cenospheres and Plerospheres

Vision for Extended use in Agriculture

Interaction of Fly Ash and water forms an incrustation of polysialate on ash particle surface in due course of time (Fig. 6.1). The polysialate rind developed on particle surface are simple Zeolites. Zeolites are 3-D network of SiO_4 tetrahedra of honey comb structure and possess numerous exchangeable sites. The dimension of the exchangeable sites in the mineral depends on the number of tetrahedral rings around (Co-ordination Number) (Fig. 6.2). A six fold Co-ordination site has a space of about 0.6 A^0, most ideal for accommodation of the heavy metals which act as micronutrient to plants. The 12 fold Co-ordination site has a space larger than 1 A^0 and is ideal site to accommodate K cations and perhaps larger anionic radicals like Phosphates and Nitrate which are essential macronutrients.

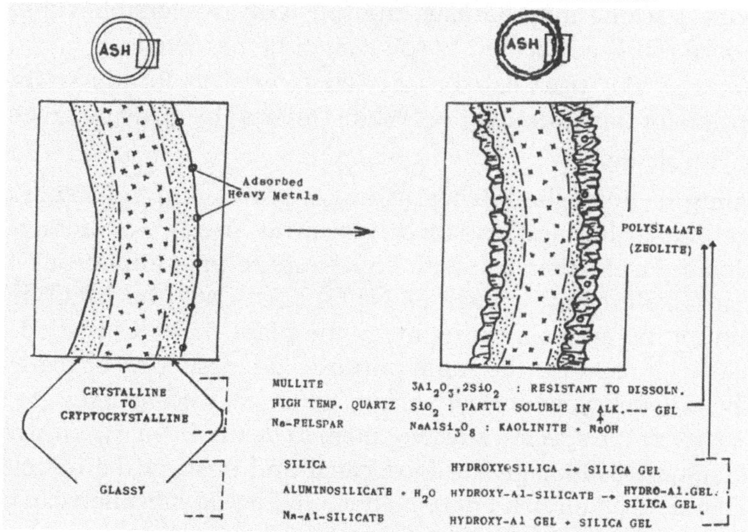

Fig. 6.1: Mechanism of Zeolite Formation on Ash

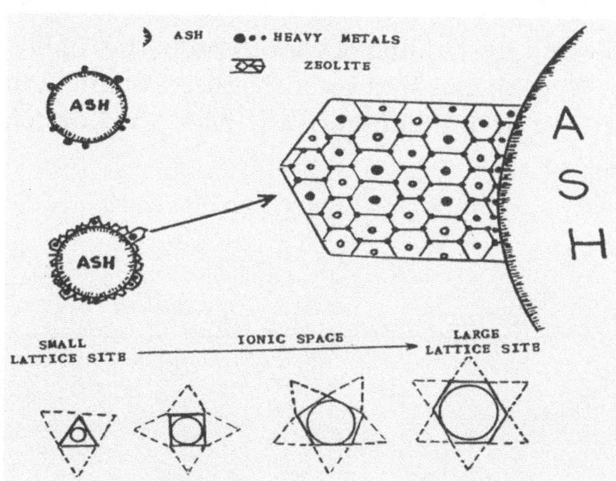

Fig. 6.2: ION Immobilization in Polysialate

Formation of a polysialate rind with such exchangeable sites makes the ash a store house of micro and macro nutrients on fertilizer application. Exchangeability being pH dependent, it is possible to prime selective intake and uptake of micro and macro nutrients in the exchangeable sites of Zeolite by controlling the pH of the soil environment. In other words, each ash particle with a polysialate incrustation becomes a mineral pump for nutrients needed by over-growing biomass. If succeeded, ash addition to soil can increase agricultural productivity and herald a second Green Revolution in this country. It is of course necessary to understand the crystallochemical properties of the polysialate and chemo dynamics of adsorption-desorption and exchange in the concerned Zeolites and simulate a series of experiments in this regard, before any large scale activity of ash addition to soil is undertaken, lest one may damage the soil with irreversible consequence. Because once ash is applicated to soil cannot be retrieved.

However, the trial can be carried over Ash Ponds without any apprehension for transforming the "White Deserts" by growing green foliage.

Ash as a Herbicide

Dusting of domestic kitchen ash over plants and vegetable crops in kitchen garden (including Tulsi) for driving away insects is a common practice in rural India. The kitchen ash with high proportion of anhydrous oxides of alkalis and alkaline earths such as Na_2O, K_2O, CaO and MgO dehydrate (dehydrolyse) the animals eating away the plant parts. Classified Fly Ash can similarly be used for the same purpose. Besides, 80 % of the ash being glassy, the fine splinters on leaf surface when chewed, is likely to damage the oral cavity of the species, starving them to death. Even, when swallowed, the splinter would damage the food canal and destroy the insects in due course. Therefore alkali rich Fly Ash after suitable classification can be use as a herbicide.

Conclusion

With proper understanding of various properties of Fly Ash and suitable modifications, Fly Ash can find extensive use in agricultural practices and ease the burden of accumulation in the back yard of coal based thermal power plants.

7

The Burning Issues of Coal

It is good to have foresight, but Man can not look beyond what he sees

–Winston Churchill

The tree in front prevents to see the forest beyond.

ABSTRACT

Coal is an important energy resource. But mining and combustion of coal to generate power produces many environmental impacts, the adversity of which is never realized by consumers of electrical energy. The paper attempts to focus the various impacts to arouse awareness for conservation of power and realize the hidden cost of electricity.

Introduction

Environment awareness is limited by the very limitation of sensory perception, but Imagination, Intuition and logical Interpretation enable humans to conceive Environment of larger dimensions in space and time. A draftsman drawing a straight line on a sheet of paper is limited by the size of the sheet or the drawing table, but imagine he endlessly extends the drawing table and the drawing sheet, his line will end up at where he started – obviously because the earth is round. In his routine life, he is aware of a flat table and flat earth only. So does a vertical line extended infinitely is considered (argued by Albert Einstein) to bend in space to join the base it started. In a relatively smaller scale, burning of a kilogram of coal or switching on an electrical appliance powered by combustion of a few Kg. of coal in a Power Plant apparently has no effect on the atmosphere or environment per se. But imagination (Hypothesis) of Global Warming due to fossil fuel combustion has come to a reality. The law of Butterfly Effect in physics may not be perceptible, but can not be denied.

The present paper attempts to condense (microfy) larger dimensions such as that of atmospheric volume, global coal mining and power generation and consuming population into visible and perceptible dimensions, virtually to be aware of atmospheric alteration by Man through fossil fuel combustion and ultimately to realize the hidden cost of electricity. The atmospheric volume of 7.67×10^{18} cubic meter(up to average 15 km. height) which stands polluted has been condensed to 100 cubic meter of a study room, the 8000 million tons of coal that is annually mined to a mere one Kg, the global consumption of electricity of 20 trillion KWH to a 100 Watt Lamp and the 7.1 billion global consumer is represented by a sole person – in this case a student studying in a 5 × 5 × 4 mt. room under a 100 Watt lamp but has no other electrical appliances at all (Most conservative use of electricity). The levels of a select atmospheric constituents emitted from burning one Kg. of coal to sustain the 100 W lamp on for 24 hours and which effect the health of the "Student" (virtually us) is focused in two stages as "Initial Air" and "Air After 24 hrs". The adverse health effects of exposure to such constituents are well known but little realized or lost in the perception of progress and development.

Discovery and use of coal in human history stands next to the discovery of fire and agriculture. It set in the Industrial Revolution with a significant jump in the quality of life and supplied many life supporting materials like fuels, chemicals, fertilizers, fibers and most importantly power through coal based thermal Power Plants. Electrical energy derived from fossil fuel burning has virtually made Man a powerful agent on earth, consequently a veritable exploiter of Nature. However, lunch is never free in Nature. The cost of coal mining has been ample and are commonly listed as follows:

- Loss of top soil, especially in strip and "Mountain" mining.
- Deforestation (Carboniferous Sandstones and Shale of Gondwana terrain develop dense forest).
- Huge Over-Burden Dumps (at least 25 tons mined per ton of coal produced), Land Despoiling, Acid leaching (Pyrites, a common mineral is oxidized in atmosphere and produces Sulphuric Acid) and Water pollution.
- Change of Hydrological Regime including diversion of local drainage channels and depletion of Water Table. The latter in turn wilts deep rooted trees.
- Land Subsidence, Accidents, Fire Hazards and Spontaneous Fires due to oxidation of Sulphides.
- Noise, Dust and Thermal Pollution.

- Habitat loss and Ecological damage.
- Displacement of people, Occupational and Cultural changes.
- Appearance of new Occupational diseases.
- Rise of Coal Mafia, Industrial unrests and Labor problems
- Green House Gases emissions and Global Warming.

Coal Based Power Plants

The principal use of coal is generation of electricity in Thermal Power Plants, which are normally sited adjacent to coal mines to avoid long distance transport of the raw material. This assumes importance when power plant coal can carry as high as 40% ash and longer transport of dead ash in raw coal is mere waste of energy. Thus Power Plants sited at mine heads add to the environmental problems in the already ecologically damaged coal fields. Common environmental problems arising out of coal based Power Plant are:

- Generation of a large amount of combustion residues in forms of Bottom Ash, Fly Ash and FGD Sulphate Sludge. They pile up and accumulate in Dumps (Dry Mounds), Tailing Dams, occupy large tracts of land creating what is known as "White Desert". Presently more than 100 million tons of Ash is generated in 110 and odd Thermal Power Plants in India. Only a small percent of the generated ash is used in cement manufacture and civil fabrications (Sahu,1991).
- The Fallout ash from stack and wind-blown particles from White Deserts combined, produce extreme degree of dust pollution resulting with wide spread pulmonary diseases among the inhabitants and extensive damage to land and foliage around. Emission of SO_2 and NO_X adversely add to the health hazards.
- Supernatant water of the Tailing Dam and leaching from Dry Dumps pollute surface and ground waters with Heavy Metals.
- Green House Gases emission from Power Plants is one of the principal sources of Global Warming.

Burning Issues of Coal Combustion

Mining of coal releases coal-bed-methane and combustion of coal produces CO_2, SO_X, NO_X, VOM (Volatile Organic Matters – Polyaromatic Hydrocarbons) and many easily volatile heavy metals like Pb, Zn, Cd, Hg, As, Se and Radio nuclides which continuously reach the atmosphere. Even the overburden materials like carbonaceous shale and sub-grade (uneconomic grade) coal, excavated and dumped on surface, on oxidation add the above harmful constituents to the atmosphere.

The carbon content of the coal varies from 60% in Brown coal to 90% in Anthracite. Lignite has a lesser amount of fixed carbon but higher amount of volatiles and Sulphur in form of marcasite (Fools' Gold) and both organic and inorganic Arsenic. Combustion of coal produces CO_2 three times its actual carbon content. Power Plants using Lignite, like those at Neyveli in TN, Kutch and Saurashtra in Gujarat, have larger SO_2 emission compared to those using Bituminous coals.

On average, coal also contains 0.34 to 130 ppm (gms/ton) of Arsenic, 0.01 to 1.6 ppm of Mercury, 0.01 to 300 ppm of Cadmium, 0.7 to 200 ppm of Lead and 3 ppm of Selenium (Pacyna *et al*, 1987), most being easily volatile and heavier than air, stay in near surface atmosphere and contribute to extreme degree of health damage.

Although the emissions from the Power Plant directly and visibly effect the local environment and are diluted in the vastness of the atmosphere and partly by the absorption capacity of land and ocean, they continuously accumulate in the Troposphere or circulate in Biosphere. The global impact of these deleterious constituents are slowly being realized by way of Global Warming or climatic changes and in appearance of respiratory, neurological ailments including wide prevalence of carcinogenesis in modern society. Heavy Metal pollution like that from Hg, Pb, Cd. As etc. commonly emitted elements in coal combustion are most effective when in lower concentrations. Therefore, their presence in low concentration in Power Plant emissions is all the more vulnerable to human health.

The Emission Factor of a coal based Power Plant varies widely depending on the quality of coal, ash content of the coal, technology of burning and efficiency of the Plant. With 40% efficiency and reasonable transmission loss, about one Kg. of coal will be needed to deliver one Kilowatt power to light a domestic lamp (60 to 100 Watt) for 24 hours. Average GHG emission of Power Plant coal for electricity generation has been estimated as:

For Indian Power Plants*	For USA (EPA)
CO_2: 0.90 to 0.95 Kg/KWH	1.1 Kg/KWH
SO_2: 6.94 to 7.20 gm/KWH (30 for Lignite)	6.5 gm/KWH
NO_x: 4.20 to 4.38 gm/KWH	3 gm/KWH

* Mittal *et al* (2014)

Guttikunda *et al* (2014) also reported estimates for emissions from 111 Power Plants of India with total installed capacity of 121 GW and burning 503 million tons of coal as:

580 Kilotons of Ash of < 2.5 micrometer (PM 2.5)

665 million tons of CO_2

21000 Kilotons of SO_2

2000 Kilotons of NO_X

1100 Kilotons of CO

100 Kilotons of VOC

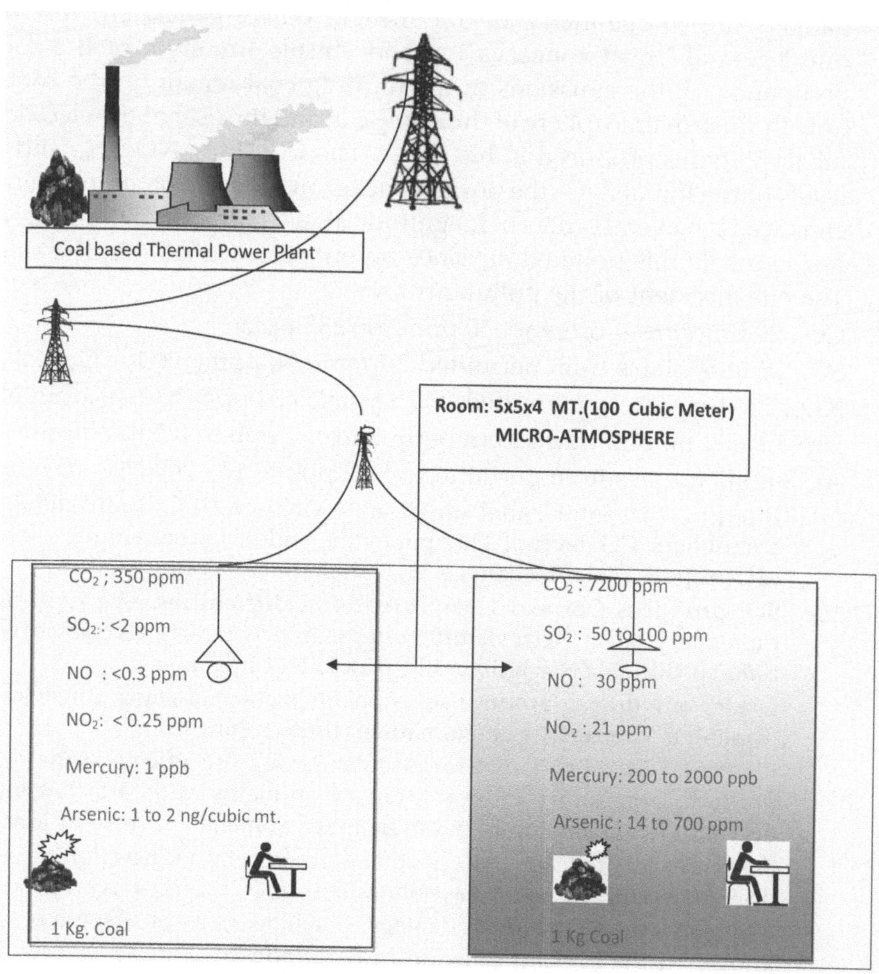

The health impact of which is estimated at 80,000 to 115,000 premature deaths and 20,000000 cases of asthma. For the average emissions of USA stated above, the health impact is reported at 24,000 premature deaths of which 2800 from lung cancer only.

Life in a Model of Micro-Atmosphere

In order to comprehend the environment impact of coal combustion on atmosphere a conceptual model is presented (vide illustration above) where:

1. The Tropospheric atmosphere which directly effects the life on earth but today stands polluted by fossil fuel burning is condensed to a closed room of 100 cubic meter.
2. An amount of one Kilogram of coal needed to generate 1 kilowatt electricity to keep a 100 watt lamp on for 24 Hrs. is allowed to be burnt to enable a "virtual Student" to study in the room. No other electrical

gadgets can be operated with the meager power generated from this one Kg. coal (most conservative and simple life style of the room occupant). All the emissions of the burning coal remain in the room - now the micro-atmosphere of the occupant, and the user of the electricity inhales what is produced in his usage. The CO_2, SO_X, NO_X, Hg and As levels of the Initial Air – the normal background levels of atmosphere is enhanced by several orders of magnitude after 24 hours and the occupant has to inhale this polluted air since no outlet is available in the room. The enhancement of the pollutants are:

CO_2: 20 times from present 350 ppm to 7233 ppm

SO_2: 25 to 50 times from permitted 2ppm to 50 ppm(100 for lignite)

NO_X: 100 times from permitted <0.25 ppm to 32 ppm NO, 21 ppm NO_2

Hg: 0.2 to 2 million times from permitted < 1 ppb to 0.2 to 2 ppm

As: 2 million times from permitted <1 - 2 ppb to 14 - 700 (Av. 300) ppm

- Intergovernmental Panel on Climate Change (IPCC) stipulates an atmospheric CO_2 level of 450 ppm by the middle of the century to avoid catastrophic climatic changes.
- SO_2 produces Corneal Haze, breathing difficulties, eye irritation, pulmonary edema, circulatory collapse and is clearly associated with asthma, chronic bronchitis in old people and infants.
- Oxides of Nitrogen produce atmospheric ozone and smog, cause lower respiratory damages, asthma, nausea, fluid in lungs.
- Elemental Mercury is neuromuscular toxic, also effects kidney and produces respiratory failure. Mercury on methylation effects central nervous system leading to paralysis (refer Minamata disease of Japan).
- Arsenic exposure leads to dermatitis, skin cancer and ingestion through drinking water, damages gastrointestinal tract, enlarges liver, produce black foot disease and brain damage. Carcinogenicity of Arsenic is well known in the present episode in Bangladesh.

Thus complex damage to the health of the occupant in the study room (Micro-atmosphere) arising out of high concentration of pollutants is a foregone conclusion.

3. There is no scope of opening of the room in any front to ventilate and dilute the pollutants of the room, because every facets open into another room which has unlimited electricity consuming appliances like, fans, air-conditioners, heaters, ovens, refrigerators, grinders, washers and what not, besides the bizarre of illumination extravaganza at homes, work-place, markets, streets, stadium and every celebrations round the year. The micro-atmosphere of the room with conservative use of electrical energy if found unhealthy to live, the immediate "mega-atmosphere" (lower region of Troposphere) ought to be more inhospitable for normal development of life. The vastness of the atmosphere, recuperation capacity of Nature, the Eco-scavengers of the

emissions such as ocean, soil and vegetation and perhaps the homeostasis of Earth (Gaia of Lovelock,1995) protect but keep the humanity limping along the evolutionary slope of modern development and progress. It is clear that the Anthropocene period triggered by the discovery and use of fossil fuel has already led to craving for a sustainable development (Search for a Sustainocene period) in human history, because the present has become a tyranny of the future.

4. The above modular analysis has been made to bring home the hidden cost of electricity and to arouse awareness that every time one "abuses" the use of electricity, the victim is none but the self. As such, as much as 60% of the world's energy used today stands abused.

REFERENCES

Guttikunda, S.K. & Puja Jawahar. 2014. Atmospheric Emission and Pollution from Coal Fired Thermal Power Plants in India. Atmospheric Env., v. 92, pp. 449-460.

Lovelock James. 1995. The Ages of Gaia – A Biography of our Living Earth. N.W. Norton & Co., 288 p.

Mittal, M.L., Shrama.C. & Richa Singh.2014. Estimation of Emissions from Coal Fired Thermal Power Plants in India. www.epa.gov/...mmital (PDF –Google)

Pacyna, Jozef M. 1987. Atmospheric Emission of As, Cd, Pb and Hg from High Temperature Processes in Power Generation. In Pb, Cd, Hg in Environment. Ch. 7 (Ed. Hutchinson & Mema). SCOPE. John Wiley & Sons.

Sahu. K.C. (Ed.). 1991. International Conference on Env. Impact of Coal Utilization, Proceeding. IIT-Bombay.

8 Solar Energy Exploitation

An Alternative but with a Cost

Worldwide, 41% of the electrical consumption comes from coal, which adds 44% of 32 GT of Carbon dioxides added to the atmosphere annually. For India and China more than 70% of the power comes from coal combustion. Blessed with huge reserves of coal China is known to add one 1000 MW thermal plant every week and India is poised to increase the same. The most optimistic projected plan to limit the global temperature rise to 2°C(3.6°F) by 2050 when the present 387 PPM of CO_2 is likely to be stabilized at 450 ppm, requires a variety of *Alternative* non-carbon energy resources. *Alternative* energy sources from Nuclear, Solar, Wind, Geothermal and Bio-fuel (Genetic Algae) have shown commercial viability and countries like France and Japan with no coal resources have gone heavily on nuclear energy.

For a stabilized CO_2 level of 450 PPM by 2050, an American Scientist Saul Griffith, quoted by Stewart Brand (2009) proposes that humanity is to lower the fossil fuel use to generate only 3 Terawatt (TW) power and produce the rest of the requirements through *Alternatives* only. The present level of 16 TW of world's annual usage of power (Average per capita use multiplied by world population) should be met by 3 TW of Fossil Fuels, 2 TW each of Solar Thermal, Solar Photo Voltaic, Wind Turbine, Geothermal, Biofuel and 3 TW of Nuclear energy if the 450 ppm is to be achieved by 2050. To produce the required *Alternatives* the following efforts and installations are necessary during a period of next 25 years:

1. For 2 TW Solar PV: 100 sq. m. of 15% efficient solar cells every second for next 25 yrs. (1200 sq. miles of solar cells a year, in 25 years: 30,000 sq. miles of solar cells).
2. For 2 TW of Solar Thermal: 50 sq. m. of highly reflective mirror every second for next 25 years (600 sq. miles a year amounting to 15000 sq. miles of mirror surface).
3. For 2 TW of Wind energy: 300 ft. dia. Wind turbines every minute (105,000 turbines a year in windy locations, continue for 25 years).
4. For 2 TW of Geothermal: Build 3 nos. 300 MW steam turbines every 5 minutes, 1095 a year for 25 years.
5. For 2 TW of Biofuels: 4 Olympic Swimming Pool size Algal Ponds for GM algae every seconds (61,000 Sq. miles a year for 25 year)

6. For 3 TW of Nuclear: A 3-Reactors, 3 GW plant every week, 52 a year for 25 years.

To add up the requirements of all the Alternatives a land mass of the size of Australia is required, covered with stuffs dedicated to generating world's energy requirements to cap the atmospheric CO_2 at 450 ppm by 2050. The *Alternative* energy land be named *"Renewsthan"* says Saul Griffith and concludes that the effort is technically possible but politically doubtful.

An Artist's Dream of "Renewsthan" (*Courtesy:* Google).

The most promising *Alternative* that stands out as the panacea of human energy need (greed ?) is Solar energy. But a new dimension of adverse impacts of "Solar Energy Exploitation" is brought out here and narrated below:

Perils of Solar Exploitation: An antithesis of solar energy exploitation. (21st Lecture Series, delivered in ESWARA, Hyderabad, 2014).

Limitation of capacity building in hydel power, radiation threat of fissile fuels and problems of carbon emission in fossil fuel burning, virtually compel the energy hungry world to go for non-conventional energy resources. Among all the non-conventional energy resources, solar energy, by far, appears to be the most favored, because its availability is unlimited and use is considered to be pollution free. Each year the sun delivers to earth more than 10,000 times the energy that humans currently use. Not only is solar energy alone sufficiently abundant to meet all the day's energy needs thousands of times over, harnessing within certain limit is not particularly land or resources intensive. Even a simple roof top solar installation on a 800 sq. ft. terrace would supply enough power to meet limited domestic requirements of electricity in a modern Indian home. Technological breakthrough for commercialization of solar energy is very much on agenda. Solar thermal technique being time specific, solar photovoltaic (SPV) technique for tapping of sun's energy with suitable storage facility has gone a step forward. Manufacture of PV-cells requires a number of hazardous materials including many chemicals and heavy metals used in semiconductor electronic industry, but the problems can be minimized by suitable technology and equipments. But the basic element Silicon, needed for manufacture of SPV cells poses a threat in different dimension that has never been hitherto focused.

Silicon, Group IV element, is a semimetal, and like aluminum, arsenic, selenium, and tellurium, it lies on the border of the metal-nonmetal boundary in the Periodic Table. Chemically in many ways, it resembles germanium, selenium and aluminum. However, unlike those three, its toxicity (metabolic impact on the organic kingdom) is least known, primarily because, native elemental silicon does not exist on the earth even if it is the most abundant element in the crust. The case was similar with aluminum until a couple of centuries ago; the metal was so scarce that the emperor of France had the proud privilege of dining with aluminum utensils. Its profuse circulation and use in modern society (aluminum is a poor man's utensil and an affluent society's wrapper) has revealed the possibility of brain damage in human beings, which is known as Alzheimer's disease.

The Pollution Index of a metal increases with its Technophyllitic Index, that is, the extent of its use in society. The Technophyllitic Index is defined by the ratio of annual global production of a metal, and its Clark value in the Crust. Pollution Index is defined by the amount of metal present in the environment (air, water, and soil) over and above the background values. Obviously, the larger the production and use of a metal, the greater the possibility of its leakage from the utility cycle into the environment. There are indisputable examples of metal toxicity consequent to prolific use of specific metals. For example, extensive use of lead for plumbing and for curing wine in lead vats is considered to have caused lead toxicity and the decline of the Roman Empire.

In view of man's demand for energy and the search for a clean, nonpolluting source, solar energy appears to be a panacea. Capture of solar energy requires use of silicon-based photovoltaic cell. Production of elemental silicon is chemical intensive, some 500 to 1000 chemicals are used for imprinting electronic circuits on silicon wafers. Production of a six inches silicon wafer results in 14 kg. of solid waste and 11,000 liters of waste water. Extensive use of silicon in most human activities is clearly envisaged in future. In all aspects, future human species will be virtually surrounded and soaked in silicon wafer to collect and process solar energy received in every possible occasions. That means an increased Pollution Index of hitherto unavailable elemental silicon. The unlimited stock of solar energy, abundance of silica on earth and ever-growing ceaseless demand of energy will compound exploitation and abuse (presently happening).

In an oxygen-dominated siliceous Crust, evolution of thousands of species of silicate minerals by polymerization of Silicon Oxygen Tetrahedra was the most probable mechanism in Nature. Development of a series of clay minerals in the crucial interphase of the lithosphere, hydrosphere, and atmosphere is a subsequent process of silicate mineral genesis. Clay minerals are considered to exhibit primeval life processes such as growth by repetition, reproduction of identical types, and absorption (eating)-desorption (excreting), etc. and show that silicon, the dominant constituent in the lithosphere, was destined to trigger and evolve into a life system (Crain-Smith hypothesis). In any natural phenomenon the daughter products (offspring) ought to bear close relationship to the physiochemical characters of the parent (source). Thus, life ought to have been naturally siliceous in a silicon-rich Crust. However, the complacency (strong covalency) of silicon in the COSY space of Si-O tetrahedral site resulted in its strong immobility. By chemical coincidence, the tetrahedrally coordinated space of oxygen has almost the same size as that of the Si4+ion (0.41A0)to put the cation in a tightest fit. In contrast, the relatively smaller carbon, although a minor constituent in the Crust and manifested in a variety of states (solid, liquid and gas as well as in a large number of organic polymers), proliferated and reigned supreme, relegated silicon to the background in the developing units of life on the early earth. Consequently, 'the aspiring to form life' Silicates merely became a substrate for organic development by versatile carbon in the primeval hydrosphere. Silicon lost and life became carbonaceous.

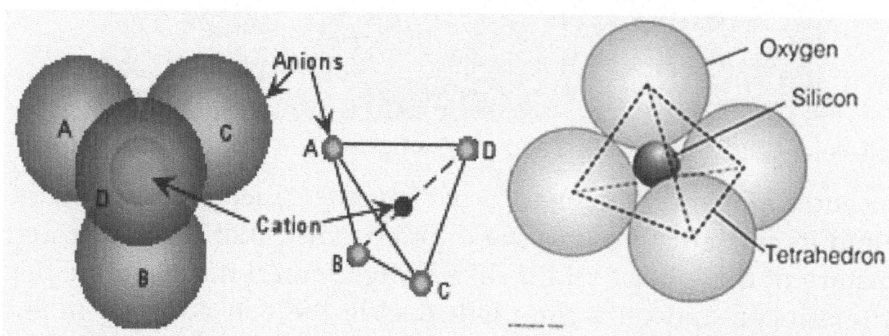

The "COSY"0.41 Aº tetrahedral space of Si in Clay mineral makes it complacent (strongly covalent) and prevents mobility unlike the Carbon atom which is only 0

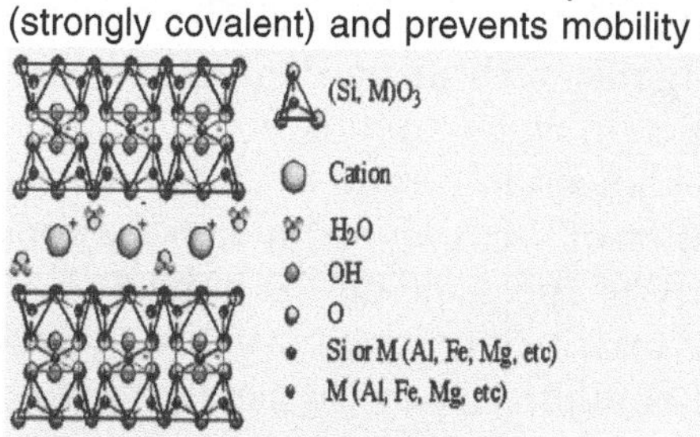

Clay mineral structure (TOT) with ion exchangeable layers

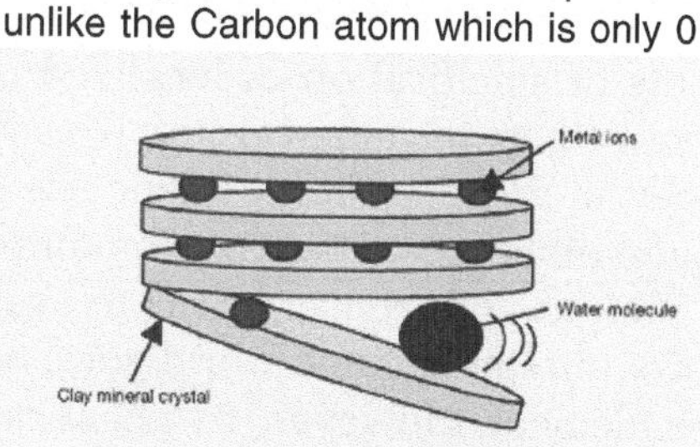

Clay minerals can "Eat" and "Excrete" Cations and Anions

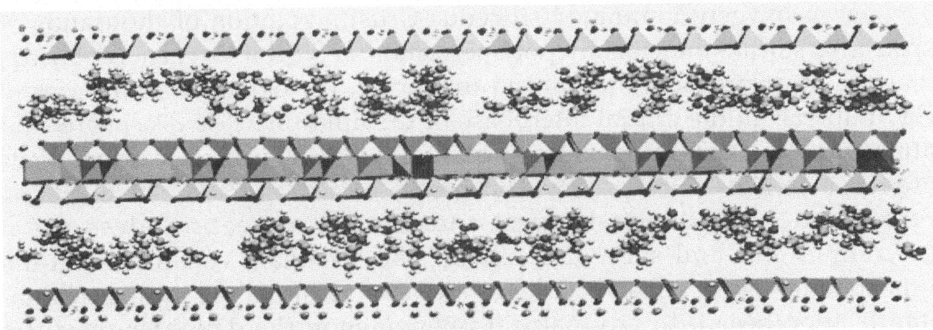

The series of triangles are Silicon-Oxygen Tetrahedra, the green strip is Aluminum-Oxygen Octahedra and the blue granules are Exchangeable ions in the ("*Food pipe*") of clay mineral.

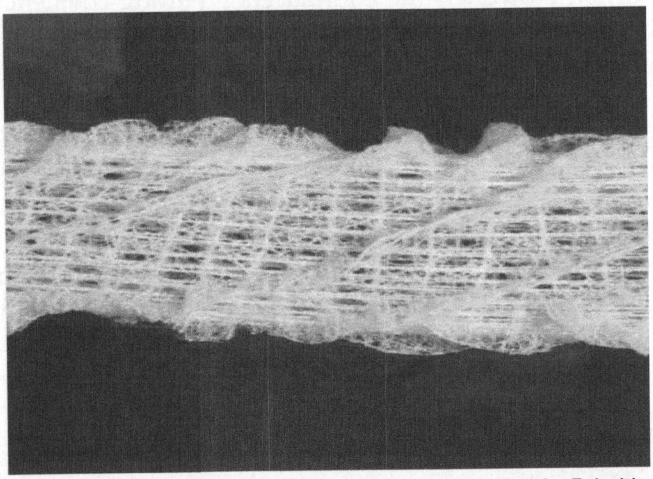

Skeletal Silica Framework Supports Carbonaceous gel in Primitive Life

The anthropogenic rejuvenation of elemental silicon for tapping of solar energy and its introduction into the organic world that has never occurred in the history of this planet will be like bringing onto the stage the defeated competitor silicon and only time will decide the consequence of such an invitation. As such, silicification of wood and microorganisms in fossils clearly reveal the replacement zeal of silicon in the organic world. There have been spots of silicification in localized organs, such as hardening of veins and bones where the impact is total destruction of the carbonaceous living tissues, albeit in micro scale. Cosmetic use of silicon in certain body parts has been found disastrous. Therefore implantation of *Very Chip* on humans for tracking, is viewed with concern. It is too early to speculate on the impact of silicon entry into the organic world since no toxicity studies have yet been done for the element. However, its chemical similarity with Ge, Se etc. shows that silicon is potentially toxic and needs to be handled carefully. Some silicon compounds are also used as a rodenticide. If Selenium toxicity is a cause of dinosaurs' extinction, Solar exploitation will be a chime of our death knell due to environmental silicon toxicity. The technology of tapping solar energy, therefore is in no way different from the introduction of atomic energy. The world is still learning to cope with repercussions of the chemical revolution and will soon plunge into the electronic age. To avoid surprising side effects and unanticipated feedback loop a more holistic view of the world and a better understanding of the kinds of connections is needed and not merely a technological option, however promising it appears to be. The search for a clean source of energy for the future world should not end by inducting an element of societal disaster.

Relevant quotations on Solar Exploitation:

— "The Light that enlightens, becomes blinding when in excess."

— "Suryat Bhawanti Bhutani, Suryena Palita Ni Cha,

Surye Layam Praptabanti, yah Suryah So Aham Eba Hi."

–Gita

—An Odia Folk song, saying : Woe of a Mother Vulture who brought a snake to feed her baby but the fodder swallowed the baby instead.

"Hari Hey, Guhari Karibi Kahaku **... (Oh' God whom do I complain)**

Chhuara Nimante Ahara Anili **... (Fetched foods for the children)**

Ahara Khaila Chhuaku **... (The fodder swallowed the children)"**

9 Electromagnetic Radiation Pollution

The Type Man Never Knew

Celebration of "World Days" for various environmental issues has been established by UNDP to bring awareness among people. For example, "Ozone Day" celebrated on the 16th Sept. every year is a reminder that in our enthusiasm for AC-comfort, fast automotive mobility and indiscriminate use of aerosol cans and bottles, we have punctured the stratospheric ozone shield that once protected earth from deadly ultra violet radiation coming out of sun. The result is our health and environment faces threat from UV-radiation pollution. UV-radiation is only a minuscule of a gamut of Electromagnetic Radiation (EMR) around us and that too is created by our enthusiasm for use of a variety of gadgets and appliances at homes and office. The environment conscious world is seized with pollution threats from pesticides and heavy metals in food and water; automotive exhausts, acid rains and global warming; waste disposals; nuclear waste, leakages and accidents, but barely aware of this new form of pollution "*Radiation Pollution, precisely the EMR- pollution*" which pervades everywhere and every when, 24 hours a day- unless one lives in some remote corner of the planet. EMR is a radiant energy of accelerated electrons or photons, travelling as waves or particles and commonly known as gamma rays, X-Rays, UV and visible light rays, Laser, Infra-red, Radar or microwaves or those under various frequencies of Radio-TV propagation and high voltage transmission. Unlike the conventional pollution which takes place due to pollutants, which are substances or organic materials like metals, plastics, gases, salts, chemicals and bacteria, Radiation Pollution takes place through energy radiation that soaks us but can not be filtered and felt, seen or smelt or even mapped and measured through PUC tests and equipments. Radiation Pollution is a passive form of pollution that has both chronic and explosive impacts on health and environment in a modern progressive society.

Depending on wavelength and frequency, the EMR can be grouped into two types:

1. The **Ionizing Radiation**, coming out of cosmic rays, nuclear fission and fusion, mining, processing and use of radioactive minerals, radioisotopes use, x-rays and to some extent the short wave UV-rays, all of which are harmful to health and environment. When exposed, Ionising Radiation

can induce burn, cancer, tumour, leukaemia, fatal foetal damage, defective births, chromosome aberration, DNA damage, mutation and other abnormalities till unknown to us.

2. The **Nonionizing Radiation**, covers a large range of wave length and lower frequency from UV to visible lights, Infrareds, Microwaves, and Radio-TV transmission, all of which are passive pollutants in the environment.

Either of the radiation types can be natural or artificial, but it is the artificial radiations which now threat the global ecology and the environment.

NonIonising Radiation------------➔...Ionising Radiation------------➔ in Mtr.

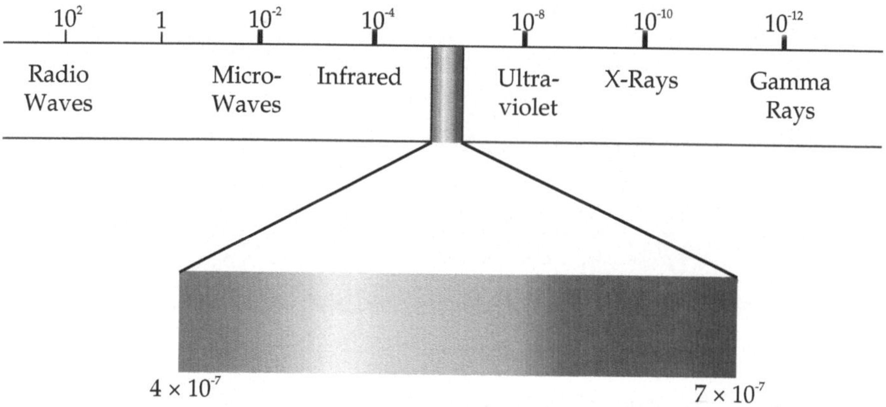

Ionization Radiation: *Cosmic radiation* originating from outer space and modulated by solar winds continuously impinges earth's atmosphere. These radiations are charged particles, 90% proton, 9% Helium nuclei (Alpha particle) and 1% electrons (Beta particles) and having energy level in the order of 10^{20} eV, when man could artificially generate a maximum of 10^{12-13} eV. But for the protection of mother earth through an umbrella of magnetic field which makes our atmosphere opaque to these high energy cosmic bullets, life on earth would have been totally ionised and blown out into the abysmal space. Earth's magnetic field is weaker at the poles where the ionization produces the spectacular glows of aurora. While the threat from exposure to cosmic radiation to astronauts during their space flight is taken care of, the common man now travelling in high altitude commercial flight faces similar threats, although in a lesser degree.

Earth has a small amount of radioactive materials evenly dispersed in crust. The spontaneous reaction (fission) of these produces enough heat to compensate heat loss by radiation and has prevented a frozen death for our planet. However, mining, concentration and production of enriched stocks of these materials generates *radioactive pollution* and background radiation in the environment and consequently, rightly resented by local residents. Man made radioactive emission has increased since 1950 and 60 because of nuclear weapon tests, various accidents, leakages and disposals of radioactive wastes world over.

Sun **Earth**

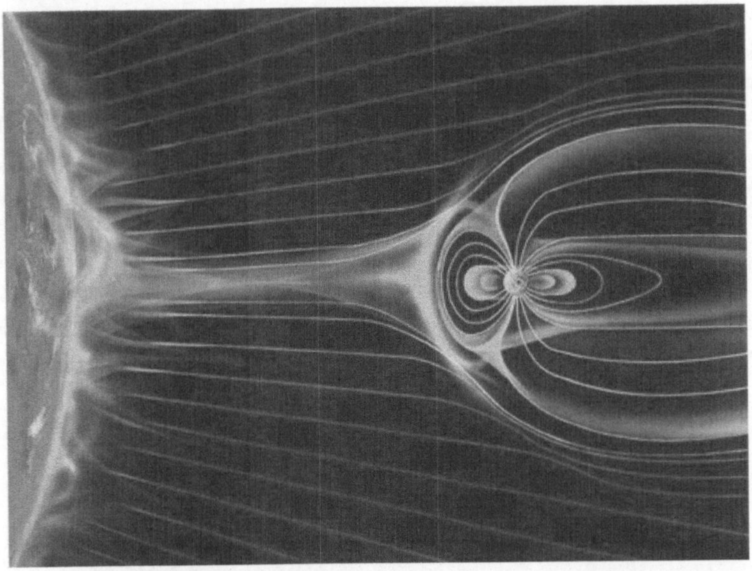

Earth's Magnetic Umbrella Protects us from Cosmic Radiation

Coal used for power generation also carries small concentration of uranium and other radioactive nuclides. A Canadian Scientist has estimated that annual mining and burning of coal world over brings out to the surface about 200,000 tons of uranium which freely moves in the biosphere and whose impact on background radiation is little understood. Similarly, according the calculation of a Project at Bombay IIT, a 2000 MW coal fired power plant using 8 million tons of coal per year (with 5 ppm Uranium) would spread about 40 tons of uranium around the plant. The apex radiation research laboratory (ORNL) in USA reports that a normal size coal fired thermal plant disperse to the environment an amount of U-235 equivalent to a dozen feeds of a nuclear reactor. Since the radionuclides accumulate year after year, a century of coal combustion in thermal power plants world over would elevate the global anthropogenic radiation to a level of "Subdued Nuclear Evening" without going into large scale nuclear warfare. No wonder, a coal based thermal plant is considered more vulnerable than a nuclear power plant when it comes to hidden fall outs. However few will like to have a nuclear power plants at their back yard (NIMBY-Not In My Backyard) but fail to realise the radionuclide pollution arising out of a coal based power plant.

Another common source of radiation pollution is release of radon gas and fission products from construction materials like sandstone, granites and fly ash that go into building of our homes and offices. Many developed countries have laid down radiation limits for construction materials, especially for homes where people spend a greater part of their life time.

Medical practices including x-rays, radio-isotope therapy, disinfection, food irradiation and disposal of radioactive products cause radiation pollution of the environment.

NonIonizing Radiation: The UV and visible lights make up an insignificant range in EMR but have significant ecological impact on life of plants, insects and animals including humans. *UV radiation* is known to damage chlorophyll in plants, kills microbes and bacteria in water purification and medical sterilization, but when it comes to humans produces skin burn, melanoma (a type of skin cancer) and cataract. In US, Canada and Australia where UV-rays entry to atmosphere is high the media publishes daily UV-Index, warning sunbathers and people working on open ground of excessive exposure to UV-radiation. The bright white light of fluorescent tubes, CFL and mercury vapour lamps carry a high level of UV component and is known to damage vision especially in growing children. Welding torch emits large amount of UV radiation and is blinding and painful to eyes. Many developed countries have changed their street lights to sodium vapour lamps to avoid UV radiation pollution.

Photons of light at various wavelengths across the visible spectrum imbibe different quality of stimuli to life. The *blue* end of the spectrum is cool- so are the colour of the ocean and our blue planet, because polarisation of light through water cuts out a large amount of energy of photonic vibration. The median of the visible spectrum is *green* and represents colour of the natural world and means growth from the word "Growan". The *saffron* tinge at the orange-red end represents dawn, purity, truth and renunciation in several religions.

Irrespective of socioecological stimulus at various wave lengths, the planetary life is greatly conditioned by the circadian cycle of day and night. Plants lose their chlorophyll, turn pale, growth and productivity retarded, so is the human pigmentation lost and production of vitamin D ceases in absence of light. Biological clock of insects, birds, animals and man are jeopardised when natural light cycle is disturbed. At least 300 insect species are known to use natural polarised light as primary source of navigation, baby sea turtles are guided to nearest water body soon after hatching. Damage of navigational instinct of nocturnal insects under artificial light pollution effects pollination of night blooms. Consistent studies have shown that under urban glows of Europe, Robins are chirping at night, where as at our door step at Hiranandani Gardens, Bombay, cuckoos can be heard singing well before dawn (for feeding and breeding). Excess, deficiency and unnatural light exposures have adverse health effects- people in night shift duty have psychological problems, sleep disorder, excess light induces loss of visual acuity, hypertension, headache, effects growth, maturity, confidence, hunger, sexual habits and increased incidence of carcinoma. Suppression of nocturnal production of melatonin hormone in body leads to added risk of breast cancer in women. Stubborn criminals are made to submit to confession under strong light beam; rapid flashes can induce epilepsy, trance and neurosis as in Javes and Discos. Scramble of insects even to the point of death around fires or lamp-post in the darkness of night is an intoxication of light pollution. The morning grave yard under the lamp post is in no way different to some of world's urban congregations, the pillar of attraction of material resources. Like any other resources, excess of which sets in pollution, light too, which enables vision can be blinding.

One of the serious impacts of light pollution is nocturnal urban haze which prevents millions of people from enjoying star studded beauty of night sky. Few urban children today behold a milky way or are capable of spotting the Pole Star in the northern horizon. Obviously, interest in Astronomy becomes the first victim, the grandeur and vastness of the universe in the growing minds is relegated to the background and replaced by a feeling of repealing darkness by artificial illumination- a sense of victory over the Nature. We lay the seeds of subjugation of Nature at the very childhood.

Urban haze not only effects astronomical observations, when considered from utilization of lighting energy, the financial implication is astronomical. The illumination lost into the atmosphere from street light alone is estimated to be about 300 MW in UK and astronomically large in some of the illuminated cities like Las Vegas and Chicago in US. Obviously increased urban illumination has not been found to decrease urban crime, but has increased it. Urban illumination not only diverts light energy to the sky where it is not needed, but in doing so add extra dose of carbon dioxide to the atmosphere and add fuel to Global Warming.

EMR pollution in the range of microwave and Radio-TV propagation has become an issue of great controversy after the proliferation of the society with mobile phones and appearance of a large number of microwave towers over the horizon for reception and propagation. Amidst the controversy, WHO, in its preliminary report denied evidence of EMR pollution but surprisingly acknowledged "its influence on environment but not on the people" and kept the issue open for further investigation. However, large number of research and studies has concluded that Electromagnetic Radiation coming out of microwave and Radio-TV masts, cell-phones, micro ovens, NMR, MRI and high tension power lines have adverse effects on health and environment. Proven effects of the EM-radiation are: cognitive impairment, memory deficiency, EEG modification, DNA damage, chromosome aberration, micronucleus formation, and foetal malformation, increase permeability to blood - brain barrier, altered cellular calcium reflux and cell proliferation. At least 33 of 35 well known international studies have made a conclusive link between brain tumour, leukaemia and other forms of cancer, auditory damage, and breast cancer in women and sperm count decrease in man. Eye strain, headache,, inability to concentrate, neck ache, irritability, depression, memory loss and weaken immune system are some of the common symptoms of Electromagnetic Field (EMF) stress.

The US Environmental Protection Agency has publicly acknowledged existence of serious threats from EMR pollution. Looking into the abuse of mobile phones, the Telecommunication Department, Govt. of India has warned young children and pregnant women to refrain from avoidable use of mobile phones. The manufacturers too have advised children with soft skull to refrain from keeping the phone close to the ear and adult to use speaking kits or radiation protection covers on the cell-phone. Many countries prohibit erection of mobile towers near school, hospitals and residential buildings. In India, for a few bit of financial support from the mobile servicers, many housing societies invite installation of mobile mast over their building at an unknown risk to health of residents of their society and adjacent buildings. A recent press report by Govt. of Maharastra says that, of the 510 mobile towers in Navi Mumbai and surrounding region, 118 are authorised and 332 are awaiting clearance, demolition or their case for demolition pending in the Supreme Court of India. Even the Government has constituted a scientific committee to go into the issue of health effects of use of mobile phones across the vast spectrum of the society. With two billion people using cell-phones world over, we are under the largest clinical trial ever conducted.

10

Jaitapur *Mon Amour*

On Nuclear Power Plant in Ratnagiri District

The Oscar winning film "Hiroshima *Mon Amour*" of 1959 was shot not on any such theme as horrors of nuclear bomb over Hiroshima but on a 36 hrs. transient love affair of a French lady with a Japanese man. The intense love scenes are dotted with memory of past flirting of the French lady with a German soldier. This title "Jaitapur *Mon Amour*" does not attempt to deal with the menace of the proposed Nuclear Power Plant (NPP) but examines the long term environmental events and socio-ecological consequences of a "determined attitude"(love ?) of a class of modernists – Scientocrats, Bureaucrats and Politicians, for setting up of a "French Tech." Nuclear Power Plant at Jaitapur, Ratnagiri District of Maharashtra.

It is true that when energy generation from fossil fuels like coal and oil is beset with atmospheric carbon emission, vagaries of monsoon bring great restriction on hydel generation and green technology of solar and wind energy has remained a pipe- dream, nuclear power is a tempting offer. India's "*Bhavaian*" legacy for nuclear research which made "Buddha Smile" during Dr.Ramana's regime and the ceaseless demand of electrical energy by industrial and urban centers of Maharashtra undoubtedly led Govt. of Maharashtra to pursue hard for the platter of Jaitapur NPP offered by the French company. Some experts feel that the French technology is new and costly and many environmental activists have raised scare-crow of Chernobyl disaster regarding the safety aspects of the Plant and opposed its intrusion into an agrarian ecology. The Govt. of India with a dedicated group of experts on site evaluation for the proposed nuclear Plant had earlier declared the Jaitapur site as the most ideal; even MOEF had given a green signal for the project, but the subsequent Fukushima episode in Japan gave a sudden brake to the progress of the project. However, intense lobbing and leadership of a technocrat CM like Prithviraj Chavan of Maharashtra, has put the derailed band-wagon back on to rails and the project appears to be on move.

A neutral analysis of socio-ecological development and long term scenario of environmental stability that revolve around the Jaitapur NPP, seems to be the need of the day.

The entire West Coast of India is dotted with industrial hubs, Power Plants, Ports & Harbors and densely populated centers, prominent among which is the city of Mumbai. The seismotectonic scenario and the possibilities of natural disasters that can trigger catastrophic tsunamis in the coastal region is intimately related to the geology and geomorphology of the Arabian Sea ocean floor (Fig. 10.2). Oceanic Ridges are major lines of magmatic exhalation/ exudation and new land accretion (Fig. 10.1). The Oceanic ridges in Indian ocean pour out hot magma from deep subcrustal zone, pushes the Indian Plate northward and produce Plate subduction south of Himalayan belt. Whereas seismic activities are common along the Himalayan subduction zone on sudden Plate movement, volcanoes and accretion of ridges at the trailing plate edge could similarly produce large displacement of oceanic water on sudden activation. As such, tsunamis and sea incursion have been reported along Makrana coast and Gujarat coast (submerged Dwaraka) earlier and future possibility cannot be ruled out.

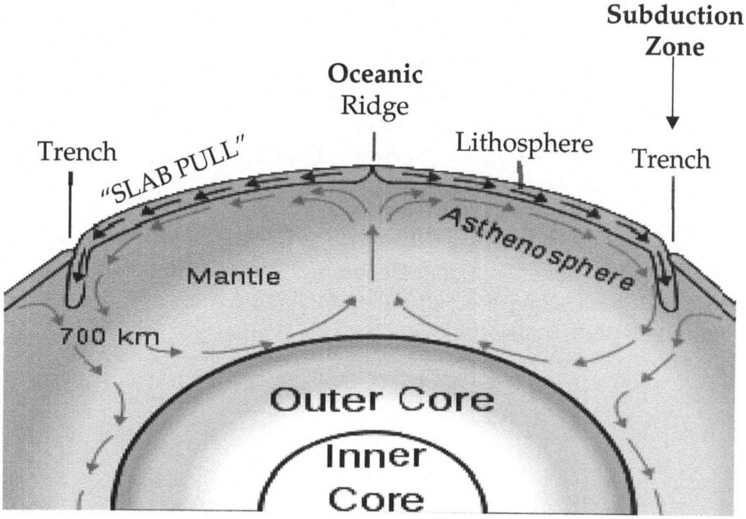

Fig. 10.1: Formation of Oceanic Ridge and Trench (Subduction Zone) on Earth

A major crustal displacement that is in progress is breaking up of a land mass in Eastern Africa, along the African Rift Valley and drifting (pushing) of the same into the Arabian Sea. Consequence of such an event in Arabian Sea in generating tsunami and impact on the West Coast of India is beyond imagination.

Coming to the Indian Shield: To most Geologists, the sharp NNW trend of the West Coast of India represents a Fault line and "Fault lines" are planes along which the crustal rocks slip and generate earth quakes. Even the various Estuaries and Creeks in Mumbai have been assigned to be lying along ten such Fault lines (Fig. 10.3). The 1998 Uran earth quake was in the junction of three such Fault line and where one of India's largest petroleum complex is located

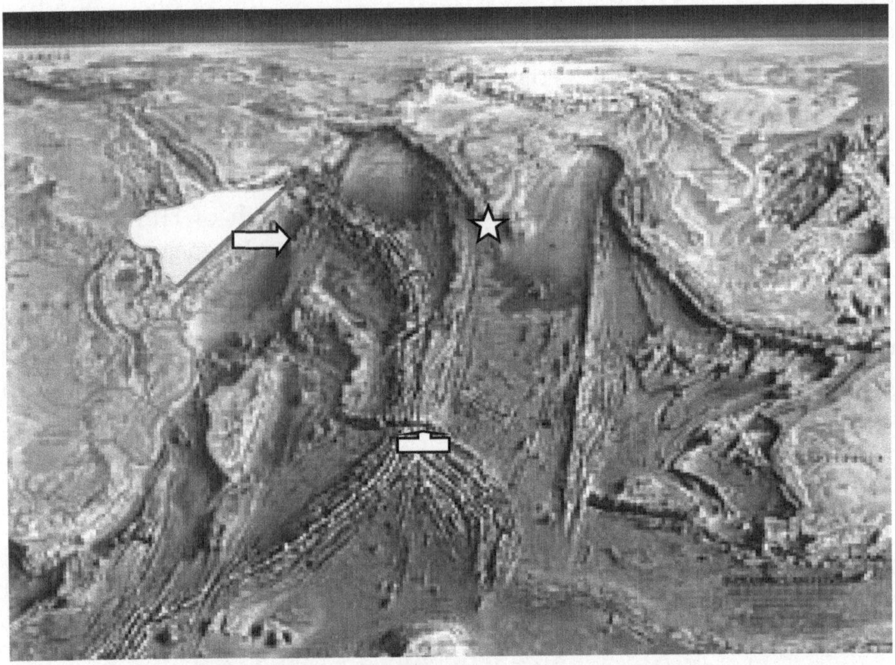

Oceanic Ridge ⇨ African Rift ☆ Nuclear Power Plant site

Fig. 10.2: The Oceanic Ridges in Indian Ocean and Arabian Sea. Land mass can brea k off East Africa along the Rift Valley (coloured pink) and generate tsunami of unprecedented scale

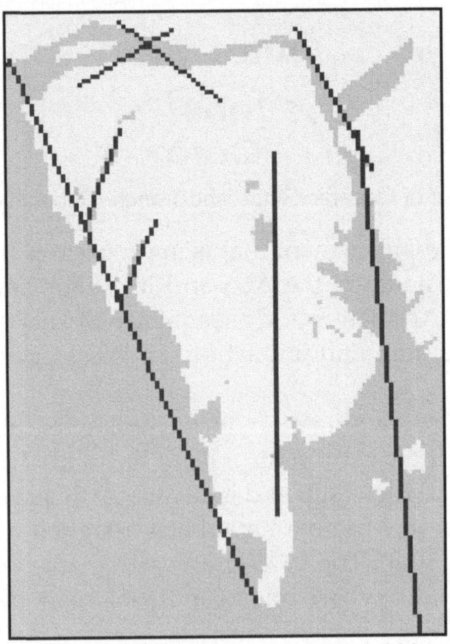

Fig. 10.3: A Fault Ridden Island City of Mumbai

A right angle bend of Koyna river and abnormally straight course there after, just south of the dam is also a clear Fault line, but was not taken seriously when the dam was constructed. The recent decision by the Ministry of Earth Sciences to drill a few Km long hole at this site to understand the seismotectonicity of the region, is a welcome sign.

The Indian Shield is known to have several Rift zones, Grabens, Fault lines and Lineaments that are known to be active in recent geological past. The Koyana and Kurduvadi Rifts below Deccan Trap Volcanic, the Narmada & Cambay Grabens and the Narmada – Son Lineament (both Narmada and Son rivers flow in opposite direction but along a perfect straight line) are some such tectonic features which are known to have produced major earth quakes in recent times.

West Coast Earth Quakes

1891, June 16th	Kutch, Gujarat	Magnitude 8
1956, july 21st	Anjar, Gujarat	Mgt. 7
1967, Dec 10th	Koyana	Mgt. 6.5
1993, Sept 30th	Latur	Mgt. 6.3
2001, Jan. 26th	Bhuj	Mgt. 7.7

Mumbai Earth Quakes

Year	Magnitude	Year	Magnitude
1618, May	9	1967, April	4.5
1832, Oct.	7	1967, June	4.2
1906, March	6	1993, Sept.	6.4
1929, Feb.	5	1998, May	3.8
1951, April	8	2005, March	5.1
1966, May	5	2005, June	3.7
2005, Aug.	4.1		

The fact that, the thick pile of volcanic rocks which once covered half of Indian subcontinent but today occupies an area of only 512 thousand sq.km. in Deccan region, represent out pouring of molten lava that destroyed all forms of life including the dinosaurs, only 60 million years before, goes to show that the Deccan Plateau is "sitting over volcanoes".

The utter ignorance of many Scientists (Scientocrats ?) and laissez faire of Geologists in particular, is the little known Panvel Flexure which extends some 250 km. from south Gujarat to Ratnagiri almost parallel to the West Coast, has a relatively thinner crust and dotted with hot springs. Presence of a hot magmatic plume below the flexure zone is considered most likely. The rise of the plume has tilted the originally horizontal volcanic layers towards west. The tilt is clearly seen around Mumbai region. Obviously the plume rise is after Deccan volcanism and its future activity or progress is anybody's guess. Any such rise along the hinge of the flexure will simply shake and slide down all contents over the entire West Coast, into the Arabian Sea – a watery grave in geologic scale. Such episodes are not uncommon in earth's history.

Recent earth quakes at Koyana and Latur have changed the earth quake zoning in India (Fig. 10.4). Indian Shield once considered a stable region, cannot be confidentially said so. So also, no expert can opine on the magnitude of the quake that would occur in an earth quake prone zone. Designing of a structure to face quake of certain magnitude is a "Commercial Astrology".

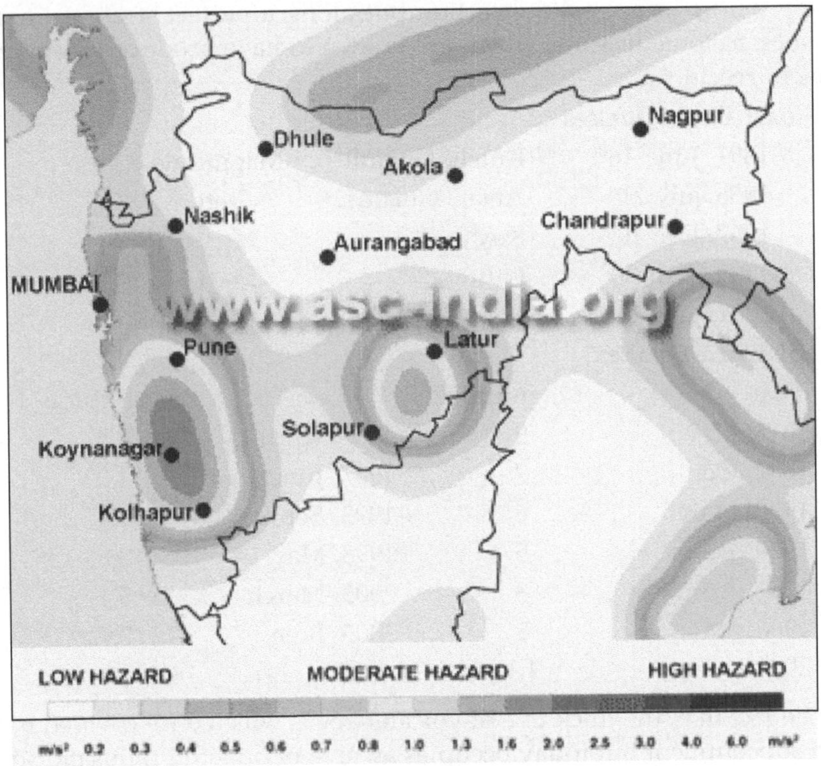

Fig. 10.4. Seismic Zones of India

In view of all that are narrated above, setting up of a NPP at Jaitapur must be examined more carefully and not by a mere determination to bring "Energy Ganga" to the thirsty urban life.

Raising of a banner of Inconvenient Truth: The present conflict in Jaitapur is not for the risk of tectonic instability of the region but against land acquisition and ecological damage. Whether it is Nandigram in West Bengal for setting up of an Automobile factory, Posco in Orissa for a Steel Plant, Vizag Coast in AP for a Power Plant, Raigad Dist. In Maharashtra for the SEZ and now Jaitapur near Ratnagiri, the industrial and urban aggression tends to exploit agrarian natural ecosystem with force and political power under the pretext of progress and regional development. The major beneficiaries of Jaitapur "Utility" being the industrial belts and the urban centers of Mumbai and Pune, the question may be asked "why cant the Plant be sited at the backyard of the beneficiaries?" After all, the fish loving Japanese and our fellow Indians, the Bengalis, maintain fish ponds right in the backyard of their home to get their daily requirements and Gandhi Ji once rightly said, if Man can satisfy his needs from the immediate vicinity, all modern problems he faces will be automatically solved. Our Technologists strongly vouch for erection of a 100% safe and leak proof Power Plant at Jaitapur and unlike the coal based Plant which are dirty and need large space for material handling, the nuclear Power Plants are clean and can be made slim, compact and smart, in which case, can be accommodated in a smaller open space like that of Cross Maidan, Shivaji Park or Aarey region of Mumbai, so that "one can lavishly use what one generates at the back yard". Obviously a small peripheral comfort of a recreation ground or open space is affordable for such an essential requirement like electricity and we do not have to evict Jaitapur folk from their ancestral land for our hunger for energy. Even the Govt. of German Republic has decided to stall the program of NPP after the Fukushima episode. The real truth however is, can we have progress and development not with "*Mon Amour*" but with "No More" of the nuclear Power Plants ?

11

About Cell Phone

What Everybody must know

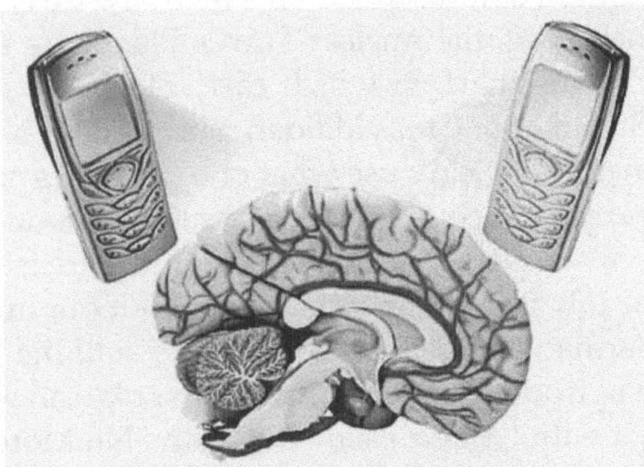

A few years before, when a controversy arose on the possible ill effects of a mobile phone hub atop a multistoried building of Cuffe Parade in Mumbai, I was approached to submit a technical report on the subject for judicial consideration. Not being an expert on the subject, I referred the aggrieved party to a reputed and competent Scientist for the job. The report was submitted and placed before the court, who sought independent comments from the Apex Authority on Radiation Regulation in India, but was informed that the Authority deals only with *"Ionizing Radiation"* and could not comment on *"Non-ionizing Radiation"* on human being. Whereas the Electromagnetic Radiation (EMR) in ionization range is known to be extremely harmful to living being, the EMR emitted by mobile or cell phones and their hubs falls in non-ionization range and little information are available on the subject.

EMR in the microwave range though non-ionizing, is very well known to have thermal effect, such as in micro-ovens, but its athermal effect on body tissues and organ remains a matter of curiosity, research and speculation.

Mobile or cell phones working in microwave range have given a tremendous boost to telecommunication facilities: increase comfort, save time, expand business and save life in emergency, but have posed many socio-medical problems amongst users. The problem is acute in India because of the sheer number of users majority of whom are children, mass ignorance and abuse, exploitation of interested parties (makers, service operators, consumer goods manufacturers, media etc.), poor or total absence of regulatory authority and the amount of money that goes behind the business. Warning people about the harmful effects of radiation from mobile phones, Ministry of Telecommunication, Govt. of Gujarat has asked service providers and makers to avoid promotional advertisements inducing vulnerable segments like children and pregnant women using cell phone. But the rules are only in its violation. With drivers on wheels, students and teachers in schools, colleges and class rooms, during meetings, conferences and discourses, in places of warship (also during worship) and in funerals (even while carrying dead body on shoulder), mobile has become a common object of use. Govt. and mobile phone companies do not want the users to be aware of the possible adverse effects simply because too much money is on line. History is full of such instances- DDT, Asbestos, Tobacco and Smoking, bottled drinks and Endosulphan spray in cashew plantation in Kerala, all harmful to public and community are overlooked through pressure from one corner or other. Specific Absorption Rate (SAR) value of mobile, mandatory to be mentioned in each set and strictly followed in USA, UK, Canada and EU, are not given in Indian phones.

A visual representation of the electromagnetic radiations (In picometer, nanometer and micrometer) not to scale:

```
                    Gamma Ray | 10 pm
                        X-Ray | 100 pm
violet    \                   |
(400nm)         Soft     X-Ray|          10nm
Ionizing. \
blue       \               UV |
green       \ ___             | 100 nm
yellow      /____ Visible     | 1 µm
orange               Infrared
Non-Ionizing
red        /                  |
(700 nm) /             T-ray  | 100 µm
                              |
                              | 10 mm
                    Microwave | 100 mm
                    Cell phone-(1mm. to 30cm.)
                    Radio/TV |  1 m
```

Although the number of mobile users has snow balled, 2 billions in world and 500 million in India, unbiased knowledge on effect of cell phone use on humans is practically not available. The reason is, no visible impacts can happen on humans in a short period of observation that the phones are on use and no experiments can be undertaken on man. Experiments on animals however show significant effects – rats whose brain cells are similar to man develop brain tumour, rabbits develop cataract. But extension of animal models to man is not possible.

Mobile phones use Electromagnetic Radiation in microwave and very short radio wave range and as per present information, normal use has little or insignificant impact on human health. But quite a few believe that if used for a long period, is likely to be harmful. Studies undertaken by a number of Scientists spread over many countries and health related information that have appeared in various media on cell phones and their base stations are summed up as follows:

Symptoms and Health Risks on long use of cell phones:

Sleep disturbances and Restlessness, Depression and Nervousness, Headache and Reduced power of concentration, Hot Spot in brain, Partial over heating and opening up of Blood-Brain Boundary to toxins, Over heating of eyes (cornea and lenses have no thermal regulation), High Blood Pressure, Impotency-Productivity problems, Exhaustion and Physiological problems, Genetic disturbances, Changes in blood formation and reduction of WBC etc.

Some authentic statements that support the above list of ailments are summarized below:

1. The first positive link between mobile use and malignant brain tumor was suggested by a comprehensive Swedish study which established 240% risk of brain tumor in heavy users of mobile phone (2000 hours of use or 1 hr. per day for a decade or so). Earlier studies made for a shorter period and on a smaller number of people had failed to detect any such link.
2. A Neurosurgeon from Australian National Univ. found 1 hr. of continuous use of mobile phone increases the risk of development of brain tumor by 2 to 4 times.
3. Young children have soft scalp and thin skull, developing nervous system and a long life ahead for exposure to radiation from mobiles, therefore considered to be the most vulnerable section of the society. "Do not let kids to use mobile- its radiation can alter DNA" warn Scientists. The National Institute of Environmental Health Science (NIEHS) finds a "weak link" between Electromagnetic Field and childhood Leukemia
4. People who have used cell phone for 10 years have 40% more likely to have Glioma (A malignant tumor on the side where the phone is held).
5. An epidemiology study in Tel Aviv Univ. showed 50% more risk for tumor formation in parotid gland (The largest salivary gland).
6. The American Society of Reproductive Medicine found significant adverse effect on semen quality and an Hyderabad based Indian Endocrinologist noted decreased sperm count, motility, viability and quantity of semen and increased risk of Testicular cancer among habitual mobile users.

7. Many well known Cardiologists feel cell phone can effect heart: Pacemakers, Implantable Cardiovestor Defibrillators (ICDs) and Impulse Generators.
8. Pregnant women and embryos are at risk from cell phone radiation and several studies reveal link to Brest Cancer.
9. Research in Human Genetic Department of Guru Nanak Univ. found DNA and Chromosome damage: "Exposure to Radio Frequency (RF) signals generated by cell phone effects physiological, neurological, cognitive and behavioral changes and induces, initiates and promotes carcinogenesis".
10. An Israeli study has detected mouth cancer for frequent speakers
11. Cell phone radiation is likely to increase Acoustic Neuroma, a tumor of the nerve connecting ear to brain (?).
12. Experiments on rats have shown brain damage, radiation from cell phone stations (hubs) effects navigation of migratory birds and for cattle grazing near cell phone towers American farmers have reported still birth, spontaneous abortion, birth deformity and behavioral problems. Moving of the cattle away has reversed declining of general health of grazing animals. No such studies have been made on human population, although Governments of UK, USA, Canada, Australia and European countries do not allow microwave hubs near schools and populated regions. In India many housing societies invite hubs atop their building for financial gain at the risk of resident's health.
13. A Canadian team detected clustering of Red Blood Cells (RBC) in the brain and hindering of oxygen supply to the blood cells when spoken over an unprotected cell phone continuously for 5 minutes. The radiation hampers movement of RBC through micro-vessels.
14. A Swedish study proposed leakage of albumin into brain via permeated Blood-Brain-Boundary.
15. Thermal effect of EMR has produced cataract in rabbit and premature cataract in humans.
16. According to a German Doctor mobile phone radiation alters cell function, increases BP, and people with the phone by bedside have poor REM sleep and decreased production of Melatonin, a cleansing chemical in blood. With larger dose of the radiation EEG and calcium value in blood changes.
17. "Ringxiety"- a psychological disease of hearing phantom sound and sensation of cell phone ring has appeared in Japan (also reported in India) among cell phone users.
18. Cell phone radiation interferes with navigational equipments; therefore its use is banned in airborne flights, also in hospitals near ICUs using life-line E-gadgets. Its use in gas stations is discouraged after it was found to have triggered a spark and ignited a filling station.

19. An IIT-Bombay EE-Professor emphasized that radiation from mobile phone not only goes to the tower, it also enters the body and organs of the user and people next to him. Unlike cigarette smoking, one can not smell, see or feel the electromagnetic radiation which permeates the immediate space and produce a new type of "Radiation pollution". Like passive smoker, people nearby become passive receiver of this "New Pollutant".
20. Although Govts. and Makers of cell phone emphasize that no significant health hazards are yet to be confirmed in normal use of the phone, yet warns for possible health hazards in its long term use. Like the "Filter Tips" in cigarette, several radiation protective devices are being manufactured and marketed to protect the cell phone users from the "ill effects" of radiation. The users are also advised to use hand free sets to avoid close contact of the phone to the body or brain.

Mobile - A Debate or Warning

The technology of EMR through mobile phones, satellite communication and micro ovens has moved very fast but the science of its impacts is least bothered or understood, rather pushed under the carpet in the name of progress and advancement. Technological innovations effect humans by various Orders: 1st. Order immediately, 2nd. Order in near future and 3rd or higher Order in distant future. Similarly, the intensity of impact varies from instant death (bomb blast), chronic illness (occupational diseases) to slow poisoning (Genotoxicity, carcinogenesis). Typical examples of the 3rd.Order impacts are: Global Warming, Ozone Holes and the down to earth history of vanquished Roman Empire because of "Lead poisoning" due to their habit of curing wine in Lead vats and extensive use of the metal in plumbing networks. Fortunately modern alert Scientists by chance recognized the "lead poisoning" in the automobile emission of leaded petrol and saved the petroholic society from the lead-hazard, which otherwise could have made the car-centered society full of Idiots. Lead on inhalation from the atmospheric aerosol permeates Blood-Brain Boundary in ppb (parts per billion) levels, effects central nervous system and produces Idiots.

EMR from mobile phones results in 3rd. Order impacts and is in no different from the plumbic idiotization of humans in long run. Few may be aware that not long before, the Indian village mother used to give a minute spec of opium to her baby every evening to make the infant sleep comfortably and enable herself to attend the house chores undisturbed. The present "mobile comfort" is an identical act of "self-stupefaction" by the user.

Today, unlike in any other advanced nation, a majority of the Indian children are glued into the mobile phones. By the time they grow to adulthood and take up the responsibility to run this country, each of them would have undergone a tremendous dose of EMR exposure. Even if with a minimal chance of adverse health effect from mobiles and hubs and which no sensible Scientists, mobile makers or service organizers will deny, future India will be run by "EMR-effected" people only. Besides, like the sprouting of cardiac and cancer treatment centers which were rare a few decades before, India must set forward a network of hospitals ready to meet the need of the new generation of EMR-effected patients in near future. It looks cell phone radiation is no more a debate to argue upon but it is a future warning for India.

12 Geosciences to Geosense

A Basic Education for Geoscientists

"The whole concept of Mother Earth shifts from symbol and myth to a dawning realization that every single one of us has feet of clays, and that we live on a parent, not on a planet."

—Lyell Watson

ABSTRACT

Geology as a Science and Science, as a type of knowledge (*Gnana*) has been explained and analyzed. Like any other Sciences, Geology too, is "bent" to serve the society for supplying earth resources. The Earth is considered a holistic system where the various subsystems, Atmosphere, Hydrosphere, Lithosphere and Biosphere continuously interact. "Bending of Geology" for earth resources exploitation for anthropocentric developments interferes with Natural Cycles. When the intensity of exploitation damages the natural processes that sustain the Natural Cycles, Nature steps in for Checks and Balances. Geologists who undertake mineral exploitation too, are at dilemma to find a bizarre of conflicts in mining and mineral industries. Based on Earth Ethics a code of conduct for Geologists to serve the society without adverse interference with the Natural Cycles may lead to developments, unscathed by Nature. This is considered a common sense or "Geosense" in Geoscience.

Geology is a Science, and Science is a kind of Knowledge

Geology, Geosciences or Earth Sciences, by whatever name denoted, is basically the study of Earth – its origin, its constituents (Products and Processes) and evolution of life during a long geological time, now estimated to be about 4.6 billion years.

Geology is not a basic science, but like any other basic sciences, it is pursued through, logics and hypotheses, theory, experiments, observation, analysis, verification and confirmation. Field component forms the core of contention in Geology.

The Colors of Knowledge
Cognition or *Gnana*
(Consciousness of Knowledge)

Special *Gnana* (***Vishes Gnana - Vignana***)
SCIENCE
A Mechanistic Knowledge
!
On application becomes
!
TECHNOLOGY
!
On empowerment produces
Powerful **TECHNOLOGIST** (Technoholic)
!
Who on being Fixed/Glued, becomes
!
A CAPTIVE of the CAPTURED
(Riding a lion but cannot get off)
!
!
With Ego
!
Exploitation of Weak & Meek
!
PLUNDER

Inquisitiveness
QUEST/SEARCH
!
Increased knowledge
!
AWE & WONDER
!
Further increase
!
INSIGNIFICANCE OF SELF
!
Leads to
!
The ***GREAT SURRENDER***
or Total Submission (***Saranagati***)
!
!
1. **To KNOWLEDGE** (***Budhi***)
(***Budham Saranam Gachhami***)
2. **To SWARM INTELLIGENCE** (Togetherness)
(***Sangham Saranam Gachhami***)
3. **To LAWS of NATURE** (cosmic Principles)
(***Dhamam Saranam Gachhami***)

Science or *Vigyan* in Sanskrit, is a special type of knowledge (*Vishes Gnana*) and on application becomes Technology (akin to Applied Geology). Technology empowers the "Knower". But power in essence, increases Ego, corrodes the "Learner" and leads him to exploitation of the less powerful, that is, the Weak and the Meeks. The problem however is, having been empowered and technologically fixed/glued, the Knower loses the freedom of choice and becomes a "Captive of the Captured".

To note:

1. Science is a sort of "Mechanistic" knowledge which requires observations, experiments, analysis and verification. In Geosciences "Field work" is the core of contention.
2. Knowledge is power, but power boosts Ego and corrodes the Knower (The Man). Therefore:
   (a) When Archimedes discovered the Lever Rules, he declared "Give me a place to stand, I shall move the Earth with a Lever" (Mackay *et al*, 1991).
   (b) Similarly, on discovery of the Focus of the Concave Mirror, he designed the "Flaming Steam Cannon" or "Burning Ray Mirror" to concentrate sun's rays at distance to burn enemy Roman ships.

   Modern efforts of Science are not different from "Archimedes' "
3. The "Captivity of the Technologist (The modern Man) can be understood by looking at the "Footloseness" (Schumacher, 1972) of the car centric society or the glued hand (Handloseness) of cell-phone users. Even the kitchen at homes stops functioning when its appliances run out of function.
4. Meeks and Weak are meant by the less powerful, such as an individual or groups of individuals, Societies, Tribes, Nations, Species of plants and animals; even inanimate natural objects or elements like Land, Mountains, Meadows, Rivers and Bays which silently bear the assault of the technological giant. The latter's are significant to Geoscientists engaged in earth resources exploitation, in which the exploitee is none but the "Mother Earth" and locally (For India), the sacred rivers like Ganga, Godavari and Cauvery. The talk of sharing the upper and lower parts of Cauvery by the two concerned States in which she flows, is obnoxious and is not different from the anonymous Graphito of Michigan University Campus in USA which writes "Mankind has an incestuous relation with mother earth" (Sahu, 2003). For the present generation, Rocks and Rivers may not have right, but the future generation has a right to see a majestic boulder, an escarpment or a "Silent Spring".
5. It is interesting to note that the Science stream of knowledge (*Gnana*) ends up with Plunder, whereas the other stream ends up with Surrender. Surrender or acceptance to supremacy is attended in three stages,

namely, (1) to *Budhi* or intelligence of the Self, (2) to "Swarm Intelligence" to progress together (*Sangachhadwam Sambodadwam Sambo Mana Si Janatam* - incidentally, this is the invocation song of IIT, Bombay, the Author's work place), and most importantly, (3). to the Laws of Nature such as Laws of Gravity, Thermodynamics etc. In contrast, in the Science stream, the knower, Geoscientists in particular, work against the Natural Laws such as in damming a free flowing river, albeit for the benefit of a section of the "Earthlings" (Man) at the cost of the Weak and the Meeks downstream.

Geology then and now

Systematic studies of Geology as a Natural Science goes back to the 17th. Century, when Neptunist Alfred Warner (1880-1930), Plutonist John Hutton (1736-1797), Stratigrapher William Smith (1769-1893) and Uniformiterinian Sir Charles Lyell (1830) recorded their views on occurrence of "Oceanic volcanism" and "Layering or Laminations", mineral assemblies and fossil finds in rocks. Most of their studies were confined to Petrology, Mineralogy, Stratigraphy and Structural dynamics in understanding the origin and evolution of Earth. Contribution from Charles Darwin (1809-1882) on Evolution considerably added to earth's Biostratigraphy and Paleontology. A variety of minerals and gems have been on use and sought after by Man from prehistoric time. Britain, where the systematic studies on Geology started is known to have abundant mineral resources like Tin & Tungsten in Cornwall, Lead, Zinc & Fluorite in Derbyshire, Coal, Clays & Limestone in plenty, but no serious study on Economic Geology was undertaken in Britain. The matter was left to the mineral hunters, Mining Engineers and Metallurgists. When "Economic Geology" was proposed as a vital branch of Geology, many British Geologists discouraged the move as "Mundane interest". However, serious studies on economic minerals and Ore- Petrology appeared in the Continent and later in USA where exploration and exploitation of mineral resources including Engineering and Applied Geology formed the major thrust in Earth Sciences and continues to be the principal aim of the present Geoscientists.

The very fact that useful metals and minerals are always associated with certain type of rocks (Geochemical affinity) and get concentrated under specific processes (Magmatic, Sedimentary and Metamorphic) in geological space and time (Metallogenic Province and Metallogenic Epoch respectively), intensive studies and extensive knowledge on Geology is a prerequisite for exploration and exploitation of earth's mineral resources.

Modern approach in study of Geology with support from all the disciplines of Science and with the aid of sophisticated equipments and techniques, is exclusively directed for exploitation of earth resources including energy and water. Remote Sensing, Space Applications, launching of satellites for assessment of earth resources and for weather forecasting to aid agriculture, are some of the latest developments in Earth Sciences. However, extra-terrestrial mining of minerals and metals for supplementation of depleting earth resources, vouched by some leading Indian "Geoscientocrats", is but figment of imagination and a gimmick of fund for search.

Besides exploitation of earth resources, Scientists knowledgeable in Geology are engaged in Seismotectonicity for study of earth quakes, in Ore-dressing and Mineral beneficiation, in Geotechnical & Engineering Geology and in Environmental problems like Geoconfinement of Wastes and decontamination of land.

The Earth is a System

The earth is a System of four components (Subsystems) or "Spheres", the Atmosphere, the Hydrosphere, the Lithosphere or Geosphere and the Biosphere, that continuously interact and change within certain limits. Cosmosphere, the extra-terrestrial region dominated by Sun has astronomical influence on Earth, but for all practical purposes, is excluded from the Earth System. The Earth System Science seeks to integrate and correlate the interactions (mutual impacts) of the Subsystems. The integrated Earth System is virtually considered a "Closed System" where no addition and removal of materials are involved. A small amount of meteorite and cosmic dust reaching Earth is considered negligible. Receipt of energy from the Sun and loss of internal heat by radiation into space, prime all intersystem reactions.

The scale and magnitude of reactions of the Subsystems are extremely variable and their imprints (Impacts) have been recorded in the history of the Earth by way of geological events.

Some Impacts of interactions among Earth's Subsystems

Of Planetary magnitude and slow.	Magmatic & Tectonic Episodes, Plate Movements, Species Evolution and Extinction, Marine Transgression & Regression.
Of Intermediate magnitude	Volcanism, Cosmic Bombardment of Jurassic, Ice Ages, Erosion & Rock Weathering, Ozone Shield formation.
Of Relatively Fast magnitude.	Desertification, Global Warming/Climatic Change, El Nino, Little Ice Age, Soil Salinity.
Instantaneous	Earth Quakes, Floods, Landslides, Forest Fire. (War, Famine and Global Terrorism when it comes to Anthroposphere).

All ingredients, water, gases, chemicals and nutrients exist on Earth in limited amounts. For life on earth to continue to function, these ingredients have to be recycled over and over. If any of the essential ingredients are used up, exhausted or seriously depleted or any Natural Cycles disrupted, the System is at a risk of disbalance and life dependent on it is in danger. For examples, the 21% Oxygen content of the Atmosphere, availability of the Liquid Fresh Water and the Soil Mantel are critical constituents to sustain life in Biosphere.

All living things on Earth function as one super organism, classically known as Gaia (James Lovelock, 1995), that changes its environment to create conditions to continue the life and made evolution possible. Thus, with a biospheric envelope, this huge ball of rocks, behaves as a single self-regulating System with its physical, chemical and biological components including Humans and is "known to suffer metabolic damage from "High temperature fever" (Global warming), Asphyxiation (Oxygen shortage), Acid indigestion (Acid rains), Ozonemia (UV-radiations), carcinoma (Nuclear Radiation damage) and "Dermatological dilemma" (Soil salinitization)".The interactions and feed-back between the components are complex but homeostatic and production of human species is considered a great step upward for the Gaia – a sort of rapid evolution of brain tissue (Lovelock, 1995).

The assumption of this planet as a single self-regulating organism automatically makes the Earth a "Holistic System" so that "When we try to pick out anything by itself we find it hitched to everything else in the Universe" (John Muir, 1838-1914). In other words, destruction and degradation of any sector of Earth affects others, at least in immediate surrounding or along the downstream region. Strip mining produces erosion, siltation and pollution of rivers.

The Earth-People System has become Anthropocentric

Making of Man on earth was neither a dictat of a creator, nor with Adam meeting the Eve in the Garden of Eden, but through 3.8 billion years of persistent evolution and Natural Selection from the prokaryotic cell to the multicellular complex Hominids. There is no denial that humans carry the signature of the primitive organism and, in odd with Genesis, is 90% Ape. Appearance of Man in the organic evolution too, is a mere flicker such that, if Earth is considered to be seven days old, Man appeared only in the last eleven seconds. But the last 2/3 rd. Second activities of modern Man, known as Anthropocene, has made him the privileged guest and the commander of this spaceship. Of late, he has become a powerful agent capable of bringing in large scale changes on earth. Modern Science and Technology has become a handy tool to produce the changes. Removal of mountains, creation of new sky-lines, diversion of river system, creation of lakes and reservoirs, clearance of Range forest ecosystem, reclamation of Bays and ocean etc. which Nature took million years to do, are made to happen in his own life time. Natural changes are slow, self-balancing and healed by recuperation. But Man made changes are sectoral and violent, therefore subject to Checks and Balances of Nature. Downstream and adverse impacts that commonly occur in case of such rapid changes are, water-logging, soil salinitization, floods and drought when hydrologic cycle of a region is interfered; land and soil degradation, water pollution in case of mining and industrial agriculture; soil and sheet erosion when forest cover is removed and coastal erosion when Bays and ocean are reclaimed. Thus, when Man takes the role of "Little God" to destroy, build or sustain an anthropocentric culture, Nature comes heavily to discipline the errand child. Since cultural changes are very fast, ethical changes are slow and evolutionary changes are extremely sluggish, almost negligible, conflict becomes a necessary byproduct. Thus terrorism has become a byproduct of modern civilization, making identical brothers on arms.

Conflicts in Mining and Mineral Industries

Minerals are primers of progress. No doubt mining, beneficiation, transportation, smelting and production, even use of minerals and mineral products bring in profound changes in environment, often of adverse nature, the activities cannot be stopped or postponed if the present developments are to be sustained. Even slowing down the activities is considered harmful and an act of conspiracy against progress. However, recent events world over have shown signs of turmoil and socio-ecological concern against the developmental practices in the mineral industries and cannot be ignored however minor the dissenting group or the opposing elements may be. The history of " Gold rush" in California or "Blood Diamond" in South Africa, cyanide pollution of Amazon river for gold extraction, the miseries of oil extraction perpetuated on Nigerian natives, untold stories of Chinese coal mining and the bizarre of agitations against mineral extraction and mineral based industries now going on in Indian subcontinent - from Rishikesh in Himalayas against the stone crushers to sand extraction in Alwaee in Kerala and limestone mining in Meghalaya to granite quarry in the Aravallis, are writings on the walls of " World Mineral Factory". An answer is due, as to why do the "Locals" rise against modern "developmental efforts" like setting up of Posco Steel Plant in Orissa, Vizag Power Plant in AP, nuclear power plant at jaitapur, limestone trading in Meghalaya, uranium mining in AP, Bauxite mining in Neyamgiri in Orissa or Radhanagari in Maharashtra and iron ore mining in Goa and Bellary in Karnataka? Over and above why is "a war against the State of India" has been let lose by a significant section of Indian natives (*Adibasi*) living in the mineral belts of the country? The roller and coaster of "Go- No go" policy in coal exploitation itself arouses doubt on sustainability of development exclusively through mineral industry. The reasons for the endogenic turmoils are obvious. Most of the mineral rich regions are environmentally pristine, ecologically fragile or rich in biodiversity and inhabited by people who generally, are poor and totally dependent on the existing land resources. The present mode of mineral exploitation in the veil of economic progress pays little attention to the environment, habitats and the very people who are affected by the ingression of the new industrial culture. Regulatory acts, damage control practices, rehabilitation measures, remain in paper or rarely practiced and compensatory doles get lost in bureaucracy and intermediaries (vide Bhopal tragedy). The resources generated from the ground are pumped out to distant places to benefit others while the PAP (Project Affected People) is left with "bread and circus". "Developments which destroy environment eventually destroy development itself", said one of the late young prime ministers of India. At the end, it is the people that are exploited, not the minerals.

Anthropocentric Development has led to Ecocide, the Fore-runner of 6th Extinction

The anthropocentric changes have also cost heavily on other living species on earth. When destruction of natural environment or loss of ecosystem of a given territory is caused to the extent that peaceful enjoyment by the inhabitants of that territory is severely diminished and survival endangered, the act is now known as Ecocide and is a peace time crime. In the present world, Ecocide is wide spread in large scale land uses such as in commercial agricultural practices, Industrial belts, urban settlements, opencast and strip mining of coal, iron ores and Bauxite and in limited cases around oil-spills and dumping sites including Green House Gases in atmosphere.

War time Ecocide, such as the ones practiced in Vietnam War by USA was considered to be International Crime. The present forms of Ecocide that prevails in all developmental practices world over, is no doubt "a crime against humanity" its international connotation is under controversy. The UN is under great pressure to consider the present form of Ecocide that prevails and practiced in many developmental activities mentioned above, as an International Crime against humanity under Rome Statute and in Earth Law & Earth Jurisprudence. Opponents oppose the move saying that this will mean criminalizing the whole human race and making business activities antidevelopmental

Geologists' Dilemma

Earth resources like minerals, fuels and water are the key materials that keep the industrial society running. Scientists in general and Geoscientists in particular are deeply involved in exploitation of earth resources for development of an anthropocentric culture. With increasing demand and depleting resources, exploration and exploitation are overstretched to the extent of compromising the environment and Natural Laws of Earth System. The 1969 USBM commandment to their Geologists said "Thou shall not tear apart the land, nor contaminate water and pollute the air but supply the requisite mineral materials to the society" (Flawn, 1970), but did not spell out how. A few instances of dilemma and dichotomy faced by working Geoscientists are described below:

1. **Ecology or Economy:** A mountain or a chain of hill range with green vegetation cover is meant to arrest rain cloud, heralds rainfall. The rain water runs down with weathered materials and nutrients released from rocks to form fertile land downstream and distribute the life sustaining precious constituents to all forms of life including humans. Demand of construction materials and occurrence of high valued minerals make the hill range vulnerable to quarrying and mining activities with consequent destruction of the mountain ecosystem followed by degradation of downstream elements through siltation and pollution. A mining and industrial settlement develops, biodiversity decreased, Ecology yields to Economy and the basic life supporting systems air, water and healthy foods become a cry of the inhabitants. Exhaustion of the mineral over the gaping hill range and depletion of rain fall consequent to denudation increases the ill effects. Ecology, the core of contention of life yields to Economy, the superficial mantle or wig of the society.

> *Only when the last tree has been cut down, (Refer Easter Island)*
> Only when the last river has been poisoned, (Refer Silent Spring)
> Only when the last fish has been caught,
> *Only then you learn that money cannot be eaten.*
> Plains Sioux.

2. **The "Go – No Go" Policy in Coal Mining in India:** Imagine an isolated territory, a Closed System of Carboniferous geology with a thick coal seam below the ground and fertile soil above supporting a rich assemblage of flora and fauna including a land and forest dependent human society. Foods, fuels, fibers, timber, medicines, fresh water and air, all that a high quality of life requires are available from the environment. The society is sustainable and time tested through continuous supply of renewable resources. Mining of the coal for energy requirements, leads to destruction of the Natural System, forest disappears, top soil destroyed, rain fall depleted, agriculture ruined and emissions suffocate and poison air, a situation what one observes in the coal-fields of Jharkhand, Orissa and Chhattisgarh, albeit, akin to a "Partly Closed System" where some support is made available by external inputs and outputs. No wonder, in an intensely welfare country like UK where people are preferred than profit, coal industry was closed during the middle of the last century. The "Go-No Go" policy of Govt. of India for mining of coal in forest rich land was a sign of ecological relief but was abandoned due to lack of vision of holistic development and greed for energy, of which at least 60% are abused in the country today.

More than75% of the coal generated in India is used in Thermal Power Plants for power generation. About 100 million tones of fly ash coming out of the Power Plants piles up around the generation site as "white desert" and only a minor fraction is utilized by local industries. Like the parent coal, the ash is rich, often enriched in toxic heavy metals. The large specific surface of ash grains and diaphaneity, combined, greatly increase the mobility of the heavy metals, making fly ash a potential source of metal contamination by aquatic leaching. Considering the magnitude of ash generation, the total toxic release from fly ash into environment is alarming. Calculation by Rubin *et al* (1999) and revelation of EPA (1998) show that the "electrical utility" release of toxic elements to the environment substantially exceeds either of the two top polluting industries, namely, Chemical and Metallurgical, and could be as large as the two combined. The Indian scenario of toxic release from coal-based power plants is least known. Tripathy & Sahu (1995) has emphasized that a super thermal power plant, using 8 million tons of coal, having 5 ppm of U, 40 ppm of Pb, 100 ppm of Zn and 10 ppm of Cd, will pump into its surrounding, 40 tons of U, 320 tons of Pb, 800 tons of Zn and 80 tons of Cd annually, the fate of which is never realized. No wonder, of late, Fly Ash is listed by EPA as a "Hazardous Waste" based on Total Toxic Release Inventory (TRI) from the electrical utility services. Like any carbonaceous sedimentary rocks, coal is a repository of Uranium. Coal mining and coal combustion annually brings out and disperse into biosphere, about 5000 tons of U, 13,000 tons of Th and many other daughter nuclides such as radium, polonium, bismuth, lead and K-40. Chakravarty (1991) reported uranium concentration in Indian coal in the range of 1.1-3.6 ppm (uniform component) and 33-46 ppm (non uniform component), where as in Fly Ash it varies from 8-11 ppm (uniform) to 55-71 ppm (nonuniform). Since the radio nuclides accumulate year after year, a century of coal combustion would elevate the global anthropogenic radiation to a level of "Subdued Nuclear Evening" without going into large scale nuclear warfare. According to an ORNL Report (USA), the amount of U-235 alone dispersed by coal combustion is equivalent of a dozen nuclear reactor fuel loadings. No wonder, a coal based thermal power plant is considered more vulnerable than a regulated nuclear power plant when it comes to hidden fall outs. Apparently by bringing out the coal from underground for power generation for an energy hungry society we have produced a "*Bhasmasur*"(The Biblical Demon which turns everything into Ash) as byproduct, the devastating capacity of which is yet to be understood by Indian Scientists, particularly Indian Geologists

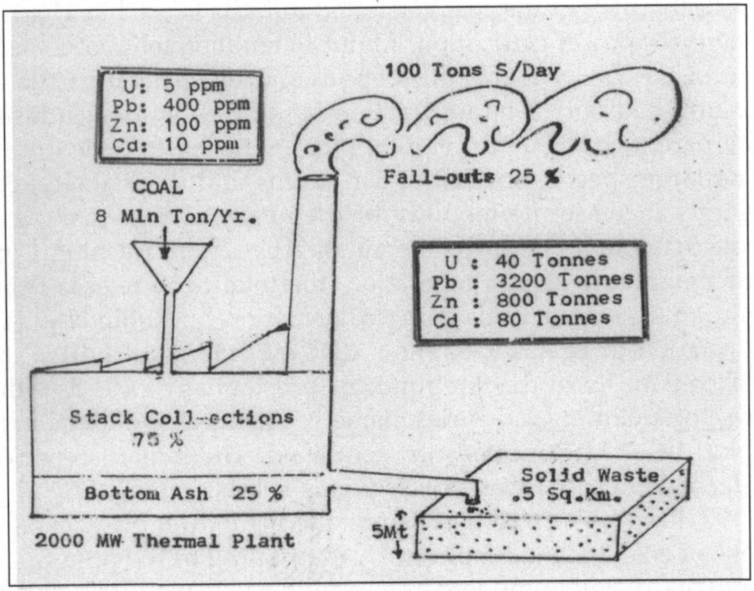

Toxic Heavy Metal Dispersion from a Coal based Thermal Power Plant in India

3. **Profession and Ethics:** The first lesson a Geoscientist learns in Physical Geology is function of some of the Natural elements, such as a River. Beside its universal role of collection and distribution of precious rain water to every ones in its path – plants, animals and Man, the river dissolves nutrients from rocks, distributes downstream, cleans up land of wastes and debris and specifically supports a vibrant human culture. The Ganges, Euphrates & Tigris, the Niles, Danube and Volga, have all done it. In short a river is an artery of the body of Earth upon which we all live. Geologists must ponder what it means by blocking of some of our arterial channels by a group of experts called Civil (?) Engineer in the name of harnessing of water resources. It is a clear discriminatory act of translocation of common natural benefits to the mighty and deprive the Weak and Meeks. A dam is a damn thing indeed (in deed) and a clear case of "Robbing Peter to pay Paul" (Sahu, 2002).

4. ***Neo-Kalidas**:** Life has arisen from rocks and the health of the present forms of life is intimately dependent on the chemistry of the lithospheric equilibrium. That is, a change in chemical equilibrium of noosphere ought to disturb the fine tuning of life chemistry. Natural compounds of Heavy Metals, geochemically known as chalcophilic elements, because they form Sulphides, represent one of such lithophilic equilibrium. Breaking of Metal – Sulphur bond and releasing the Metal to native state is a process of destabilization of the lithospheric equilibrium, which, Nature in principle would tend to reverse. The detached metal would tend to seek Sulphur atoms to return to original Sulphide. Man is a store house

of Sulphur atoms in the disulphide bridge of protein molecules, therefore vulnerable to this metallic attack. Heavy Metal toxicity has already registered its presence in human body in an alarming scale. It is a surprise that Geologists, the leading Natural Scientists are instrumental in an unnatural act of destabilization of Natural equilibrium and harming the very people they intend to serve. Have we become *"Neo-Kalidas"* cutting the branch on which we sit?

**(Kalidas was a famous poet, author but "Idiot" in ancient India).*

5. **Responsibility absolved:** Technophilitic Index (Frostner *et al.* 1973), that is, the amount of minerals and oil consumed, is an indication of progress and development of a society. However, Pollution Index of material is defined by the magnitude of leakage of the material from the utility cycle into air, water and soil. Since leakage is proportional to the amount of material used, Pollution Index too becomes directly proportional to the Technophilitic Index. (Nikiforova *et al.* 1975). Thus the basic life supporting systems stand polluted by the very culture of mineral consumption, obviously primed by supply of mineral resources to the society. Can the Earth Scientists absolve themselves from this genocide? "It is the Musketeer that kills not Musket".

It is a common observation that whenever the great pontiff, Pope Paul visited a country, climbs down the aircraft and stepped onto the ground, his first action was to prostrate on the tarmac to kiss the Earth. For "Rest of us", rampant digging of Earth for mining, constructional activities, lying of communication lines, etc. are acts of development and progress. The larger the bite of a shovel, the more advanced we are considered. However the "Rest of us" (The Earth digger) long to reach the feet of the pontiff (The Earth kisser) with reverence. It is of course true that plants shatter rocks to extract nutrients, animals burrow earth for shelter and Man has been ploughing land for agriculture, all for survival, like a baby growing on mother's breast. But a baby never "Milks" the mother as modern Man does onto the (mother) Earth. Earth is not for digging but for living.

> *Throughout history, tribes and nations have been fighting against each other with arms and ammunition. Modern man fights against earth with chain-saw, bulldozer, shovel, explosives and excavators.*

Whenever we dig, we dig for our grave

The crust of the earth has 8% Ferrous Iron which is being continuously oxidized by our oxidizing atmosphere producing red soil (laterite). All forms of digging expedites the process by uncovering underneath materials. Oxidation of each atom of Ferrous Iron to Ferric state takes one atom of oxygen from atmosphere. Only 300ft. of crust if oxidized will strip out all the oxygen of the atmosphere. Therefore, whenever we dig, we dig for our grave.

Ethics in Geology

In an opinion poll among Earth Scientists, the American Geophysical Union found that 50% of the economic Geologists, employed or funded by fossil fuel industries disagreed on "Human factors" responsible for Global Warming. The Australian Broadcasting Corporation sharply commented on this "Climate Skepticism" by saying "It is difficult to make a man understand something when his salary depends upon not understanding this."(John Cook, 2011, ABC). For a professional Geologist working hard to supply resources to the Society, the conflicts in mining and mineral industries and impacts on Natural Cycles has become demoralizing. An ethic or code of conduct in mineral exploration and supplies compatible with protection of Nature, territories, inhabitants and tribes, will help to preserve the social, cultural and economic fabrics and clarify dilemmas faced by the Geologists. A group of awakened Geologists (Matteucci *et al.* 2012) have proposed that introduction of an Ethical Code of conduct that follows the example of Hippocratic Oath of Physician will help Geologists to acquire a binding awareness of their professional and social responsibility.

A Hippocratic Oath for Graduation into Geology Profession (Proposed)

The Earth is my Home,

Her Air is my Breath, Her Water is my Blood,The Biosphere is my Flesh,

And the Rocks are my Bones.

The Mountains are my Inspiration And Rivers are my veins And the Soil is my Mother

*(Matti is My Ma' ti)**

To Preserve and Protect them is to Preserve and Protect my Self.

(In Sanskrit ***Matti*** = Soil, ***Ma' ti*** = The Mother.)

REFERENCES

Chakrovarty, S.K. 1991. In Int. Conf. on Coal Utilization, IIT-B, Procd., pp. 103-109, Ed. K.C. Sahu.

EPA. 1998. 1996 Toxic Release Inventory, Public Data Release. US-EPA, Washington, EPA-745-R-98-005.

Flawn, P.T. 1970. Environmental Geology. Harper & Row, 213 p.

Forstner, U & Muller, G. 1973. Heavy Metal Accumulation in River Sediments a Response to Environment Pollution. Geoforum 14, pp. 53-62.

James, Lovelock. 1995. The Ages of Gaia – A Biography of our Living Planet. W.W. Norton, 288 p.

John Cook. 2011. Australian Broadcasting Corpn. Env. June 28, 2011.

Mackay, Alan Lindsay. 1991. Archimedes ca. 287-212 BC-A Dictionary of Scientific Quotation. Taylor & Frances, p 11.

Nikiforova, E.M. & Smirnov, R.S. 1975. Technophilitic and Technogenic Anomalies (Abs.), Intn. Conf. on Heavy Metals in Env. pp. C 94-96.

Rubin, Edward. 1999. Toxic Release from Power Plants. EST, 33(16), 3062-3067.

Ruggero, Matteucci *et al.* 2012. Hippocratic Oaths for Geologists. Annals of Geophysics, v. 55, 3, pp. 365-369.

Schumacher, E.F. 1973. Small is Beautiful, 288 p. Bond & Brigs. London.

Tripathy, S & Sahu, K.C. 1995. Morphology and Mineral Chemistry of Coal Ash from Talchir Thermal Power Plant. Erth. Sc. 22, pp. 137-148.

13 Sustainability of a Georesources based Development

A Critical View

Georesources are classified into two types, the Nonrenewable and the Renewable. Nonrenewable, like minerals, fossil & fissile fuels, fresh water, soil and building stones are finite elements of Nature, subject to depletion and exhaustion on mining and degradation on use. Their stock or reserve can be extended by innovative methods of exploration and extraction, by utilization of the lower than the lowest grade, by recycling of scraps, by remediation and restoration of soil and water table, and by developing substitutes, but only to a limited extent. Utilization of low grade minerals means use of extra energy and faster depletion of the fossil fuels and accumulation of larger dumps and wastes, innovative methods may cost more than the recovery, remediation leaves toxic residues, resource materials when frozen in utility goods may not reach recycling market and substitutes are more often than not environmentally unfriendly. For example, substitution of biofuels and gasohol for petroleum has already started invading into production of food grain and crops like corn and sugarcane. Similarly, substitution of Aluminium for Copper in electrical transmission is inappropriate because unlike Copper, Bauxite mining results in larger area of land stripping, Alumina smelters emit Fluorides, generate Red-Mud, production of Aluminum is electrical energy intensive and extensive use of the metal is known to cause Alzheimer disease.

Renewable resources are also limited by the very nature of their dependence on Nonrenewable supports like fertile soil, nutrient, water and undisturbed habitats. Therefore, except the solar energy, the tapping of which too, needs nonrenewable material support like Silicon, the earth is virtually a close system for all types of resources used for progress and development. Extra-terrestrial importation of "elements like Ca and Ti from moon" is a scientific lie. Thus when it comes to classification of georesources, the distinction between Nonrenewable and Renewable is flimsy and the "Limits of Growth" and development is decided by the limits of physical availability of georesources, particularly Nonrenewable.

The probable life of known rich Nonrenewable Georesources on Earth

Coal: 2300 years	Aluminum Ores: 100 years
Chrome Ores: 420 years	Iron Ores: 240 years
Cobalt Ores: 110 years	Copper Ores: 30 years
Zinc Ores: 23 years	Lead Ores: 21 years
Gold Ores: 11 years	Petroleum: 31 years
Natural Gas: 38 years	

Use of minerals by Man goes back to Stone Age time. The Stone Age did not end because of exhaustion or paucity of stones, so did the subsequent episodes of Iron Age and Bronze Age in the history of human civilization. The specter of energy paucity like exhaustion of fossil fuels in near future is a stark reality. The Fossil or Fissile Fuel Age presently we are in, is not likely to be different from the earlier ones, so also will be the Age of Nonconventional like the solar energy. History clearly shows that it is not the exhaustion or paucity of earth resources, Nonrenewable or Renewable that determines the decline or limits of development of human race, but their use or abuse (end use) brings the "Limits to Growth". For examples, the carbon emission due to fossil fuel burning has ushered global warming, the threat of nuclear arsenals and cyber terrorism (Star War) of the future pose danger of total annihilation of civilization of Man. It is significant to note that the end use, over use (or abuse) of georesources comes out of increased knowledge of exploitation and decrease of wisdom and altruism. Even immediately around and in day to day life, the most useful and versatile material like plastic has become a curse on misuse, and proliferation of the Internal Combustion Engine (Car) that has greatly facilitated mobility, has made urban air unfit for inhalation. The automobile has made Man immobile (belted onto the seat) and foot-lose. A lesson is waiting to be learnt of the Cell-phone Age, when the impact of this "clinical test", the largest of the kind that humans have imposed upon self, appears in various forms of cancer in a few decades ahead. Already the Cell phone has made us "hand-lose".

For sustainable development, the role of Renewable is time tested, at least in the life span of humans. With population explosion, their use only expands and until greed does not take over the need, balance is always maintained. Exhaustion of Nonrenewable pushes the society to the edge. Fear of depletion of oil in America heralded Iraq war. Even if substitutes are likely to be invented, gestation period of their economic appearance in the market is always long. Besides, generation of high value Nonrenewable resources like minerals, oil, timber, fish and flesh (live stock) when damage the Renewable resources like air, water, soil, forest and biodiversity, sustainability is relegated to mere dream. When both Renewable and Nonrenewable resources do not compete and destroy but co-operate and complement each other for development, sustainability becomes a reality. In this case the famous Supreme Court judgment on Limestone mining on the Himalayan slope near Dehradun is historical. The honorable Court preferred to preserve the beauty of Doon Valley, although the market value of the mineral to be mined outweighed the revenue that would be earned from tourists who would visit Doon Valley to see the beauty of the mountain. The Court felt, Ecology can not be given an economic tag, as much as calculation of the cost of survival is perverse.

Sustainable development of a system, be it a Society, a Project or a Body, requires (a) Continuous supply of energy and materials (Georesources) and (b) Assimilation, absorption or removal of waste outputs which are normally harmful or toxic to the original system. In the later case, the assimilative capacity must not degrade or weaken the future capacity of recuperation such as self cleaning capacity of a river or mopping capacity of forest and sea water for carbon dioxide added to the atmosphere from the developmental activities. To be specific, when production of Iron & Steel and fossil fuels at great cost of deforestation, is preferentially diverted for manufacture of chain-saw, a powerful machine for forest clearance, for making of "Skyscrapers and Sea Link" or for manufacture of armament, sustainability of development is jeopardized.

For energy or material inputs, if Renewable, the rate of harvesting or usage must not exceed the rate of generation if sustainability is to be maintained. For Nonrenewable, the rate of consumption or depletion has to be matched by new discoveries and development of substitutes. Regenerated materials and energy must be environmentally benign, ecofriendly and do not strain the system more than the act of original removal had inflicted. For example, tractor is a poor substitute to traditional plough because, tractor needs fossil fuels and spare parts, generates pollution and unlike the bullocks does not give dung, so useful for the agricultural society. No wonder a cattle based culture sustains a well-knitted society (also a family) where as a tractor based industrial culture generates unrest and atomizes family. In spite of fast and visible results shown by the substitutes, the development can not be considered sustainable.

Fortunately, the earth is endowed with all those minerals man needs and if used judiciously, are in enough stock, though at various levels of concentration. The scare-crow of resource crunch arises out of maldistribution, unequal sharing and greed of the consumerist society which today, as per WHO Report abuses 60% of the earth resources and in doing so has invited the wrath of global warming. It is paradoxical to note that while people living in mineral rich belt are found to be poor, and for those who consume maximum of the earth resources the quality of their life is not desirable. That the excessive use of mineral resources let release an automatic brake to the development of consumerist society is evidenced not only by global warming and societal disorders but also by increased pollution of the basic life supporting systems like air, water and soil. For example, any substance after removal (mining) from earth's crust, when moves along the utility cycle, always leaves traces of it in the environment (Air, Water and Soil). Leakage of resource materials from the utility cycle into the environment is otherwise known as Pollution, which increases with increasing use of the material concerned. Thus, the Pollution Index of a society is directly proportional to the Technophillity Index, that is, the amount of georesources it uses.

Epilogue

The appearance of modern Man on a habitable earth is a long story of 4 billion years of evolution against all odds of floods, fires and celestial bombardment. An equitable global temperature to keep the water liquid, a belt of magnetic umbrella (Van Alan Belt) to ward off cosmic radiations, a stratospheric Ozone shield for protection from UV radiation, an atmosphere with optimum levels of Oxygen to breath and Carbon dioxide to keep warm, abundant fresh water, fertile land and of forest, fruits, animals, birds and insects, combined, made it possible for the descent of the most innovative species to "rule the Ocean, Mountain and Sky". Besides the planetary protections, the earth is also endowed with a variety of mineral resources to provide added comforts to the privileged child. There are building stones and cementing materials to build comfortable homes, fossil and fissile fuels to generate energy, a variety of minerals and metals to run industries and even gold, gems and jewels to display vanity and pride. In spite of having been bestowed with Nature's bounty the cry of "Resources crunch" in the modern society is a paradox of plenty and the "Limits to Growth" is merely a hype. With Greed taken over Need, the search of sustainability of development is a futile search of self identity.

14 Dance of Water for Bio-incarnation, Sustenance and Apocalypse

Introduction

An apparently inert seed, dormant for years, sprouts into a sapling when comes in contact with water and in due course develops a majestic green canopy of inner and outer world of life. Cascading stream carves out intricate pattern of curvaceous potholes even in hard rocks and erosional force of water develops diversity of land forms of mountains, valleys, plains and shore-lines on earth, attired with a cover of green vegetation. From the impact of rain drops to sheet flows on land, physical and chemical weathering by water pulverizes rocks to release mineral nutrients and feeds a diversity of life awaiting along its course of movement. No wonder, the earth surface quenches thirst and becomes alive soon after a shower. It is this hydrated biosphere which envelops the planet earth exactly as the skin, flesh and blood do over a skeleton, prompted some Scientists to address our planet as a Living Earth or Gaia. Similar idolization of the planet as *Dharitri* in Indian mythology and as "Mother Earth" by the modern generation whenever natural calamity descends, is also common.

The magic of water to stimulate or trigger activities in inorganic or organic materials at molecular to global levels has prompted search for extraterrestrial liquid water as a precursor to presence of life outside the earth.

"Water molecule in aqueous state consistently rotates and translates in an intricate movement (Dance) that imparts its critical properties, many of which are anomalous but underlie essential processes in the areas ranging from biology to atmospheric chemistry" and in scores of industrial processes.

The Water Molecule

+ ve

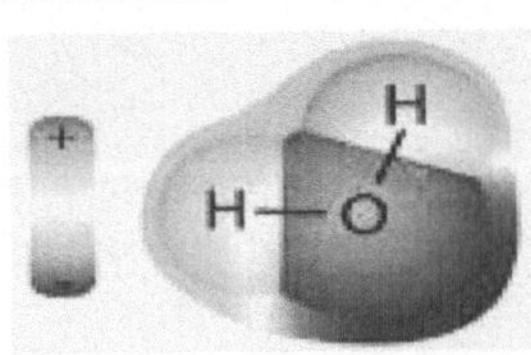

– ve

A molecule of water, H_2O with one bivalent Oxygen and two monovalent Hydrogen atoms, at once appears to be an ideal "home" of balanced electrovalency. But two sets of intramolecular discordance that perturbs the "valentine" balance in the molecule are:

(a) Two of the Hydrogen atoms bound to the Oxygen are squeezed to 104° and not at 109° of the normal tetrahedral disposition and being of same charge repel each other but held back by strong arms of covalency of Oxygen.

(b) The isolated lone pair of electrons on the other end of the Oxygen atom develops a negative field and in constant search of extramolecular relationship with protons (H or similar ions) and get temporarily attached through hydrogen bonds.

The negative charge of the lone electron pair at Oxygen end and the net positive field in the Hydrogen end, impart a strong bipolarity to the water molecule. The mutual repelling of Hydrogen pair at one end and longing for extramolecular relationship of the Oxygen at the other end are interconsequential and produce a turmoil which makes the water molecule to rotate and translate continuously. In other words, this movement can be described to dancing "Trios" (each Oxygen holding two Hydrogen) in a ball dancing hall, who harmonically move around and change Hydrogen partners between themselves or pick up from similar groups seated in nearby tables in a dancing floor.

With this scenario of primeval motions due to hydrogen bonding and "distending" Hydrogen partners', water develops many anomalous properties including a strange varying density, large heat capacity, high surface tension, universal solvency, bipolarity etc. and can strip or cleave, zip or unzip, fold or bend, inorganic and organic molecules and trigger the leap from a nonliving to living state, design the shape of planet and life, continues to sustain the biodiversity and probably can be an Apocalypse of destruction and mass extinction.

Water the Elixir of Life

Present knowledge of existence of life revolves around carbonic and oxygenated environment. Discovery of abundance of life forms around "Black Smokers" in deep ocean showed that anoxic and sulphurous environment which prevailed in the primordial juice of early earth could also give rise to living materials. Convincing arguments on abiogenesis has been given by a Scottish Scientist from interaction of water with silicate minerals which make up the crustal rocks of the earth. Clay minerals, a byproduct of water rock interaction, display primeval properties of life such as, eating and excreting (adsorption, desorption and exchange of cations and anions), high fidelity replication (reproduction), symmetrical growths and species variation etc.

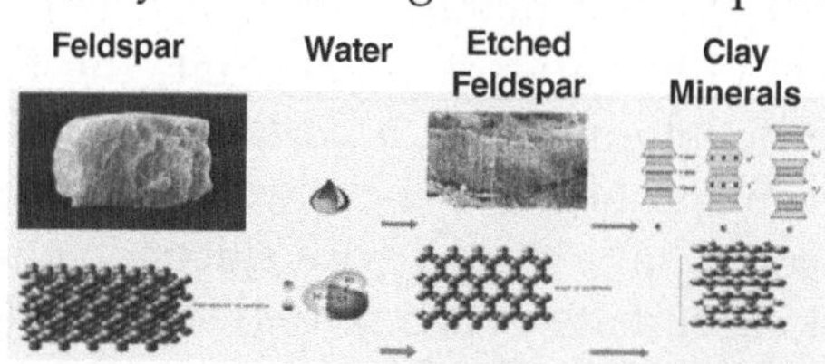

Sketch showing Feldspar Water Reaction to Produce Clay Mineral

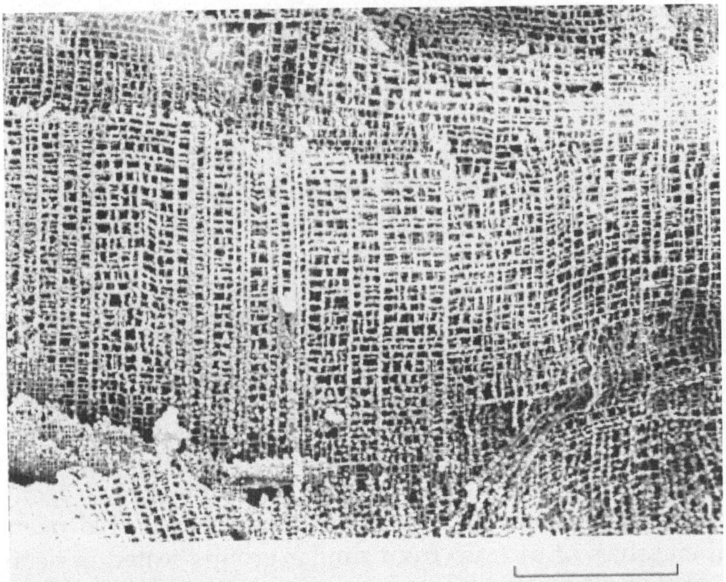

Resin Cast SEM of Water Etched Cleaved Microcline (K-Silicate)
(Bar Scale 20 micron)

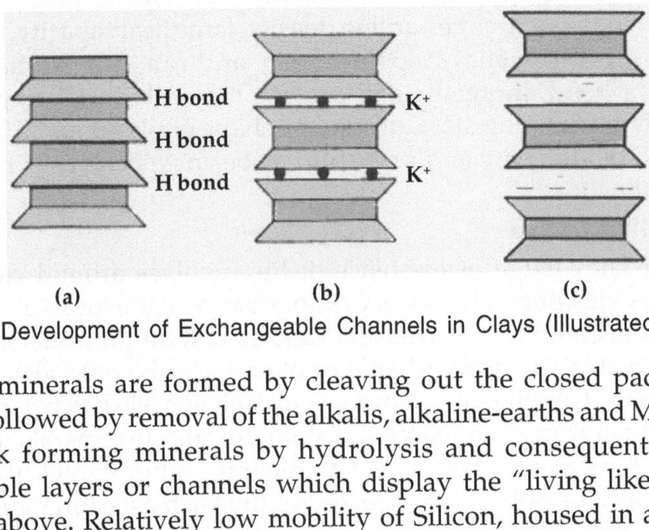

Development of Exchangeable Channels in Clays (Illustrated)

Clay minerals are formed by cleaving out the closed packed silicate structure followed by removal of the alkalis, alkaline-earths and Mg-Fe cations of the rock forming minerals by hydrolysis and consequent creation of exchangeable layers or channels which display the "living like" properties described above. Relatively low mobility of Silicon, housed in a tetrahedral Oxygen net-work in the mineral prevented further evolution of the "primitive silicic life" as against the high mobility and unlimited polymerization capacity of Carbon with H-O-N network, such that, the former became a mere substrate for the development of a carbonaceous life. The Stromatolites preserved in ancient proterozoic rocks and planktons with silica skeleton indicate that life could have started with silicon in an aqueous environment. However, in the long run life which started siliceous (obviously because of a siliceous parent earth) became carbonaceous.

Stromatolites

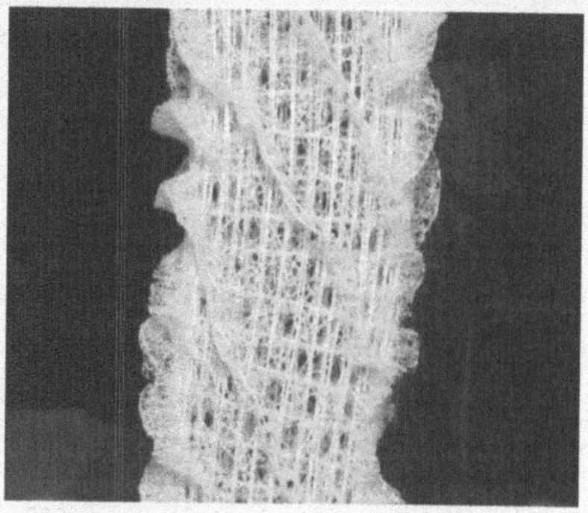

Silica skeleton in plankton

The size of a water molecule is about 3 Angstrom and the average size of protein molecule is ten times larger. But the charged ends of the bipolar water can split, zip and unzip, fold, bend or fix-up larger biomolecules of nucleic acids, lipids and proteins to form complex and diverse patterns of the organic world and shaped the various forms of life. Therefore, water is known as "The designer fluid" of the "Devine Architect".

Water Sustains Life

Having designed and kick starting a living system, water continues to control and maintain the living world through its anomalous properties.

- Its strange varying density, highest at 4° C makes cold water sink and ice float, thereby protects all aqueous life from freezing to death. The sinking melt water of Greenland ice sheet primes the thermohaline pump of Gulf Stream and keeps N. Europe warm.
- Rain drops, frost and hydrolysis break down hard rocks to form fertile soil and make agricultural practices possible while "universal solvency" of water mobilizes and transports nutrients and minerals in plants or animals, remove and excrete unwanted toxic chemicals, failing which growth would be stunted and living endangered. Natural rain detoxify saline soil and industrial urban lands equally and makes earth surface habitable, while the vast blue ocean accepts the harmful elements as a great sink (Ref. Hindu mythology of *Nilakantha*).
- High Surface Tension and capillary rise enables water to reach even the tip of tall trees and fine arteries and veins for nutritional transport and toxic exudation.
- Large Specific Heat (heat storage capacity), long range of stability of liquid water (0° to 100° C) and large Latent Heats at Melting and Boiling points maintain a variety of conducive thermal environments including homeostasis in body temperature, Sea Surface Temperature (SST), cooler ambience near and above water bodies, "Air-conditioning effect" of trees and cooling through perspiration.

- All natural processes like cloud formation, rain, slits, lightening, hurricanes and typhoons at global and local scales are consequences of peculiar molecular properties of water. Similarly, many industrial processes like sol-gel transformation, emulsion and suspension, ion-exchange, Permutit or osmotic processes and floatation of ore-minerals are controlled by the "dancing" water molecule.
- Cleaving and unzipping of large biomolecules to hydrophilic and hydrophobic units enables selective entry of "good" and rejection of "harmful" nutrients across cell membrane, the pore opening of which in turn is controlled by "bending" of the cell-wall proteins by the charged water molecules.
- By mere universal availability in the cosmos, abundance and stability of its liquid form through a large temperature range (0° to 100° C), water encourages proliferation and growth of life. Conversely, its paucity diminishes growth and diversity. Thus, proliferation of life in rain-fed equatorial region is high and in arid, desert and ice clad terrain, life is stunted, restricted and rare.

H_2O Apocalypse

Geological history of earth is punctuated with at least 5 known extinction of life, all due to episodes like marine transgression and regression, floods and droughts, climatic change such as descending of Ice Age; the last 5th one by cosmic bombardment which in turn heralded extreme climate. An earlier event, prior to these 5 extinctions, not recognised in Geology, is the transformation of the early ocean from anoxic to oxic environment due to appearance of photolytic planktons, annihilating the first anoxic life. Some of the well documented Holocene extinctions since Man appeared on earth are, the last Ice Age when large mammals like Mastodons vanished, burial of Mahenjodaro-Harappa in aquatic sediments, end of Maya civilization in central America due to drought and agriculture failure, Dust Bowl Disaster in America and Little Ice Age in Europe. Ecologist Edward Wilson reveals that half of world's higher life forms will be extinct by 2100 (in the hands of Man). An invisible 6th extinction, known as Anthropocene extinction, which started with Industrial Revolution, is considered to be in progress. The cause invariably centers around water. Large scale deaths due to water pollution and water borne diseases, flood, drought, famine and starvation (food grains, beef and milk are virtual water), national and international conflicts for water share, desertification and ecological migration, production shortage of electricity and industrial goods, wild fires and social unrest at dam site or municipal water tap, are microcosms of the 6th episode. Interestingly, this Anthropocene extinction is Man made and the "Inconvenient Truth" is that genotoxic effect of water pollution and consequence of Global Warming make Man an endangered species.

Thus the dancing water molecule which kick started life and continues its sustenance can very well be the root cause of destruction:

- By its excessiveness (floods);
- By its absence or deficiency (drought, famine and dehydration);
- When abused (pollution);
- By our misdeeds such as interference with natural hydrological cycle; and
- When misappropriated (exploitation, privatization and commoditization).

Volumes can be spoken on each of the causes to bring home the *Inconvenient Truth.*

15 Human Environment Relation, its Synergy in Ganga Basin
A Coincidence or Consequence

ABSTRACT

Traditionally Man effects environment in a variety of ways but very little information is available on environmental changes effecting Man. Environment not only effects human behavior but also has serious impacts on cluster of human beings, that is known as society. Ecological abuse or ecocide is known to end up with collapse of many ancient civilization and culture.

Human – Environment relationship is best understood in an Earth-People system, ideally represented by a fresh water ecosystem like that of a river basin, wherein many ancient civilizations evolved, flourished or even collapsed due to ecological abuse. The Ganga, Yamuna and their tributaries, the lifelines of the Gangetic basin are polluted beyond recuperation and their waters appropriated upstream through dams, irrigational diversion and industrial use. The pristine environment of the basin has undergone complete transformation through intensive agricultural activities, industrialization and urbanization, worsened by population explosion and their gubernatorial habits. Intensive degradation of the fresh water ecosystem of Ganga watershed is considered to have a synergistic effect on the human habitats of the region. An unhealthy parenthood, deficient upbringing and degraded environment cannot but give rise to a deficient progeny.

The Indo-Gangetic plain boasts for a reputed ancient Vedic/Upanishadic culture but presently pervaded by a group of "Failed States", best described as BIMARU States, where kleptocracy reigns over democracy in the entire region. This observed synergy of environment and human culture in the Gangetic basin during a period of about 5000 years, from Vedic period to the present time, is a coincidence or consequence, is the bone of contention of the paper.

Human - Environment Relationship.

Man made changes in environment began when the hunter-gatherer man settled down for farming, fishing and family raising. The anthropocentric changes of earth's environment became significant and alarming after the Industrial Revolution and now Man has become a significant agent of global changes, equivalent or at times larger than the natural processes. GHG emission, generation of erosional fluxes from mining, civil engineering constructions and mechanical agriculture, diversion of river courses and creation of lakes and reservoirs, transformation of landscapes, mobilization of "civilizational" heavy metals, nitrogen fixation in soil, deforestation and defaunation, urbanization and industrialization are some of the glaring changes, for which Science, Technology and global engineering practices have come as convenient tools. Vitousek *et al* (1997) quoted by Sachs (2008) estimates human domination, alteration and appropriation of several major components of Earths' system as, Land transformation, including photosynthesis: 50%, Atmospheric CO_2 concentration: 25%, Water use: 60%, Nitrogen fixation: 60%, Plant invasion: 20%, Bird extinction: 25% and Marine fisheries: 67%. Scientific literature is flooded with data and information on environmental changes and the impact is even quantified by the famous "Eye-Pat" equation:

I = PAT, where

I = Impact, P = Population, A = Affluence, T = Level of Technology.

- *A more plausible equation of estimation of Impact on environment ought to be: Im = PACT, where, Im = Impact, P = Population, A = Affluence, C = Consilience (Inverse of Resilience), T = Level of Technology*

Commercialization of the impact is found in the routine EIA and EMP *mantras*, practiced in various developmental projects that involve drastic changes in local and regional environment.

Man Changes Environment

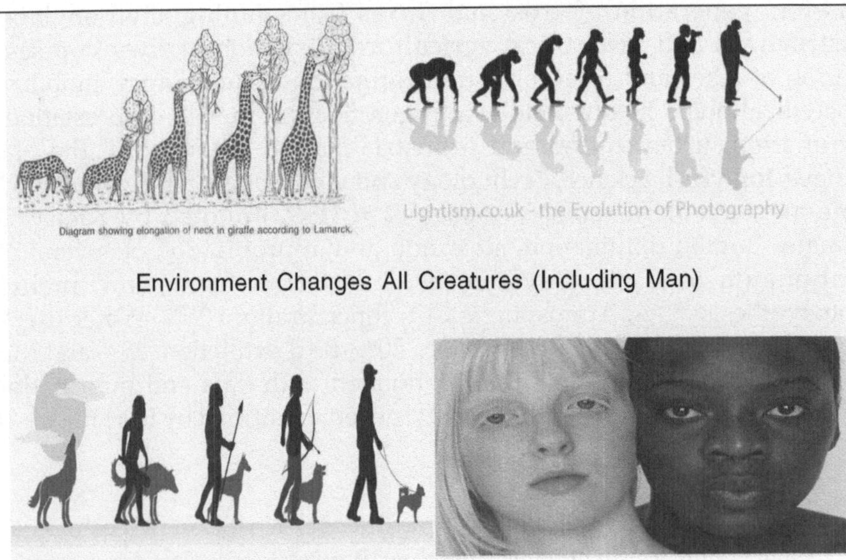

Environment Changes All Creatures (Including Man)

While human effect on environment has been a common theme of studies, little information is available on effects of environmental change on living creatures, particularly on humans. History of evolution unequivocally demonstrates major morphological changes in living creatures, including their extinction, with changing environment, albeit through geological time. Development of lungs in amphibian in place of gills in fish to enable the creature to venture from aquatic to terrestrial environment, evolution of extraordinary long neck in giraffe to reach receding foliage for food (Lamarckian theory), the lizards taking up wings and the arising of homoerectus from the quadruped hominids to use fore-legs for gathering food, for holding baby, for using tools, even for fighting, are some of the glaring instances that needs and environmental changes apparently effected morphological development of living creatures. Change in environment, even in a relatively shorter period affecting behavior of animals is found in domestication of animals, particularly by transformation of wolf to dog. Intense exposure to sun light or lack of it has strong effect on skin color of man and even pollution is known to result in various metabolic diseases and genetic disorders. Evolutionary change proposed by Charles Darwin was focused onto human beings by his cousin Francis Galton with the statement that "nature is all that a man brings with himself into the world, nurture is every influence that affects him after his birth". Environmental change effecting cluster of human society leading to collapse of several ancient civilizations are on record in human history. To mention a few, these include the Neolithic Chinese civilization along Yangtze and Yellow rivers, the Indus valley civilization of 3300-1300 BC, the Egyptian civilization of 3152-332 BC, the Mesopotamians of 3100-549 BC, the Mayas of Central America (1400 BC -800 AD), the great statue builders of Easter Island and the Angkor of Cambodia.

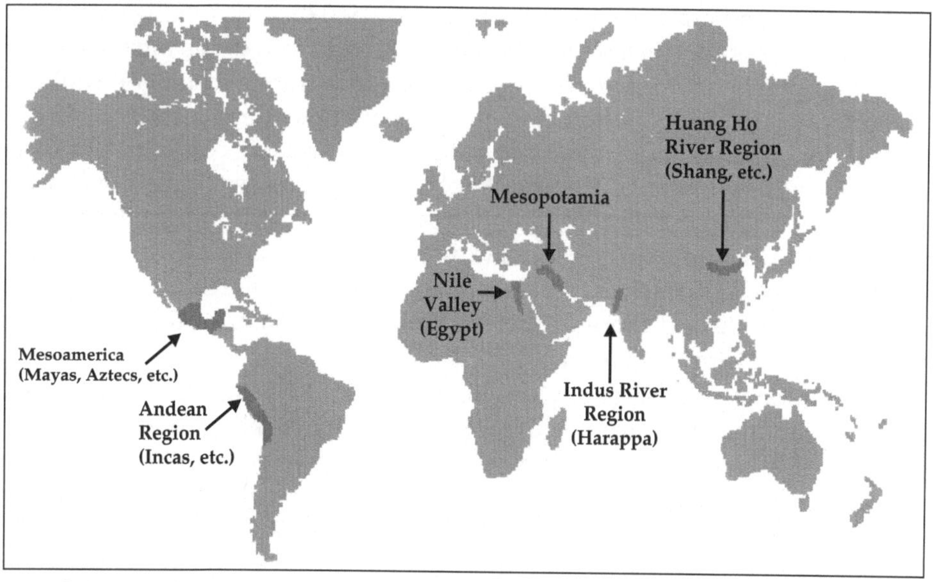

Collapse of some Ancient Civilizations due to Abuse of Ecosystem Services

Our life is identified by what is around us and what is happening in time and space – this was the rule of Nature from primate to homoerectus until we considered ourselves as "double wise" and started controlling Nature, modified environment and bend the ecosystem services to suit our comfort and convenience. This ability to control Nature and environment enabled man to survive in most regions of the earth, pole to equator and in fresh to polluted environment and now poised to extend our settlement into ocean floor, but has resulted in unforeseen feed-backs, the impact of which being slowly realized in the modern stressful society through various signals of failure. We are now in search of a "sustainable development" and knocking at the doors of different planets.

The science behind biological determinism is that "our genes are fixed but their expression is highly dependent on what our environment throws onto us". The basic assumption is that, at birth, the human mind is a blank slate – "*Tabula Rosa*", and this gradually gets filled up as a result of experiences that are "nurtured" through environment. "*Give me a dozen children ... and I can produce any specialist as I want*"- the famous controversial statement by the behavioral psychologist John Watson in 1930, triggered the debate of "Nature versus Nurture" in relative contribution of genetic inheritance and environmental influence in development of human behavior. Biology can determine the ability, but when it comes to man, what one does with the ability is decided by Free Will.

The physical features can be identified as identical to the parents but not necessarily the talents. The environment where one grows up may have a lasting effect and influence on the way one talks, behaves and responds to the things around him. Abstract attributes like, personality, intelligence, social orientation, likes and dislikes are not gene coded in DNA. The nurture theory holds that environment factors are the real origin of human behavior. Children living along highways, where the ambient air is loaded with lead aerosol from automobile exhaust, are known to have lower IQ compared to those living away from the road. Deprived upbringing increases the risk of deviant behavior in adulthood. Environment stress leaves mark in the body, shorten telomeres and alter epigenetic brain processing, crucial during brain development – 3rd trimester of pregnancy to end of adolescence. Modern life with more people and more gadgets certainly seems more stressful than the life in the past (Frank Vereeckon, 2012).

Traditionally physical environment effects human thought, feeling and behavior. Conflict and struggle among people at a trickling municipal water tap or supply tanker, dispute among States for river water share, even war among adjacent nations are signs of water stress environment at different scales. The first victim of overcrowding (for example, in local trains of Mumbai) is mutual respect to each other and that is what population explosion does. High consumption can put strain in environmental resources and can have serious effect on society, because "consumption exacerbates inequality and accelerates poverty-inequality and environmental nexus", generates waste residues that are centers of pollution and heralds transmigration of pollution across States. Ecological issues of people's relationship to their environment, has assumed crucial importance to our quality of life, sustainability of development including maintenance of peace among communities (Oskamp & Schulz, 1998).

Water Stress Environment

Stress from Overcrowding

Recent research lays more emphasis on human activities on environment, whereby historical changes in society consequent to environmental changes have little attention. "Historical study of human society pursued as scientifically as the study of dinosaurs' extinction will profit to our own society today by teaching us what shaped the modern world and what might shape our future"(Jared Diamond, 1997).

Human society responds to environmental signals through multiple pathways including collapse or failure, migration or creative inventions through discoveries. Extreme drought has triggered social collapse or ingenious management through irrigation, such as in Israel. Between 14th and 18th century, Western Europe responded to environment crisis by innovations, intensification and adaptation and avoided collapse. Resilience and readoption depends upon identified option, improved understanding, cultural solidarity and fresh ideas (Buitzer, 2012). Society on the edge becomes brittle, lose resilience including ability to adopt social values, make them more susceptible to the impact of potential perturbation of several kinds including climate change, political corruption, war and terrorism.

The disturbing fact in the history is that the primary cause of collapse of many civilizations has been the destruction of the environmental resources which they depend upon. Deforestation and habitat destruction, soil problems like erosion, salinitization and fertility loss, water mismanagement, overhunting and fishing, introduction of invasive species, overpopulation, climatic change, building up of toxins in the environment, energy shortage, limits of photosynthesis capacity of land, are considered to be some of the factors that lead to collapse of a State (Diamond, 1997). The collapse of Indus valley civilization, the great statue builders of Easter Island, the Mayas of Central America, the Pharos and Mesopotamian civilizations, the Fertile Crescent of Middle East and Angkor in Cambodia, are all considered to be due to unrealized and self inflicted ecological damage. Today it is known as Ecocide, a suicide of society.

Human–Environment Relation (Earth-People System) in a River Basin

The ideal method to understand effects of environmental changes on living kingdom, particularly on humans, is by a system approach, where earth and people make a close knit system. The Earth – People System can be focused onto a visible scale of space and time in a river basin or watershed (Riverine system), where actually human civilization started, flourished or failed in course of historical time.

Land and water are ecologically linked in a natural system called catchment, drainage basin, watershed or river basin. The basin also includes habitats such as plants and animals, including Man, which live in it, and all other things which have been added to it, such as roads and rails, buildings, dams, factories and farm lands. Everything we do affects the water basin and vice versa. "The truth is, we live downstream of someone and upstream of someone else". That is, we are all connected through the water basin ecologically, economically and socially. The river basin is a web of life, a virtually living body, the streams, channels and rivers are like arteries and veins coursing with life and are crucial to sustain it (WWF).

Soil is a basic watershed resource, but when polluted by chemical fertilizers, pesticides and industrial pollutants, gets degraded in course of time, affecting the very habitats it sustained in its natural state. Plant cover operates in the basin in a major way – intercepts rain cloud, increases precipitation, harvests solar energy, provides food to the food-chain, controls temperature, prevents evaporation and dust formation, fallen twigs and leaves supply back nutrients, absorbs carbon and supplies oxygen. Removing the native greens from the catchment (Deforestation) is disastrous to the whole life system (ecological death) especially to humans.

River basins are characterized by processes resulting from complex climatic, biotic and land use interactions. Climatic change results in change in temperature and in the elements of hydrologic cycle such as precipitation, evapotranspiration, runoff, ground-water storage etc. Changes in hydrologic characters lead to changes in food production, environment, health and hygienic conditions as well as, in long terms, on culture and civilization.

Degradation of the watershed or watershed-elements is loss of ecosystem services. Loss of ecosystem services is catastrophic to human evolution. Historically loss of ecosystem services has led to collapse of many societies. Typical of the societies collapsed for ecological abuse, otherwise known as ecocide, have been mentioned earlier.

Ganga Putras, the Principal Habitat of Ganga Basin

If abuse of ecosystem has led to historical collapse of many ancient civilizations, and Indus valley finding at our doorstep is not an exception, the complete transformation of the Gangetic basin through intense agricultural practices, industrialization and urbanization, pollution of the fresh water ecosystem including the principal rivers Ganga and Yamuna and depletion of the water-table by 100 to 150 meters, need to be critically examined for the future fate of the present human habitat of the Gangetic basin.

Arising in Himalayas and emptying into Bay of Bengal, Ganga flows a distance of 2500 km. and drains an area of one million Sq. Km., one fourth of Indian territory.

The Ganga basin supports 500 millions people and has been a cradle of successive civilization from Mourya empire of Asoka in the 3rd. century BC to Mogul empire founded in the 16th. Century AD. The pre-historic Vedic/ Upanishadic period in the Gangetic basin dates back to 5 to 10 thousand years and forms the substratum of the Indian culture.

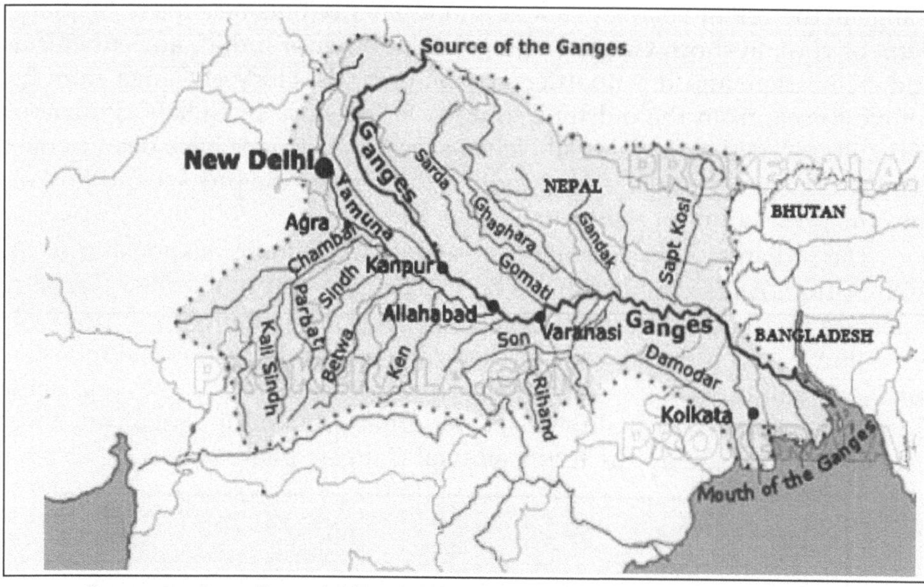

Ganga basin, a Potential Fresh Water Ecosystem facing Extreme Abuse

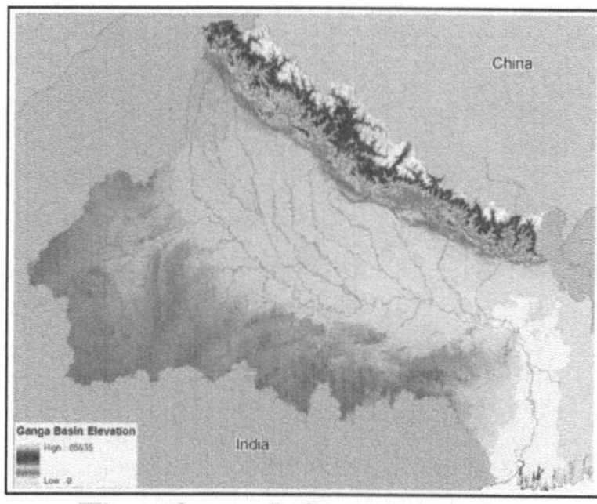

The "Green" Ganga basin

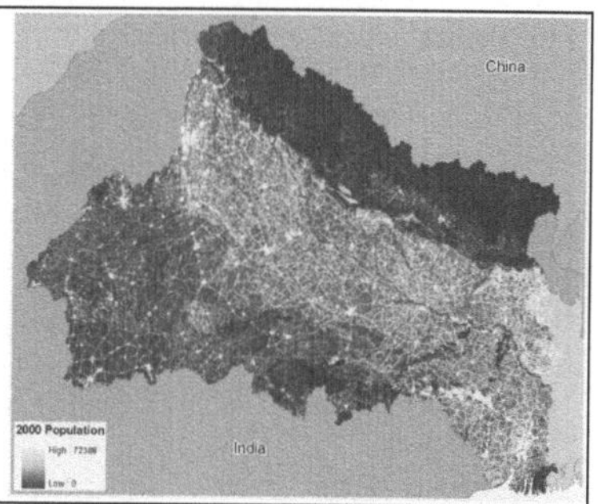

The urbanized Ganga basin

The fertile alluvial mantle of the plain, besides supporting an agricultural society had once a dense forest with large animals like elephants, bison, rhino, Tigers and lions, most of whom have disappeared and the entire basin is intensely cultivated or urbanized. The river, once a rich source of fish and life line for survival of the ancient *Kaivartas*, the tribal river folks who worshiped the river as *Adimata* (the primordial God) and treated themselves as progeny of Ganga (sons of Ganga or *Gangaya*). The Mahabharata famed Satyavaty is virtual Ganga Devi, born as a mortal woman in the world, in a *Kaivarta* hamlet in Ganges valley. The Aryan king Shantanu met the fisher women while on a hunting spree and married her. The offspring – the *Ganga Putra*, otherwise known as Devabrata or Bhisma in later days, represent the most exemplanary character of human values in ancient Indian culture. The essence of all that stated above is that, Mahabharata gives a human form to

Ganga in the veil of Shantanu's wife and mother of Bhisma – the noble *Ganga putra* of yore. In short, Ganga is the virtual mother of India's ancient culture and civilization, and it is no exaggeration that "the story of Ganga from her source to sea, from the old time to now, is the story of India's civilization and culture", and as Jawaharlal Nehru says "The Ganges have been to me a symbol of memory of the past of India, running into the present and flowing into the great ocean of the future".

The Indian system of belief is based on an intimate relationship of life with Nature. An offshoot of this is reverence accorded to the river Ganga as a gesture of acknowledgement of her life-supporting ability for a primarily agricultural society. In an ancient society that depends on seasonal monsoon for its agricultural needs, the perennial nature of Ganga was a God send. Ganga also dumped rich alluvial soil, a veritable boon for agriculture along its course and made up the fertile alluvial Gangetc plain.

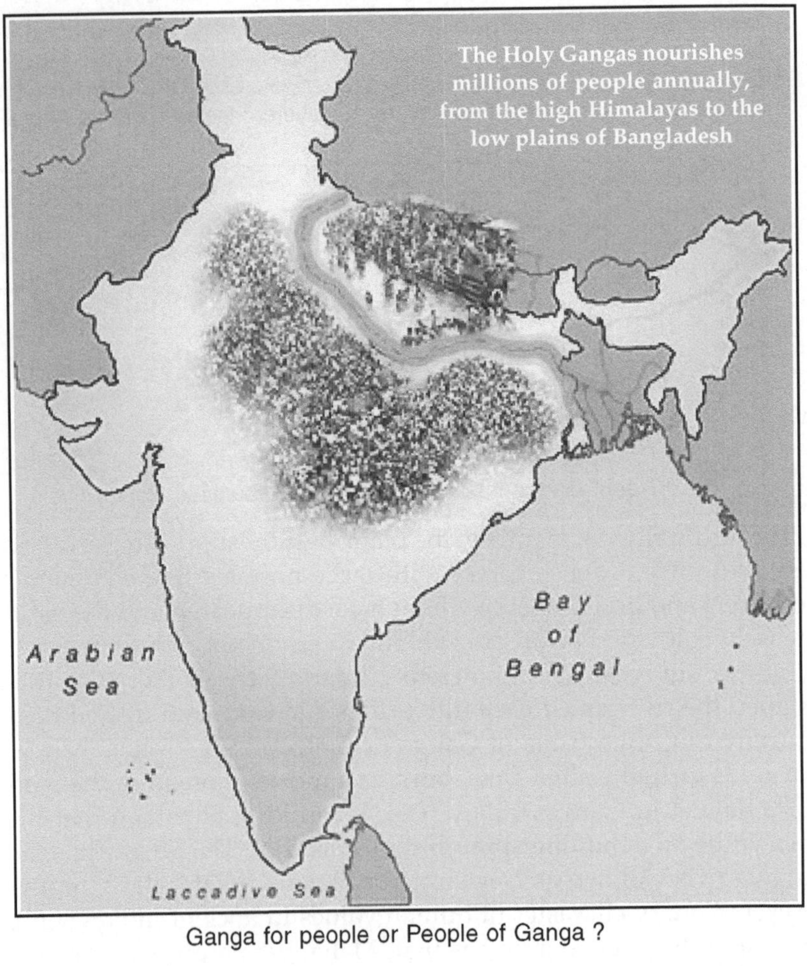

Ganga for people or People of Ganga ?

The Indian subcontinent, specially the Gangetic valley, having a glorious start of Vedic civilization has undergone waves after waves of changes in terms of invasion, influence and insurgence – first with conquest and plunder, then through colonial rule and lastly the tide of Industrial revolution in the last two centuries. The post-independent scenario, where *Kleptocracy (corrupt Govt.)* reign over democracy, has devastated the society and the transitory success of industrialization and modernization has been carried onto irreversible ecological collapse. Scores of major industries discharge effluents upstream, rendering once the pure water, polluted with harmful ingredients, dams appropriate the waters on highland, throttling the flow downstream, diversion of water for irrigation robs of the precious water from the downstream people, plants and aquatic life, even the famous Ganga dolphin *Susu* has lost vision and has become blind because of turbidity and pollutant in the river. The barrage at Farakka prevents migration of Hilsa upstream. 1.6 billion liters of sewage from 30 cities, 7 towns and thousands of villages along the course of Ganga, and 260 million liters of industrial effluents containing heavy metals like mercury and hexavalent chromium reach the river every day. Several million tons of fly ash, otherwise known as "Bhasmasur"(Sahu, 2014) from Badarapur, Indraprastha and Rajghat power plants in Delhi, enter the Yamuna water. Six million tons of chemical fertilizers and 9000 tons pesticides go into the land annually for agricultural use. Only 40 % of the fertilizer applicated is taken up by plants and the rest ends up in the water. Fertilizer and herbicide residue poisons the agricultural runoff when it returns to the river again or contaminate the ground water and soil of the region. While the population increase and their consumption residues have added to the human discharges into the river, the ancient culture of river worshipping makes millions of folks flock into pilgrimage towns along the river round the year. Discharges of the ceremonial rites including that during festival times like *Kumbha Mela*, and cremation remains of semi-burned bodies degrade the river beyond imagination. The modern day Ganga and Yamuna courses have become victims of modernization, industrialization and cultural sacrileges.

The Indian history depicts through epics, mythology, archeological and historical records, a high quality of ancient civilization in the Gangetic basin. The philosophical thoughts of Tirthankar and Gautama Buddha, the Vedic and Upanishadic descriptions, the principles of Ramaraya and the deliberations in the battle field of Kurukshetra (recorded in Gita) and the series of institutional sites like Hastinapur, Taxila, Nalanda, Pataliputra etc. that appear in the historical map of India, stand support to the existence of an extremely high quality of human civilization in the Indo-Gangetic basin. "Ancient India had an amazing wealth of science that had its beginning around 3000 BC. It had specialized among others in cosmology, mathematics, astronomy, aerodynamics, medicine, surgery, agriculture, yoga – the science of body and mind, besides language, grammar and communication.

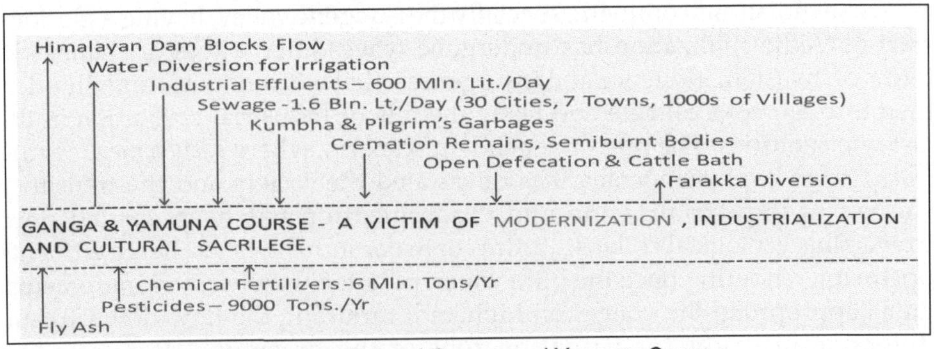

The Present Fate of Ganga and Yamuna Course

State of Pollution of Ganga

"Ganga Tu Baheti Kyun ?", Sings *Bhupen Hazarika.*

The scientific knowledge was used only for the service of mankind and preservation of the Nature and no scientific research that is inimical to Man and his environment was encouraged or allowed. The demolition of the great culture of India by foreign invasion have left the country in shamble by the mid-twentieth century". (T.Ramakrishna of ESWARA, -personal communication).

Human civilization, born and developed in the Indo-Gangetic basin for several thousands of years – the relationship was benign and symbiotic. But things changed during the last couple of centuries when population growth, industrialization, economic development, Green Revolution led to unprecedented transformation of the fresh water ecosystem and consequent biodiversity loss.

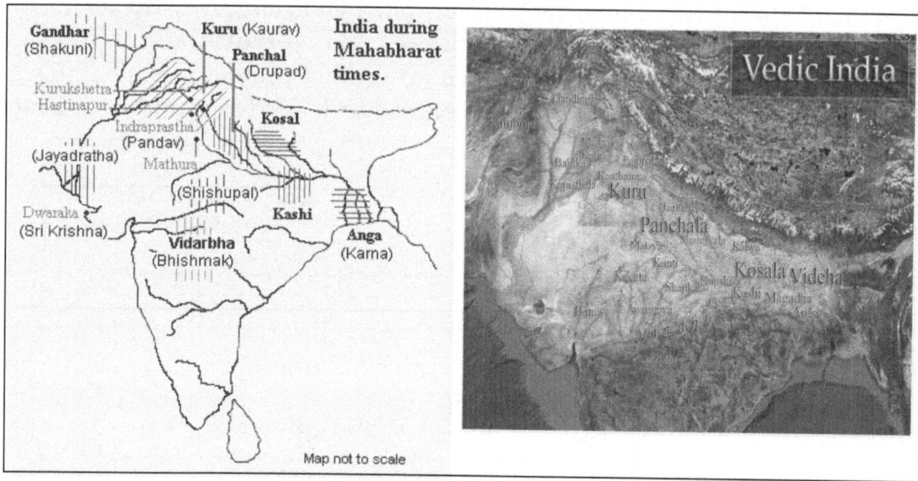

Ancient Civilization in Northern India

Ganga Basin vs. the BIMARU States

The Gangetic basin spread over an area of one million Sq. Km. coincidently includes the BIMARU States of Bihar including Jharkhand, M.P., Rajasthan and the erstwhile U.P. (Ashish Bose,1980). Going by the specific aspects of governance and growth, such as law & order, primary health and population control, primary education, literacy, agriculture, consumer market, investment scenario, budget and prosperity, the BIMARU States and their offshoots occupy conspicuously lower position compared to any other Indian States. Delhi and Haryana in west, lying in the Yamuna basin and W.Bengal lying in the east, downstream of Ganga basin, though not included in the BIMARU criteria of Ashish Bose (1980) because of industrial development and education respectively, excel in law and order problem as compared to other Indian regions. Political unrest and corruption, failure in governance, mass exploitation through religion, caste and creed, land, sand and mining mafia, industrial unrest and violence have rapidly increased in all the States that make up the Gangetic basin. These States have been rendered virtually ineffective and unlike other Indian States in the South, not able to enforce their laws uniformly or provide basic goods and services to the citizens because of high crime rates, extreme political corruption, impenetrable and inefficient bureaucracy, judicial ineffectiveness, mafia influence in politics and cultural situations in which traditional leaders wield more power than State over most areas of governance. Consumerism – Poverty – Inequality – Environment nexus has pinnacled social and ethical violence. Extreme poverty in some of the tribal but resources rich regions has exhausted governing institutions, depleted resources, weakened sober leadership, crushed hopes – fueling a volatile mine of depression and instability. Poor fragile State can explode into violence or implode into collapse … as livelihoods are crushed, investment flies, people migrate to other States and ungoverned territories become a spawning ground of threats like terrorism, trafficking, environmental degradation and disease (after Lael Brainard, *et al*, 2007). In short *kleptocracy* has replaced the hard earned independence and democracy in the entire Gangetic basin.

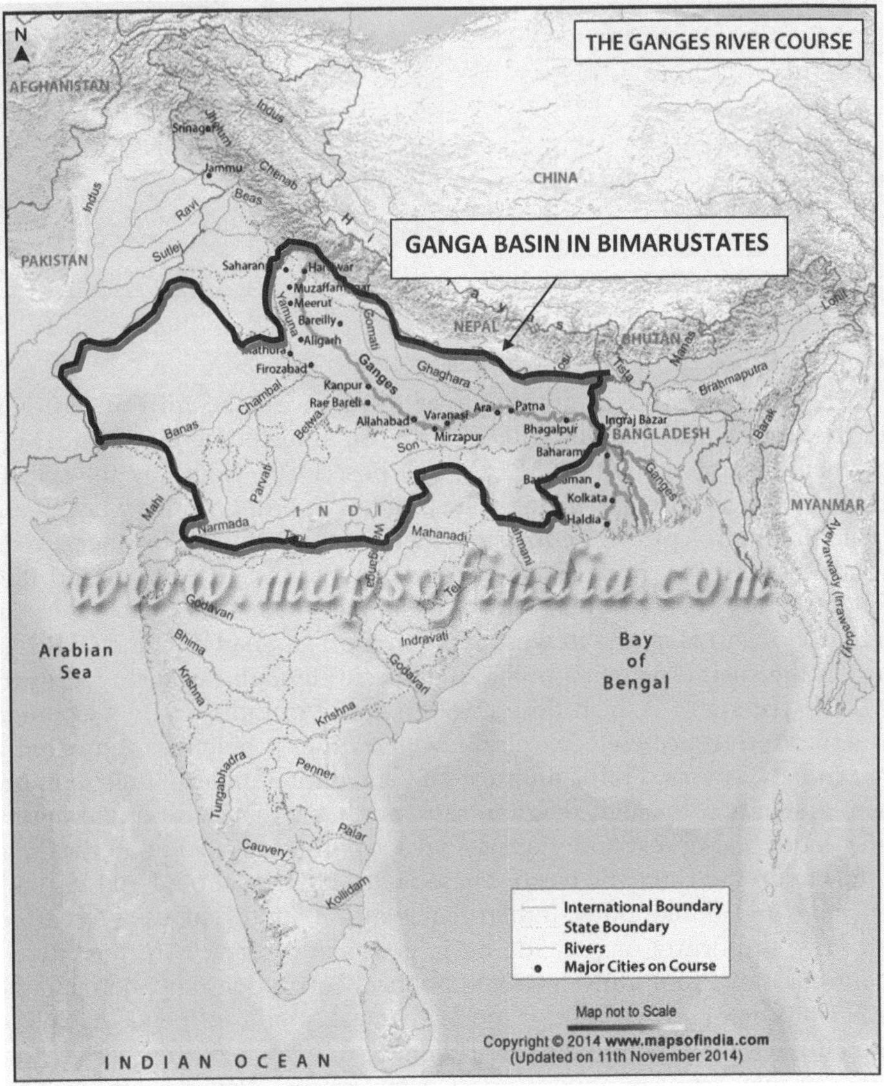

Education in Ganga basin – Yesterday and Today (Mass copying in Bihar-right).

Transportations Yesterday and Today

Present Law & Order situation in the Gangetic basin (BIMARU State)

Coincidence or Consequence

This remarkable observation that a river basin which once held a supreme habitat of ancient civilization, nurtured and sustained by an *aviral* Ganga, transformed into a group of "Failed State" and through which flows the same river in a bewildered state of pollution. This synergy of human – environment relationship is a coincidence or consequence, needs serious scrutiny by experts from various specialties to prevent collapse of Indian culture and civilization in the Gangetic basin. A pertinent question is, "if *Bhagirath* brought the Ganga from the mountain to quench the thirst of 60 thousand people in the plains" (now it is 500 million), how long the river will survive when the Himalayan glaciers are first disappearing due to global warming, human appropriation of its water upstream throttles the downstream course and pollution has far exceeded natural recuperation. The contribution of post-independent developmental approach has so far been negative because the governing model has been exploitive. When all the elements of the fresh water ecosystem in Ganga watershed has changed – soil Salinized, water polluted, climate changed, population exploding, fertile lands urbanized, aquatic life thinned out, species decimated and forest denuded, can humans be left behind? An unhealthy parenthood, deficient upbringing and degraded environment cannot but give rise to a deficient progeny. No wonder, the modern *"Ganga Putras"* of Ganga basin, instead of surviving on the nectar of the mother, seems to have started milking her violating the very system, which has sustained them for generations. With the violation of Ganga the basic structure of Indian civilization stands endangered in the very basin where it flourished. Besides questioning "For whom the Ganga flows ?" or searching for the *"Brhama Dravya"*, the enigmatic substance that once kept the Ganges water pure, the viable solution will be in a course correction in our ecological relation with the sacred river.

PRINCIPAL REFERENCES

Diamond, Jared (2005). Collapse – How Societies Chose to Fail or Succeed. Viking, p. 502.

Diamond, Jared (1997). Guns, Germs and Steel –The Fate of Human Society. Norton, p. 480.

Ganga Wikipedia: The Free Encyclopedia.

Oskamp, S, Schulz, P.W. (1998). Environment Issues: Energy and Resources Conservation in Applied Social Psychology, Princeton, pp. 205-228.

16

Interlinking of Indian Rivers

*An Open Letter (Pt. A)

The 5000 years old Harappan civilization ended due to drying of the Saraswati river and shifting of the Indus towards west, obviously because of the uplift of Aravalli region. This uplift, even today, shifts Yamuna course towards east.

1. Before 12th Century AD, Bhagirathi and Hooghly were the main distributaries of Ganga flow. Padma was a minor channel. Between 12th and 16th Century, flows in Bhagirathi, Hoogly and Padma were more or less equal. After 16th Century, Bhagirathi and Hoogly got increasingly choked and by the end of 18th Century, Padma became the main distributary of Ganga. Consequently came the Farakka Barrage to flush Hoogly and save Calcutta Port. It means, the easterly region of Ganga is tilting (Sinking). As a matter of fact, it is this easterly tilt of the whole gangetic plain, that controls the course and flow of Ganga river.
2. Analysis of all seismic events in Himalayas points out increased activities in two regions – one in NW, north of Delhi Ridge and where Aravalli Wedge abuts against Himalayas, and the other in the Eastern Himmalayas, where subduction of Indian Plate is considered to be faster.

Answers to the above three basic observations can be found by analysis of the geodynamics of Indian Plate as it moves north and rotates anticlockwise, collides with the Tibetan Plate, abut at Aravalli Wedge and subsequently subducts relatively faster in the eastern region. (vide Figure).

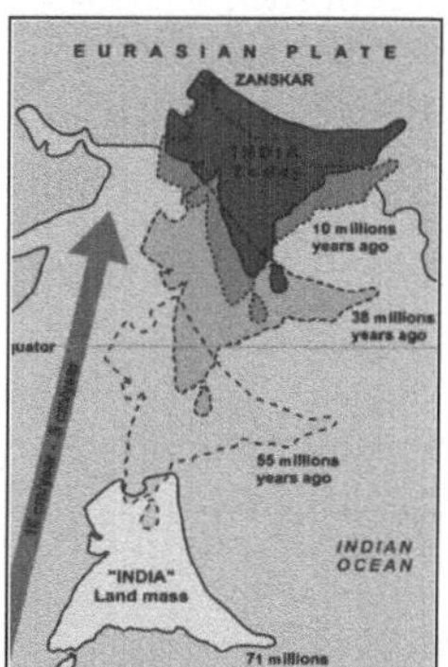

Rotation of Indian Plate

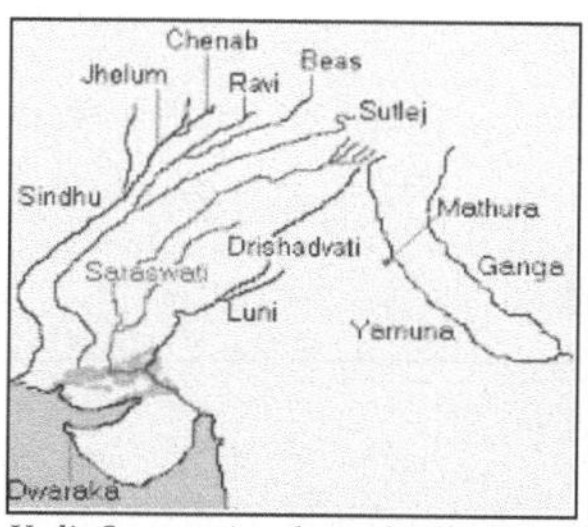

Vedic Saraswati as drawn by Shridhar

Saraswati Lost

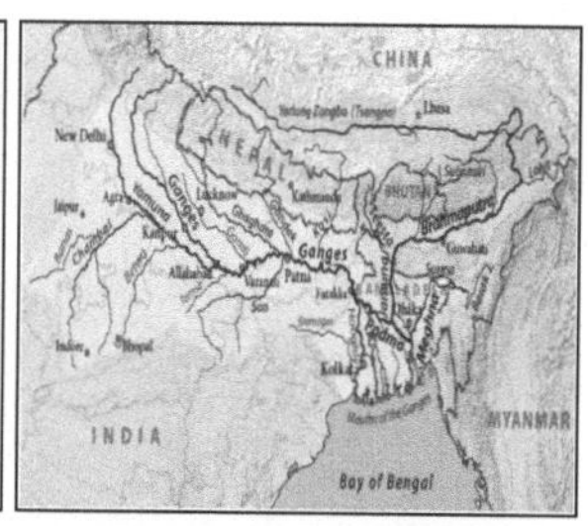

Padma Flow Increases

The above analysis ought to be understood by experts and supporters of the River Linking project since major quantum of water movement in the project is from East to the West, where as, the entire Gangetic plain is Naturally but slowly tilting towards East. Nature seems to be against us. Sustainability of the Project stands questioned.

Besides the problem of Plate geodynamics, a few minor issues that will arise in implementation of the project are:

1. Extensive excavations will increase sheet erosion and choke large sections of water courses in the country. As such, coal mining in Jharkhand has killed Damodar river. Iron ore, Limestone, Bauxite and Coal mining in Orissa and Andhra Pradesh has choked Brahmani, Mahanadi and Godavari deltas in East Coast.
2. While Ganga flow is sustained by melting of Himalayan ice caps, Global Warming threatens the very existence of the ice sheets. Ganga flow is today abstracted to the extent of 60% in the upstream regions by Dams, Barrages and Canals. Where will be the surplus water for transfer through the new Link Canals? To many, the rain water floods are wastage into the sea. But it cleanse the land and river equally, sustains deltaic and near shore ecology, but for which there will be Dead Zones in Bay of Bengal with economic loss in fishing industry.
3. Today Water disputes between States abounds It will increase with coming up of the River Linking Project.
4. Water from Brahmaputra is not guaranteed in future because its collecting source is mainly in Tibet.

Author's appeal: Let us concentrate our efforts in cleaning and Healing Ganga before carving a pound of flesh from her.

**Submitted to Parliamentary Committee on their open invitation for comments.*

PS: The latest knowledge from NASA report is that the Brahmaputra-Ganga delta is subsiding due to heavy sediments receipt, which supports the theory of sinking (depressing) and agrevating the subduction of the eastern zone.

17

Interlinking of Indian Rivers
Comments and Suggestions (*Pt. B*)

1. A river basin is a natural system produced by interaction of land and water through a period of time. Each basin has its own characteristics controlled by underlying rocks, overlying soil, rainfall pattern and a consequent habitat dependent on the rocks, soil and rainfall. Interlinking two or more basins of different characters needs careful scrutiny and matching of fundamental characters for a stable future as well as to avoid adverse downstream processes, rather than immediate benefits to be incurred by the present generation
2. Success of a few minor linkages cannot be taken as granted since the fundamental natural setups of each basin is different and the successes are not time tested too. Political and societal factors which may be autocratic, democratic or even bureaucratic, weighs heavily in the consequences of undertaking a river-linking project. One set-up overrides human rights, suppresses sufferance of a section of people, another "shares and cares". The adverse effects of the so-called successful linkage projects have been overlooked.
3. Most of us including educated and qualified Scientists and Technologists see monsoon flood as a waste of a huge amount of water that merely runs down to sea and create flood havoc. It is necessary to understand that while rainwater breaks rocks to fine particle and releases nutrients, the byproducts (sand, soil and nutrients) have to be washed down. Drip irrigation cannot do this. In other words, large runoff is required to (a) transport and distribute the byproducts of soil formation; (b) flush out generated sediments to ocean; (c) clean land surface of "poisons" now we apply and accumulate (pesticide, fertilizer residues, chemicals and heavy metals of industries); (d) provide water to downstream habitats including humans and finally (e) sustain the coastal brackish water ecology by dilution. Dwindling discharges from rivers due to anthropogenic withdrawal and high fertilizer residues have already increased the nitrate level in Indian coastal water, the impact of which is slowly surfacing on the health of the people. *Let us remember that this land (we call mother earth/India) having taken a monsoonal bath with a variety of soap and shampoo of pesticide, chemicals and fertilizers, the wash water is needed to be drained out.*

4. The Ganga-Bramhaputra basin (to be called the "Fore-Deep"), which is the focus of major linkages is an extremely dynamic stretch of land. The fragile Siwalik and the Himalayan foothills contribute a large amount of sediment through Yamuna, Ganga (with its tributaries) and Bramhaputra and continuously fill up the Fore-Deep. The Punjab wedge (submerged Aravalli ridge) in the west combined with sediment flux from the middle zone of Himalayas through Yamuna, produces an easterly shift of the river. The northerly movement of Indian plate (4 to 6 cm. per year) into this Fore Deep virtually confines and directs the entire water flow on the Gangetic plain towards east. The anticlockwise rotation of the north moving Indian plate produces the "Bengal neck" where sediment accumulation is maximum. This large accumulation is apparently the cause of chronic flood in Bihar. All the linkages and transfer of water proposed on this Fore-deep are apparently in skew if not against the dynamic landform and natural flows. Therefore, the linkage may provide temporary benefit but is destined to be a failure in long run.One will spend more energy in lifting the water across a rising terrain to make the linkages survive, than generate power from the linkage. It will be like some beaurocratic set-up in India where the revenue collection is less than the expenditures incurred in the collecting process.
5. All flood prone zones in India coincide with zones of maximum sediment deposition. (Name it in UP,Bihar,Bengal,Orissa,AP or TN). Increased sediment deposition is due to (a) intensive agricultural activities involving deep ploughing, (b) mining, stripping and land development and (c) deforestation in the watershed region. Coal mining and discharge of coal combustion products (Ash) become prominent locally, for examples in Yamuna, Damodar, Bramhani and Godavari. No wonder, all the life lines of India carrying life supporting water have become "Rogue" in our "developing land"(vide map). Large-scale excavations in linkage activity will add to the country's sediment generation.
6. Linkage will transfer pollutants to apparently nonpolluted areas, produce more extensive soil salinitization than what we have seen along some regions of minor linkages due to different rate of evaporation and soil-water interaction, in some cases produce water logging and consequent change in aquatic habitats (refer snails in Niles, algal bloom in N.Queensland, Australia).
7. The concept of water surplus and water deficient regions is a misnomer since there is no democratic use of water resources of a basin. The richer and powerful lobby/State/farm can siphon (steal) the water by dams, canals and aqueducts (examples: Mumbai, Teri dam, Narmada project etc.).Such plunder or sequestering of natural water resources has started appearing on Indian horizon even from the stock of atmospheric moisture by way of cloud seeding and artificial rainfall.

8. There will be more interstate dispute making a mockery of the Constitution and increase in disobedience to the supreme judiciary, and this has already surfaced. Thus with the increased professional activities of "Earth Engineers", the legal profession will have a boon too. Had we got Indian States organized in conformity with basin or sub-basin of rivers, things would be easier.
9. While large-scale linkage of major rivers presents a frightening scenario, honest effort can be made in a few noncontroversial intra-basin transfers. Let the future generation observe the impact of such "honest attempts" before undertaking major linkage. After all, the future is theirs. We need not burrow from the future to "beat our drum" nor are we the saviours of the future, not even the stewards.
10. The Task Force does not have a visionary Environmentalist and Ecologist, not even a Scientist conversant with earth, land, soil and plants, or a Sociologist/Tribal Expert in that matter. The members are Bureaucrats, Scientocrats, Technocrats (Earth-Engineer) and Financier, most from ivory tower.
11. Apparently, it appears at once, that the project is a conception of a syndicate of Politician, Bureaucrats, a section of Earth-Engineer, Bankers, Financiers (IMF, WB not excluded), all in a stampede to increase their professional activity (*Bread and Circus*) which will ultimately damage the ecology and environment of this land of *"Milk and Honey"*(at least once it was) in the name and game of playing with Nature. "Elephants do not play chess", "Gods do not throw dice", but it appears, we intend to play against Nature not knowing that the dice is loaded and is of "Shakuni".

18

The "3R" Factor

Reduce, Recycle and Reuse

(Reduce, Recycle and Reuse was the topic of discussion by the Young Environment Program, Powai, Mumbai, to celebrate Earth Day on the 22nd April, 2008. I had the privilege to present my views on the occasion, an aftermath of which was published to out-reach more readers.)

A common man's requirement of materials for daily use comes from the primary resources of the earth. The earth resources can be categorized as:

1. Nonrenewable resources such as, Fossil fuels – coal & oil, metals, cement, stones etc. Even our adjacent hills and lake can come in this category.
2. Renewable resources such as, timber, foodstuffs, solar energy. For India, even monsoon is a great resource for water.

Strictly, the renewable earth resources are strictly not so, since generation of timber and foodstuffs etc are dependent on the nonrenewable. Even, monsoon has been unpredictable (man made)

The appalling fact is that "Earth people are consuming earth resources beyond the ecological endowment of the earth" and that too when only 20% of world people in developing nations are consuming 80% of the earth resources. If the rest of the 80% of people in developing or poor nations aspires to follow the foot step of the fortunate few, and it is difficult to desist or persuade them not to do so, we need at least 3 earths to meet human needs. Even God cannot help. That means, sooner or later world is likely to face a paucity of basic resources and the burning example is shortage of fossil fuels – coal and oil, if not the life sustaining material called "water".

It is not only the paucity or exhaustion of earth resources alone is an outfall of consumerism, the residue and waste generated in their conspicuous use, has threatened the very earth to turn into a junk yard. "Consumerism has made a trash of the planet", Stephens Hawkins, the Nobel Laureate once remarked. Look on to the ground around. Not only the sprawling municipal dumping grounds, the entire city of Mumbai has risen out of reclaimed materials and we stand over our discardants. There is no "virgin soil" over any part of the city.

But the dilemma is, consumerism is now an index of socio-economic progress and we need to progress to be civilized.

Recycle and Reuse are terms of an affluent society who are afraid of exhaustion of resources or accumulation of waste around. Besides, Recycle and Reuse do not stop consumerism; they only extend it in some form or other. Although provide local relief in environmental and economic fronts, Recycle and Reuse have several global crisis. Typical examples are:

- The colorful toys, furnitures and household goods made from recycled plastics carry harmful toxic substances like heavy metals (Refer: banned Chinese toys).
- India has become the largest junk yard of imported used electronic goods (e-waste) bringing in toxic substances like mercury, lead, arsenic, cadmium, etc.
- The ship breaking industries at Chittagong (Bangladesh), Alang in Gujarat and Darukhana in Mumbai, the only places in world where redundant ships are dismantled at great cost of environmental damage and contamination, are world's most polluted locations.

It is but typical of the modern technology to assure society to devise curative measures to overcome paucity and exhaustion of resources by providing substitutes and alternative materials or by extension of the resources stock by innovative methods. For examples:

- Aluminum has been substituted for copper in electrical cables, but production of aluminum is (electrical) energy intensive, bauxite mining is harmful to land-ecology and use of the metal is supposed to be the cause of Alzheimer disease.
- Tractor is a poor substitute to bull-pulled- plough in traditional agriculture. Because the former requires fossil fuel and spares, generate pollution but the later needs little, even gives dungs while in service.

Extension of the resource stock too, is ridden with unforeseen problems such as:

- Emergence of Bovine Spongiform Encephalopathy (Mad Cow Disease) and vanishing eagle species who feed on cow carcass are due to feeding of animal protein to increase calf-muscle (beef) and injection of oxytocin to extract maximum milk from the cattle respectively. Accordingly, the avian flue of today is a symptom, something scientists must ponder about.
- The health of the soil consequent to Green Revolution to extend agricultural yields is far from satisfactory.
- The temptation to appropriate fertile lands for biofuel in place of food-crops, may supplement fossil fuel, but is likely to end up with world hunger.

The real danger of excessive use of earth resources however comes from (a) waste generation, that is, residue left over and (b) pollution. Because, pollution is caused by leakage of material (resource) from the utility cycle, the larger the amount of its use, the larger the leakage and hence the greater the pollution. Pollution is known to be a fait accomplice for a society on wheels of consumerism.

The most important and essential earth resources which do not need reduction, recycle and reuse are:

1. The air in the atmosphere
2. The water of the hydrosphere and
3. The soil, which produces food in the pedosphere.

However, the quality and quantity of the constituents in each of the resources are fixed for optimum development of the quality of life on earth. Change any; the human life is adversely affected. For example, a small increase in carbon dioxide level in atmosphere will increase global temperature and set in severe ecological change. The perception of modern man to this three basic life supporting system of earth resources, appears to be perverted because our consumerist attitude has:

- Polluted the air – vide the air over Mumbai, ozone holes over Poles and Inconvenient Truth of Al Gore for global warming,
- Contaminated the water to the extent that there is no natural potable water left in any rivers or lakes,
- Degraded and damaged the soil, leading to accumulation of pollutants in our foodstuffs that grow over it.

With such a scenario around, we need to be aware of a *Panchsheel* that:

1. Earth is a limited body and carries a limited stock of resources.
2. Earth is a home for many other family members besides Man, to share resources and responsibilities. The lower forms do, Man does not.
3. Earth is not a motel, but a home and needs to be maintained clean, not by any extraterrestrial scavengers but by us only.
4. Man has become a terror to other forms of life on earth, made trash of the earth due to excessive use of resources. It is time we reduce it.
5. Man is but a privileged guest, merely a steward (captain) but not the owner of this spaceship.

19 Decriminalisation of Homosexuality

The Dynamic of Gender Bending Chemicals

Judiciary decision on July, 2009 to decriminalize homosexuality in India was greeted with jubilation by a section of urban activist but raised eyebrows among a vast section of Indian society and Government in particular. The Govt. remained shy and left the matter to the judiciary but the Indian press continues to mastigate the issue.

Nature's effort to perpetuate life by procreation started by simple cellular division followed by asexual vegetative propagation as in potato, and ended up with complex modes of sexual conjugation in higher animals and man. By the process of Natural Selection two distinct streams, males and females evolved, characterized by fundamental structural units like X or Y chromosome pairs in homo sapiens. Homosexuality or transexuality is but an aberration of this natural law and the cause can be traced back to environmental, social and cultural factors. We analyze and speculate below first hand examples observed in plants and animals and discuss why the aberration in Nature has come into place.

1. **The case of a Temple tree (*Kath Champa*) in the garden, next door:** *Kath Champa* blooms throughout the year with white or red flowers, is normally nonfruiting and propagated by planting a piece of its stem (vegetatively). During last 12 years, one such plant nurtured from a stick to a full grown tree with sewage water in the said garden, has for the first time bore a few pods from its flower atop the tree. A vegetative plant showed sign of fruiting perhaps under intensive sewage water application. Its exclusively white bloom also turned reddish in some of the branches. In manicured gardens, flowering plants like Hydrangea are also made to bloom flowers of desired colour simply by addition of chemicals in the feeding water. This year, the TESCO departmental store in UK sells a variety of black tomato known as *kumato*.
2. **The womb of an Apple:** While on a visit to USA, I cut open a large American apple during breakfast and was surprised to find one of the seeds embedded near the skin away from the kernel of the fruit. I showed the abnormality to my Microbiologist daughter sitting by my side. She remarked, American apples are grown with heavy chemical treatment.

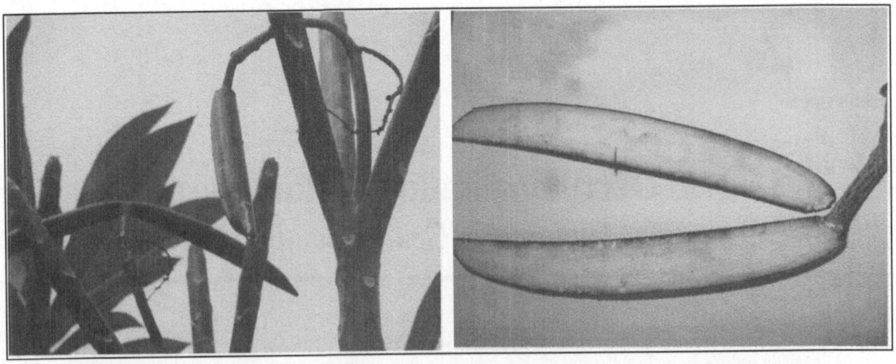

Vegetative Champa Tree Sprouts Fruits but the Fruits do not bear Seeds

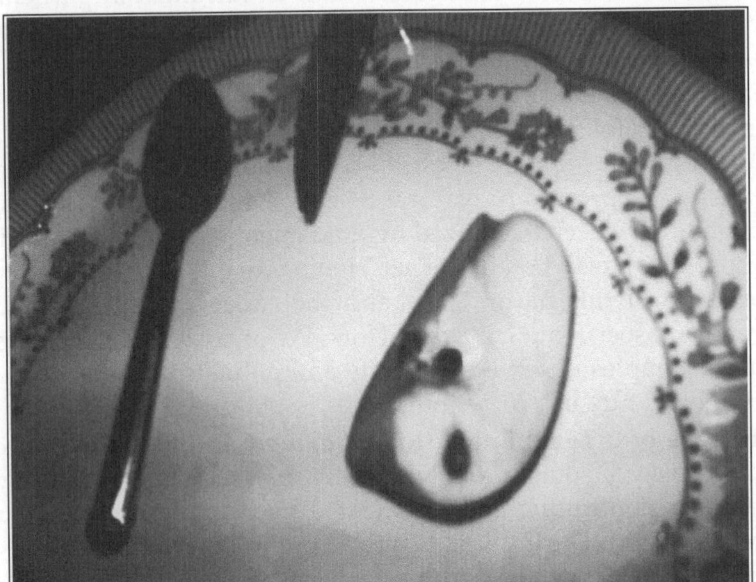

Displacement of a Seed from the Ovume towards the Skin in an Apple

3. **False pregnancy:** I had a female pet dog who was let out of the house only on leash during morning and evening walks. On growing up, she was found getting restless in the balcony of the house whenever a stray male dog appeared near the balcony. Once they were found "nosing" each other through the small holes in the railing. In a few weeks the dog showed enlarged mammary organs and to my surprise, even the vet-doctor on his next monthly visit declared the dog to be pregnant. But it was merely a false pregnancy, apparently due to hormonal changes consequent to stress of conjugal isolation (very cruel on the part of the Master).
4. **Egg from a caged parrot:** In Bhubaneswar, we had a parrot in a cage. During our lunch or dinner time the cage is opened and the little bird

would run to get fed by the side and on finishing would return to cage of itself. One day the bird was found chattering heavily and while rushing off the cage for usual feeding, stopped low for a moment, dropped an egg and continued to reach the dinner site. Only then we realized that the parrot was a female and laid an egg without mating any male parrot. The elderlies in the house remarked "Such thing happens".

5. **Parsi Dairy:** We know cow can be made to yield milk throughout the year by injecting hormones like *bovine somatotropin* (rBST). The injected chemical is known to cause mastitis and infertility in cows. Similar chemicals are also used to target the reproductive organ of women to induce labor pain or abortion and also in Viagra for arousal of penile tissues in man. The residual hormone in case of the milking cow remains in her body. After the death of the animal, when vultures feed upon the carcass, the toxin is transferred to the scavenger birds whose egg shells turn thin and fragile. The vulture population dwindles. Of late, the problem is keenly felt by the Parsi community because of the birds not available around their "Tower of Silence". Extreme abuse of the chemical to fasten the growth of female girls for immoral trafficking has been reported in media.

6. **The Pimp Papaya:** In earlier days, *Gaunti* papaya (Papaya brought from village firm) on cutting used to pour out a large amount of slimy seeds and the entire fruit was uniformly sweet. Now a days, the size of the fruit coming to the market is larger, often seedless or carry a single or few scattered seeds, the sweetness differs in different parts of the same fruit and often there would be malignant growths of knots and blocks in the fruit. Most modern papayas are grown with heavy dose of chemicals.

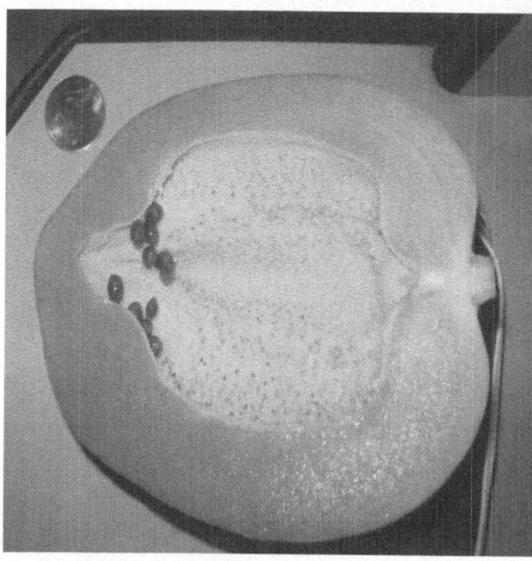

Papaya with less or no Seeds

Fruits in Stalks of Feminised Tree

Also one can transform a papaya plant from male to female and produce fruits by piercing a wooden plug through its stem at the base. Plant Scientists feel that the piercing plug imbibes a shock of hormonal change in the male plant. Fruits from transformed plant do not carry seed; at most have a lone or only a cluster of few seeds.

7. **Chemicals in Environment:** Man has invented and uses hundreds and thousands of synthetic chemicals and continues to add more every year. Today, we have some 100,000 such chemicals which virtually bathe us in our daily course of life. Added to this, we are soaked with Electromagnetic Radiations (EMR) from a variety of modern equipments and instruments, used at homes, offices, work places, the most talked about one is our daily companion the Cell-Phones, over and above the increased quota of UV-Radiations reaching through the punctured Stratosphere. Few are aware that the UV-Radiation in our Aqua guard does not kill the microbes in the water but destroys their proliferation capacity so that the water we drink from it remains safe. EMR and the bizarre of chemicals are apparently useful to us but are Endocrine (hormonal) Disruptors (EDC) and are also known as Gender Bender Toxins because they directly target the sexual and reproductive organs of plants, animals and Man. It may be chemical fertilizer which increases the seeds and reduces the stalks in rice or wheat plants, may be the technology of genetic manipulation which decimates seeds in grapes, papaya, changes color of flowers and stimulates fertility or infertility in animals (and Man).

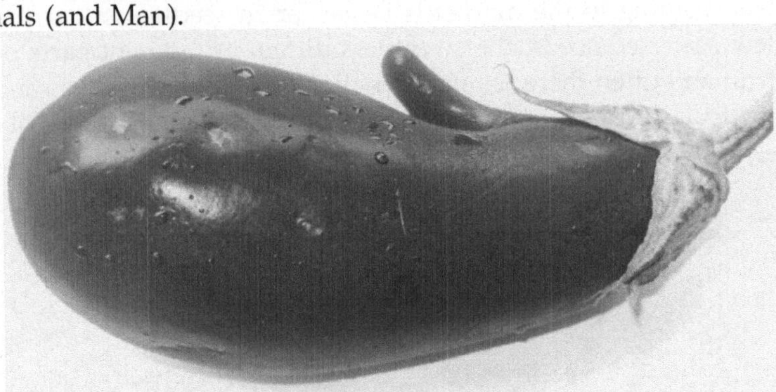

Aberration in Growth of Brinjal

Whatever enters the grass, vegetables, fruits and animals ultimately reaches man through food chain. Man is the biomagnifier of all toxic substances that enter the environment. No wonder, what affects the lower forms of life does the same in humans more effectively. We are not aware of it because the changes are small, slow and sluggish and camouflaged with terms like progress, modernism and cultural changes.

Take for example Phthalates, a chemical which makes plastic pliable, goes into manufacture of toys, medical equipments, paints, hair sprays, deodorants, cosmetics, toothpaste, soaps, vinyl and many more, is known to block action of male sex hormone Testosterone or mimic female sex hormone Estrogen. Boys born to mothers exposed to Phthalates have been found to have smaller penis and show genital feminization. Chronic low level exposure of many such EDCs starts feminizing boys at womb. Sperm counts in man have been dropping in many industrial societies which use large amounts of synthetic chemicals like PCBs, heptachlors, dioxins, DDT and heavy metals like lead, cadmium, chromium, mercury etc. A study spreading to 20 developed countries showed that during last 50 years the count has dropped from a normal value of 150 million per milliliter to 60 million per milliliter. Most synthetic chemicals have been with us for less than one half of human life span; this is far too little time to evolve defense against them. Hermaphrodite male fish have been found laying eggs in polluted Potomac River of USA and half of all fish population in British low land rivers changing sex due to pollution (BBC-report). Even changes in environmental temperature has impact on amphibian gonads - crocodile eggs buried in sand mounds hatch out girls in cool sand and males in warm sand. Every human males, child or adult ought to have noticed his scrotal sac carrying testicle recedes in cold and extends out in warmer condition – a fact that goes to show the sensitivity of gonads to environment.

8. **Social and Cultural factors:** In traditional and cultural isolation of males and females, such as in boarding schools, hostels, defense services, religious institutions demanding celibacy, and industrial urban society where family life is curtailed, the hidden cost of homosexuality is a historical fact. The spectacular grooming activity of conjugal seduction by male in plant and animal kingdom, for instance the dance of peacock, to attract females has now been reversed in humans of modern era by commercial exploitation of women with textile & fabrics, cosmetics, jewellery and "body care solutions and surgery". In the post-modern era, the culture of "Women on the Top" in the veil of their liberation too has far reaching consequences on the aberration of the Natural Laws particularly on Gender Bender Dynamics.

   Natural Evolution is being distorted by pollution, which damages genitals and the ability to father/mother offspring says a study in "Independent Science". This distortion or aberration is not "Natural" but is anthropogenic, the consequence of which can neither be left in the hands of a few "Gay enthusiastic", Socialites or ill informed Judiciary. It affects the evolution of life on this planet.

20 Resources Curse

A Paradox of Plenty, with Example

—*"While people in mineral rich countries are found to reel under poverty line, for those using maximum of it, the quality of life is not desirable."*

—*"World's largest blue diamond, the Hope is known to have brought death and ill fortune to a series of owners on its trail."*

Minerals are the backbones of all modern developments. They usher economic growth and prosperity. Our settlement in comfortable homes, materials and appliances of daily use, sustenance of modern agriculture, transport and communication networks, fueling of power plants and industries, all requirements of defense and armaments, even display of vanity with gold and jewelry need a variety of minerals. Fortunately the earth is endowed with all those minerals we need and if used judiciously, are in enough stocks, though at various levels of concentration. The scare-crow of "Resources crunch" arises out of misdistribution, unequal sharing and greed of a consumerist society which today, as per WHO Report, abuse 60% of earth resources and in doing so has invited the wrath of global warming.

Mineral exploitation, mining, processing, extraction, transport and use are interwoven with a bizarre of ecological, economical and societal problems. Ecological problems in mining cannot be averted or diverted because minerals have to be mined where they occur and cannot be relegated to a place of our choice, and mining, processing and smelting always degrade and pollute environment. However, adverse economic and societal impacts can be averted, at least reduced by good governance and introduction of social and environmental safeguards.

Most countries or regions endowed with massive mineral wealth are poor, economically backward and are virtually exploited with cruel labor practices, violation of human rights, conflicts, even war and the resources mobilized and pumped out of the ground at a great cost of environmental damage, are siphoned to more developed and richer nations who enjoy the benefits of the new found wealth. Thus the French exploited the bauxites of New-Guinea, the Britain exploited the rich diamond finds of S.Africa and Netherland took the diamond and copper resources of Congo. The sub-Saharan African countries such as the oil rich Nigeria, diamond, gold and copper rich Congo, Sierelona and Gold-Coast, the oil rich countries of

Venezuela in Latin America and Arab nations stand witnessed to the fact that mineral resources have not improved the life but have brought untold misery to the native people. History of diamond extraction and trade in Africa is based on gruesome violence and terror. "Blood Diamond campaign" against diamond industry has appeared in many world capitals to arouse awareness underlining the misery among diamond workers. In India the mineral rich belts of Bihar, Orissa, Chhattisgarh, MP and parts of Andhra Pradesh and Maharashtra too face similar fate. Absence of environmental safeguards, poor governance, emphasis on corporate and foreign interests, neglect of local and project affected people, lack of public policy in post-conflict situations, human-right violation, corruption, bureaucracy, delay in implementation, intermediary brokers and mine-mafias are some of the causes of sickness of mineral rich nations or regions listed above. This is known as Resources Curse, a paradox of plenty and is also called the *Dutch Disease*, which amounts to societal degradation, an opposite of Development and has led many economists and sociologists to propose "How not to develop a country" in the present style. The present turmoil in development of mineral industries in Odissa are symptoms of this illness that plague the State.

An example: (Refer Chart)

A bright example of the Dutch Disease is the history of development of Chhotnagpur Plateau that has come to light by analysis of events during last half a century. Soon after independence, to improve the fate of native population of the region, Damodar Valley Corporation (DVC) was formed to harness the flood prone Damodar river by a series of dams to generate power and use the water for irrigational purpose. A parallel activity was to exploit the abundant coal resources to supplement energy requirements. Reservoir submergence and coal mining transformed the land dependent tribals to industrial laborers, coal mafia sprouted and politics of a separate Jharkhand State began (and finally achieved) for the benefit of a favored few. Decrease of flow in Damodar river and the vast amount of erosional fluxes generated in coal mining, silted Hoogly river, hampered incoming large ships to Calcutta port and at the same time created back flow of Calcutta sewerage. Calcutta Municipality was blamed. A major part of the port activity from Calcutta was diverted to Diamond Harbor followed by development of Haldia port, which earlier had a sprawling settlement of East-Bengal refugees. The refugees, having been uprooted migrated to National Capital and located in trans-Yamuna sprawl east of Delhi. Race riot, disease and death plagued the sprawl in 1991 and the matter reached Indian Parliament. Some of the uprooted refugees from Haldia reached Dandakaranya only to lay foundation of the Naxalite movement. To ease out Hoogly river discharge, Farakka barrage was constructed across Ganga to divert a part of Ganges water which obviously aroused Indo-Bangla dispute of water sharing, while fisher folks upstream of Farakka lost their precious catch of Hilsa fish which stopped migrating upstream. The intention of improving the lots of Chhotnagpur tribals is not a matter of dispute, but the series of adverse impacts that have surfaced during last half a century in translating the intention to reality is a matter of concern. In fact the developmental effort was nonholistic (unholy) and became a curse of earth resources exploitation.

A Bewildering Flow Chart of Development

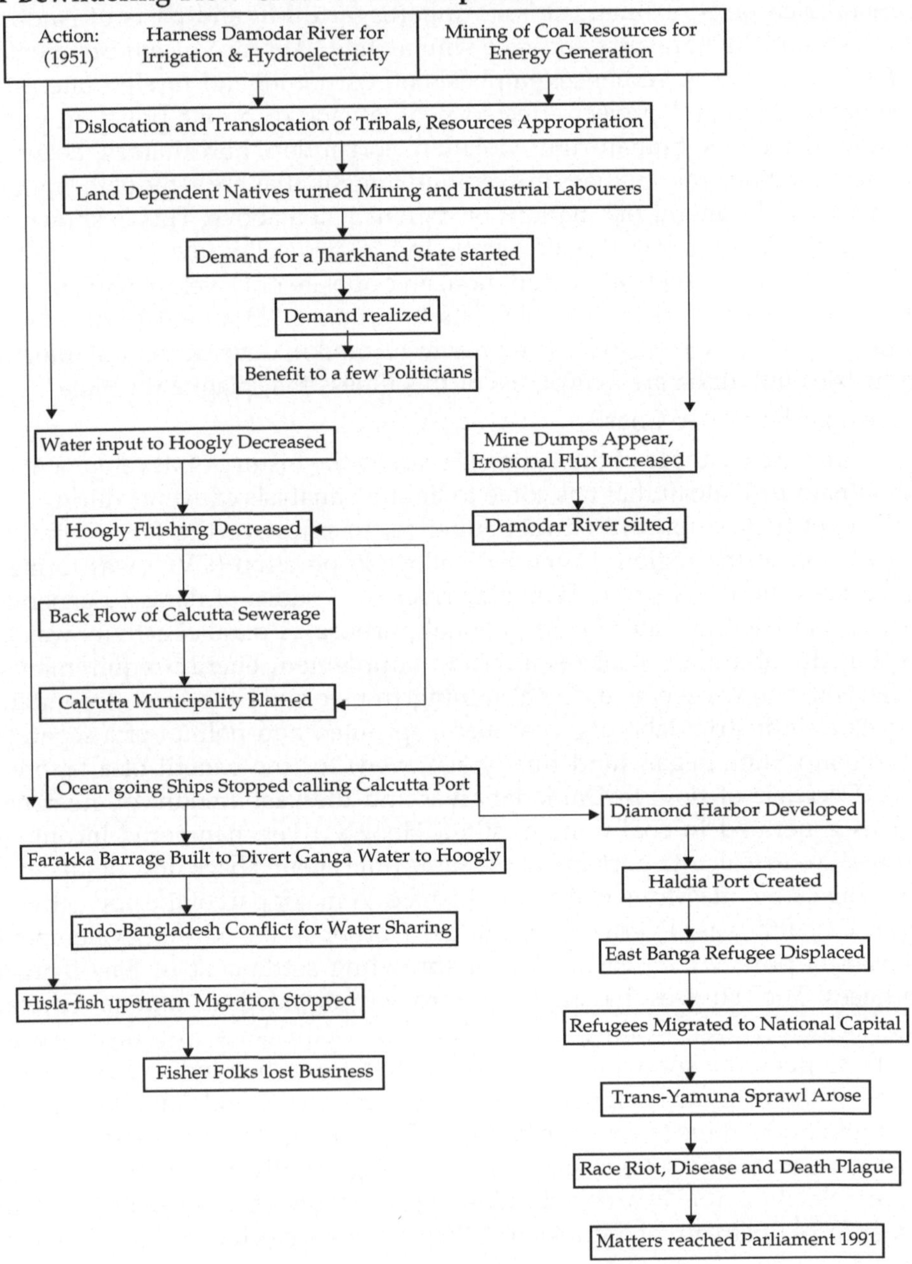

21

Enviornmental Ethics

Basics of Environmental Ethics

Basic scientists define Environment as "Aspects of Physics and Chemistry of Air, Water and Soil". Life scientists define environment as "Physics and Chemistry of Air, Water and Soil, where living things live". But when it comes to humans, the definition also includes "Social, Cultural, Political and Economic aspects". The amendment of the definition of Environment from basic fundamental principles, through a spectrum of living kingdom to human world, greatly changes the values and perception of nature, therefore, the environmental ethics. The metamorphosis also brings in polarization and contradictions to the spirit of the definition, because, the "human aspects" themselves are variable, myopic and bias.

The Cosmocentric concept based on primary rules of nature of basic properties (Dharma) of matter and energy, runs the universe, all the phenomena of time and space including the extraterrestrial and terrestrial motions, electrical, magnetic and gravitational pulls, evolution of life, changes of season and movement of electrons. The boundary of living and nonliving has little importance because one is same as the other, though of different kinds. "Tat Twam Asi", "So Aham".

The Ecocentric and Biocentric ethics weigh heavily on the earth and living system as a whole and emphasizes a symbiotic relationship, "Vasudeba Kutumbakam". All equations in these systems function under a rule that everything is connected to every other things for mutual benefit and sustenance. The relation among the rocks, the soil mantle, growth of trees and nesting birds over, all primed by hydrologic cycle is a simple example. Symbiosis automatically presupposes interconnectedness. A deeper sense of interconnectedness, not normally realized is, the elemental transfer and cycles such as oxygen, carbon, phosphorus, etc. among soil, plants, animals and humans. As a matter of fact, the Gia theory of James Lovelock, which considers the earth as a gigantic living organism, exemplifies the ideal ecocentric concept.

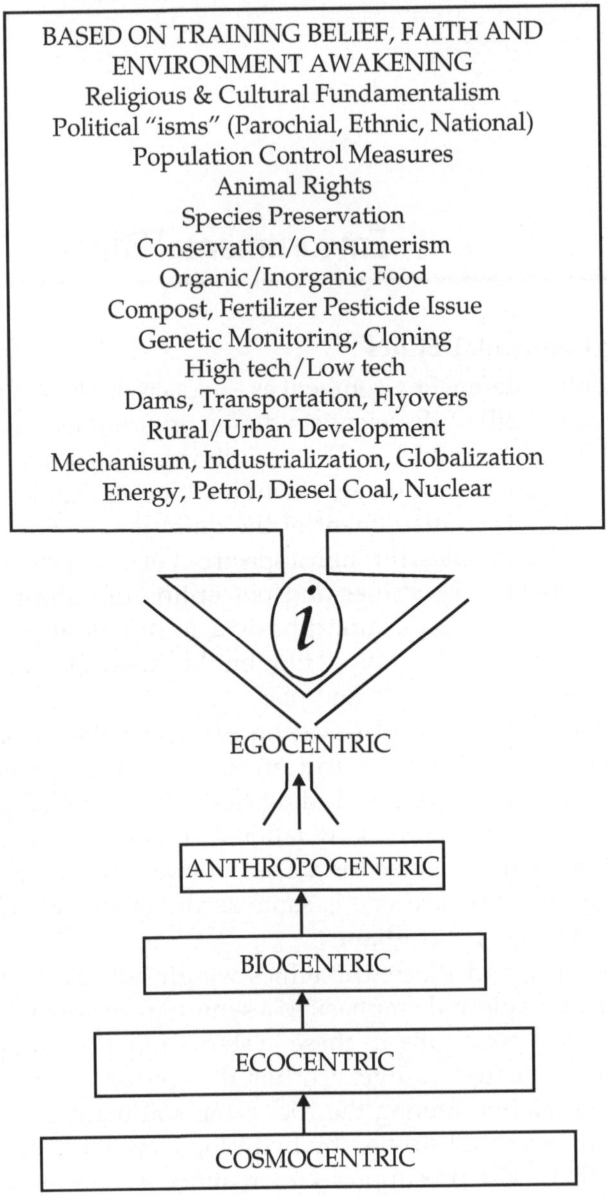

TOP HEAVY ETHICAL PYRAMID IN ENVIRONMENT

Approach of Environmental Ethics

Anthropocentric ethics is architected around the needs and comfort of man. Here the "rocks have no right", "animals are created for man" forest is our cellulose bank and even the rivers, that have been flowing long before the appearance of humans are bent to lose their instinct of gravity flow. No wonder, when the "Civilized Explorer" from Europe descended onto the

New World few hundred years before, the local inhabitants, the Red-Indian (now coated with a respectable title – the American Indian) had the same ethics to face as man do unto natural elements today. However, of late, sanity has dawned on a section of the people that, although a single tree or a single cow may not have the right of survival, the plants and cows as species ought to be preserved, so also a hill range, a coast line or a dancing stream, so that our future generation will not have to go to museum to stare at a majestic Banian tree or the beauty of a mountain slope. Therefore, the earlier judgment of Supreme Court of India banning limestone mining near Mussorie to preserve the beauty of Himalayan slope is a silver lining on patches of dark clouds such as quarrying of hills in Mumbai and assaults on granites around Hyderabad. The dilemma, however is, will the revenue generated from tourists who will flock to Mussorie to enjoy the beauty of Himalayan slope be more than the value of limestone that would be raised in mining, moreover the benefit of downstream developmental process such as cement production, building activities, road paving etc.! The latest move in such anthropocentric evaluation is to design on Environmental impact Analysis (EIA) through "experts" (Environmental Traders) for a cost benefit ratio of the operation, knowing very well that the "effected" in downstream process are neither a party nor presently available for protest or opinion. The project burrows heavily and blindly from the future generation. Anthropocentric ethics put Environment in the market; the earth is for sale. In an anthropocentric culture the saner elements of the society finds it hard to push the economic concepts of "multiple choice" into the frame work of ecological protection. Ecology and Economy, though have the same root mean different through a polarized ethics.

The conflict of economic development and ecological protection in anthropocentric ethics arises out of our perception of nature and natural elements as "objects". Objective point of view colours our personal relationship with nature. Objectification treats even us as goods or material. For example, in a factory "goods are polished and beautified but man (workers) comes out degraded". Similarly medical research names a rat as a specimen, which can be injected with poison until it expires and the data generated is published as "tolerance level". It may be any pollutant. The "lethal dose" is extrapolated to humans (you and me – specimen equivalent) after winning a qualified approval, permitting its use in nature at lower levels. We end up spraying the poison or injest us with the permitted dose through food chain. No information is given on bioenhancement, cumulative doses of various poisons and their interaction, accumulation over time and collection by us as predator on the top of food chain. In fact objectification of rat is an objectification of self and is indeed, a contradiction to our title that we are Homo Sapien meaning the intelligent one. Has objectification of nature, a backbone of anthropocentric ethics, produced a "Neo-Kalidas", a matter to ponder over. Because, the "Limestone Mining" synonymous to any earth resources utilization be it fossil fuel burning or fertilizer application on land has clearly resulted in despoiling the basic life supporting systems such as air, water and soil.

Anthropocity Justified

Among the estimated hundred million species in the living world, mammals make up only 4,500. The lone mammalian species known as Homo Sapien (Humans), though make an insignificant number one, has evolved to steward this spaceship. Supramacy of the human species cannot be ruled out or doubted because they have evolved through a process of "Natural Selection" and through a stiff competition for "Survival of the fittest" in a course of eons of evolutionary process. Nature, even the hardcore agnostic scientists define as "The minds of God", can not be wrong. Man " Created from the rib of the Father" (evolved by nature) and appointed to steward the earth, is but natural to rule the earth and therefore anthropocentric ethics appears to be a planned design of Nature (the minds of God) and is legitimate.

Aberration of the Ethics

However, earth's historical observations show that humans are but a privileged guest, arrived only 10 to 50 thousand years ago in this ancient home (earth), which was built some four billion years before and where two to three billion living species have come and gone and which still has 100 million living species. "Stewardship", the literary meaning "Caretaker" of a functional estate (originally applied to a piggery farm) assigns a great responsibility on humans, at least for the 100 million living occupant species. An ecocentric ethics which takes care of the entire ecosystem appears to be the rule of the nature and anthropocentric ethics is but an aberration. It is estimated that at the present rate of destruction of life supporting system and utter disregard to other species, 50% of the living species is likely to be extinct by the middle of this century, that means, the sixth extinction has already started, this time not by natural climatic changes and asteroid impacts, but by man himself.

Drawbacks of Anthropocentric Ethics

Environmental ethics tend to give a suitable value to various components in a system for functional continuum. When this functional value of a component is disrespected, the system gets degraded. The system can be conceived as a class-room, an educational institution, a family, an ecosystem or even the whole of the earth. Environmental degradation is basically disrespect of the naturally assigned (god given) role of any component in a system. Appreciation of this assignment by individuals or groups of individual depends on environmental awakening, which varies considerably in space and time. This makes anthropocentric culture slowly slides into egocentric ethics. One can, however, have an esoteric consolation by "thinking globally while acting locally".

Anthropocentric culture suffers form autogenic negative feed back loops, which sets in classic checks and balances by Nature. It is also nonhollistic (therefore unholy) and can not therefore be applied to a holistic system like natural environment. Science and Technology has come up as a powerful tool to support this neoculture. Application of S & T has solved many problems for survival of mankind, produced a variety of comforts and expanded the frontiers of knowledge. But, its very solutions and success have adversely effected the life supporting systems and threat to man's continued existence. It has placed guided missile in misguided hands. The only consolation is that if ozone hole is created by burning of fossil fuels, harness of alternative energy is capable of excluding the use of fossil fuel and stall the negative feed back pressure and continue developments. In other words "man not only cuts trees for his use and comfort, but also can plant seeds and cultivate a forest".

Anthropocentricity to Egocentricity

A normal trend of anthropocentrism is to slip into egocentric ethics which is heavily primed by, education, training, belief, faith and environmental awakening of individuals or groups of individual who happen to be the caretaker of the system or stewards of the society. These may be the various professionals, experts, politicians, religious leaders, "demigods" etc. The anthropocentric ethics is further polarized for sectoral benefit. Thus issues, such as construction of dams and reservoirs, flyovers, industrialization mechanization, population controls and religious fundamentalism have always arisen in society. The ideology also trickles down to breed experts like "petrotites & dieselites", "coalites & nuclearites" etc. in energy usage. Lower level environmental awakening is very much responsible for extreme degree of polarization of environmental ethics. Cases like judicial diktat on noise pollution only around a court building during working hours, " proposal to destroy stray dogs because some VIP's are disturbed in sleep", although environmentally justified are but polarized and egocentric ethics. Every sane individual must remember that "We are not alone, nor the earth for ourselves alone". Classical modern solutions have not given satisfactory response. We need to have a different mode of development and progress than have been doing so far.

Group - B

Earth Matters

22

History of Earth Unscrolled

Earth's historical time scale runs in terms of thousands of million years, where as that of humans, only in hundreds of years. For comprehensibility of relationship of the two, the history of earth has been condensed and presented in a time period of seven days (one week) and in that case human history comes within measurable units of a time clock. Accordingly, the birth of the universe (the Big Bang) happens three weeks before the present.

Earth History Unscrolled

1st week. Sunday:	Big Bang – Birth of the universe	13 billion yrs. (13,000000 000) ago
	Monday to Saturday:	Cosmic events continue
2nd week	Monday to Saturday	Cosmic events continue
3rd week	Sunday: 12.00.Mid-night:	Birth of Earth 4.6 billion yrs. (46,000 000000) ago.

Monday: Formation of solid earth, creation of primitive crust, ocean and atmosphere.

Tuesday: 8.00 AM: Evidence of bacterial life and single cell organism in sea.

Wednesday: Little fossil records.

Thursday: Evolution of life continued.

Friday: 4.00 PM: Sexual production by microorganism.

Saturday: 1.30AM : First marine animal noted on fossils.

9.30 AM: Plants appear on shore	425 million yrs. ago.
11.30 AM: Amphibians and Insects on land	410 million yrs. ago.
4.50 PM: Great Reptile – Dinosaurs appear	300 million yrs. ago.
5.30 PM: Mammals appear, subjugated by Dinosaurs	200 million yrs. ago.
7.15 PM: Birds fly in air.	150 million yrs. ago.
9.45 PM: Death of Reptiles-Dinosaurs extinct.	65 million yrs. ago

10.00 PM: First primate seen
11.00 PM: Monkey appears.
11.40 PM: The Great Apes.
11.52 PM: The Erect Apes.
11.56 PM: First Homo sapiens recorded (Homohabilis)
11.56,30″. Homoerectus.
11.59,30″ Archaic Homo sapiens
11.59,49″ Modern Man in Africa. 200,000 yrs. ago.
The great Mastodons extinct. 11,000 yrs.ago.

Earth created for Man (Genesis,) 23rd Oct. 9 AM: 6004 yrs. ago
11.59,59.33″. World written human history (2/3rd. Sec.from midnight).

The Period of Upanishad:	5000 yrs. ago
Lord Buddha:	2500 yrs. ago
Aristotle:	2300 yrs. ago
Confucius:	2260 yrs. ago
Birth of Christ:	2000 yrs. ago
Little Ice Age (UK):	600 yrs. ago
Charles Darwin:	160 yrs. ago
M.K. Gandhi:	150 yrs. ago
2nd World War:	80 yrs. ago
Foundation of UN:	75 yrs. ago
Cloning of Dolly the sheep:	20 yrs. ago

In this time span of 4.6 billion years of earth's history and evolution of life from a single cell organism to modern Man in course of about 3 hundred million years, at least five wide spread Global Extinction of living species have been recognized. These are:

1. 440 million before, when 25% of the marine families died and got extinct.
2. 370 million before, when 19% of animals – Fish and Invertebrates got extinct.
3. 250 million yrs. before, when 54% of the species were lost, mostly Trilobites and Insects.
4. 210 million yrs. before, when23% of Reptiles and Invertebrate died, but Dinosaurs flourished.
5. 65 million yrs. before, when 17% of the species lost, Dinosaurs got extinct, but Mammals survived.

The great mastodons vanished in the Pleistocene period at the hands of hunter-man. Scientists have noted an alarming rate of extinction of modern species of animals and plants since Man appeared in the scenario, more so, after the industrial revolution. At least one million species of the presently estimated 3-9 millions have succumbed during the last quarter century. The earlier five extinctions were caused by natural disasters such as, marine transgression or regression, floods, draughts, climatic change like Ice Age and meteorite bombardment from space. But the latest one, now known as the sixth extinction is man made and primarily by pollution, "Islandization of animals and plants", exploitation of habitats and resources and vanity. Since some types of pollution are genotoxic, man himself is exposed to the ill affects of his own achievements. "The Inconvenient Truth" of Global Warming is only one of the indicators of a sixth extinction.

The two third second activities of modern man in its eleven-second life span on the earth apparently make him a privileged guest and also the commander of this spacecraft. But appearance of the sixth extinction in the history of earth points out that "Man is not only a dangerous animal (to other animals) but himself an endangered species".

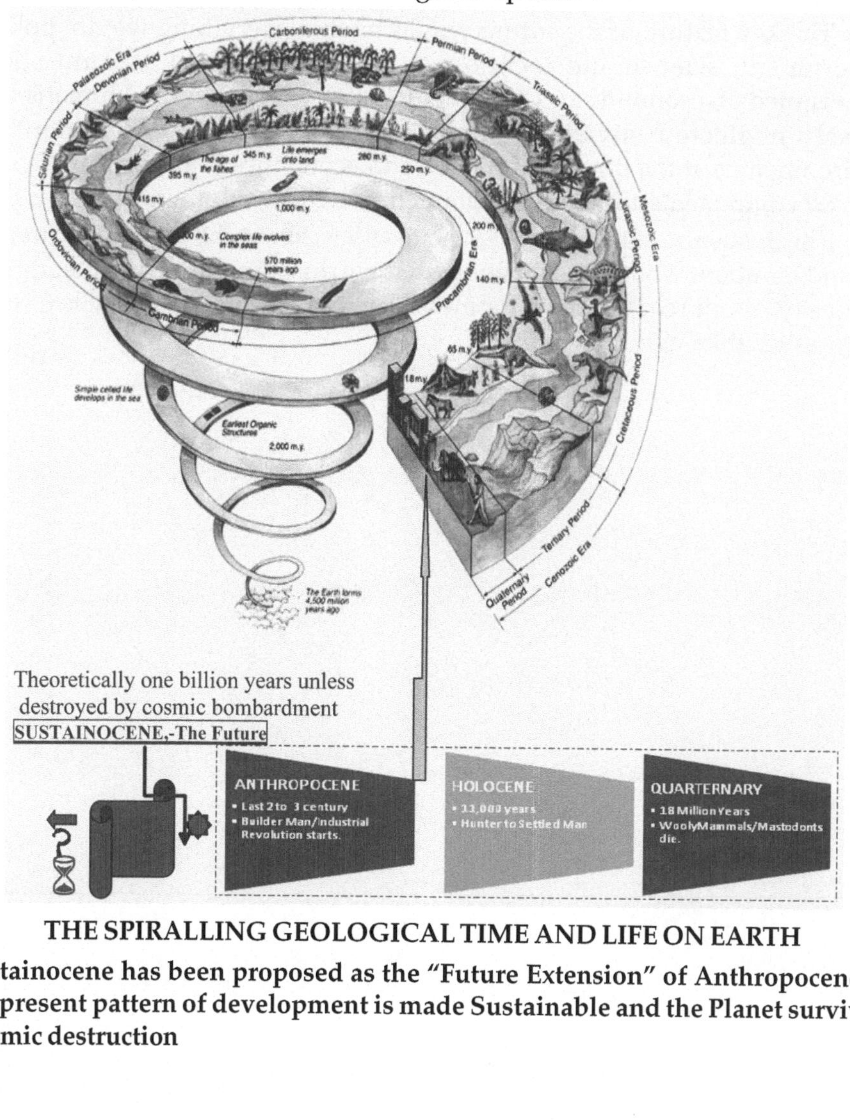

THE SPIRALLING GEOLOGICAL TIME AND LIFE ON EARTH

Sustainocene has been proposed as the "Future Extension" of Anthropocene if the present pattern of development is made Sustainable and the Planet survives Cosmic destruction

Anthropocene Unrolls to Sustainocene in Future

According to the International Union of Geological Sciences (IUGS), the professional organization in charge of defining Earth's time scale, we are officially in the Holocene ("entirely recent") epoch, which began 11,700 years ago after the last major ice age.

Anthropocene has become an environmental buzzword ever since the atmospheric chemist and Nobel laureate Paul Crutzen popularized it in 2000. This year, the word has picked up velocity in elite science circles: It appeared in nearly 200 peer-reviewed articles, the publisher Elsevier has launched a new academic journal titled *Anthropocene* and the IUGS convened a group of scholars to decide by 2016 whether to officially declare that the Holocene is over and the Anthropocene has begun.

The key feature of the future would be that everything we do, politics, government, science and technology, would take into account social, environmental, economic and personal lifestyle sustainability. Humans have grossly neglected environmental sustainability. At the moment the environment is at the bottom of the list and economics is at the top. We need all four components to work in conjunction with each other.

The Sustainocene is about being conscious, about the plants and animals around us, about what we eat, about what we do, about the gross inequalities in society, about real human happiness. The crux of sustainability is to work with rather than against nature.

23

Earth is a Gigantic Organism

Can you stand on the roof of a car speeding at 1250 miles an hour? Definitely not, you will simply be thrown out of it. But all of us apparently stand comfortably on a ball of rocks, the Earth, rotating at that speed and not aware of the danger of being thrown out into the space. Our stay on the earth has been possible only because the earth (like the mother monkey jumping from tree to tree with the baby stuck onto her) holds us tightly by a force known as gravity. This force of attachment does not distinguish between humans, animals or plants. No wonder, Earth is traditionally known as *Dharitry,* that which holds all equally. The ancient Greeks also regarded Earth as a goddess and called *Gaia.*

Rational analysis and logical arguments equally suggest that the planet Earth is a self-regulating coherent system of life, at least an envelope of living matters.

James Lovelock, a British Scientist first proposed that the earth is a gigantic living organism and called it *Gaia.* His *Gaia* could not fit into any form of a living object that science or Scientists are familiar with. But in his book, "The Ages of Gaia", he explained in great details that the *Gaia,* named after the Greek goddess of Earth is like a living body, has basic capacity of homeostasis and is subjected to metabolic damage from "High temperature fever" (Global warming), asphyxiation (Oxygen shortage), acid indigestion (Acid rains), Ozonemia (UV-radiations), carcinoma (in nuclear radiation) and "Dermatological dilemma" (Soil salinitization). Only a couple of centuries before, Leonardo Da Vinci, the great Architect and Engineer (better known as Artist and Painter) described the soil layer on earth as the skin of the planet. Modern Scientists do not deny that this layer, like human skin, continuously erodes, grows afresh from below, breathes, cools the body and is subjected to damage by contamination. A pinch of soil carries more than ten billion microbes and bacteria in symbiosis and that, the soil can be looked upon as a community and not a commodity. Soil, known as *mitti* or *matti* in vernacular is virtually the *Ma'ti* (The mother) for a variety of lives. Lovelock, however, took over from Da Vinci's "Soil skin" and warned that, with 60 to 70% of this skin damaged by way of degradation and deforestation, the health of our planet is in peril.

Algore, in his Inconvenient Truth mentions about annual increase and decrease of average carbon dioxide content of the planetary atmosphere due to seasonal global variation of plant foliage and calls it the breathing of Earth.

James Hutton, a reputed Physician and Geologist of 18th.century compared cycling of nutrient in soil and movement of water from ocean to land with circulation of blood. In the 1785 meeting of the Royal Society of Edinburg he proposed that geophysiological investigations of earth as a super organism are needed to recognize degeneration. Today the health of the earth is most threatened by major changes in the natural ecosystem. Resources exploitation, among others, stands foremost, which brings geophysiological changes. "Earth Doctors" and "Planetary medicines" have appeared for environmental cure.

The ancient religion and culture of India assigns a status of sacred motherhood to the "Earth". This concept, in practice, has sustained a time tested land dependant civilization, where astronomical bodies (The Sun and the Planets), mountains (the Himalayas), rivers (Ganga to Cauvery), animal habitat (Cows, Elephants to Snakes) and oxygen nourishing plants (*Banyan, Neem or Tulsi*) are worshipped. Gaia hypothesis goes back to fundamentals, to Genesis and to the Vedas of earliest Indian culture.

The doctrine of non-violence in Jainism extends into the inorganic kingdom, even to the destruction of a landform like mountain. Modern ecology unequivocally asserts the death of mountain habitats – plants, animals, birds and insects, whenever a mountain or hill is flattened for mining, land development or urbanization, although to perpetuate a new generation of life called the "modern man" in an urban sprawl. Supported by powerful tools of Science and Technology, this urban sprawl rapidly spreads like the ill famous algal bloom, to adjacent region. The material hunger and gubernatorial culture of the "new species" change, swallow and gulp all that was once natural and primeval. Therefore, many thinkers speak of urbanization as planetary cancer and man of becoming a terror to the planetary life. Because, of the present 100 million known species on earth, 30 millions have been lost since man appeared in the scenario and at the present rate of destruction of the life supporting systems and utter disregard to other species, 50% of the living species is likely to be extinct by the middle of the century. The "High temperature fever" of earth or "Global warming" alone will eliminate one out of every four land animals from the earth. That means, the Sixth Extinction has already started, this time not by natural climatic changes or asteroid impacts, but by man himself.

The doctrine of a living planet was ultimately brought into focus by the first space traveler Neil Armstrong when this planet was observed from outside the earth, changing hues, rolling and wobbling in space with a coherent system of life. The notion of a living earth is designed to inspire respect and admiration of a planet carrying this coherent life system.

It is true that microbes living inside our minute body cells can not conceive the magnanimity of human body and mind, so are the humans, incapable of understanding the grandeurs of a living planet like the earth, except by Para-sensory concepts and not by experiments, observations and comparisons which are the classical methods of knowing through sensory organs.

Today's "Biosphere", earlier described by Vladimir Vernadsky as the envelope of life or the area of living matter, can be regarded as the topmost layer of earth crust occupied by "Transformers" which convert cosmic radiations into effective terrestrial energy. Thus, the earth is not just a "Rock-ball" to be rolled around by today's Planetary Engineers; it is a living statue of a celestial motherhood whose body and attire (Air, Water and Soil) ushers reverence, admiration, protection and preservation. The future of humanity depends much more upon a right relationship with this celestial motherhood than with the never-ending drama of human interest to usher geophysiological changes in the name of progress and development.

24

Mother Earth ! Whose Mother Indeed ?

The Inconvenient Truth

With environmental stress raising head and natural disasters descending upon the stressed sites more often than before, there have been a spate of sermons in many national and international forums to "save the Earth", more specifically, the Mother Earth. If this realization is true a few points immediately arise.

- If the earth is viewed as a mother, it has to be a living organism.
- All species of living things such as, Man (Homo Sapiens), Monkey to Cattle; Frog, Lizard to Crocodiles; Birds, Insects to Ants; Fish, Crabs to Whales; Plants, Grass and Algae or Worms, Mushrooms and Microbes are "Children" of the Mother Earth. She is not likely to discriminate any of the above kinds, rather is likely to be kinder to the Weak and Meeks for a living in Her home.
- The Earth is being assaulted by one of the prodigal offsprings, her "family home" is under turmoil and the weaker members endangered, decimated or extinguished by the latest arrival who appeared only a few thousand years ago in the 3.8 billion year span of her productive life.
- Natural catastrophe and disasters are but Checks & Balances of Nature to settle "domestic ethics" of her home and are correctionary measures to discipline errand offspring.

Man is an Infinite Minority

The human species, Homo Sapiens, makes up only one of the 1.7 million fully known and described species of living things on earth. Insects alone make up one million species with 10 quintillion individuals and at any times there are 200 millions of living insects for every individual human being. Even in terms of biomass, the earth has 300 kg of insects for every kg of humans. The ants (a type of insect) alone equals to the total weight of the 6.7 billion humans (of 50 kg each) which presently live on earth. Besides the one million insect species, there are 5490 number of species of Mammals (of which humans make only one), 9998 species of Birds, 9084 species of Reptiles, 6433 species of Amphibians and 31300 species of Fish. The actual number of living species may be as high as 8 million as against 1.7 million that are very well known.

As against 6.7 billion humans, the earth has 240 billions Livestock, 60 billion Land Birds, 1000 billions Land Mammals, 1000 to 10,000 billions each of Reptiles and Amphibians and 10,000 billions Fish.

Out of the 1.7 million species, the plant kingdom of 0.3 million species, make up a biomass 560 billion times the biomass of animal Carbon and annually add 100 billion tons of primary Carbon by way of photosynthesis.

The essence of the above statistics is that the Mother Earth has such a large variety and number of offsprings that proliferate the biosphere that Man is an infinitely small minority. Besides, the appearance of Man on earth is a flicker of a mere 0.05 million years compared to 3.8000 million years of organic evolution in the 4.6 billion years old Earth.

Is Earth a Living Organism ?

Observation of the nine planetary members of the solar system, of which, Earth is one, at once negates the concept of a living earth. Earth is just a huge ball of hot metals and rocks with a veneer of biosphere where living things live and unlike a living organism which replicates offsprings, this planet has not produced any, except a Moon which in no way resembles the earth.

Mythological and philosophical connotations describe the planet as a living earth and many Scientists, pioneer among whom are James Hutton and James Lovelock, have proposed it to be a gigantic living organism and called her Gaia, after the Greek Goddess of earth.

Earth has a highly dynamic system of Core, Mantel and Crust, over which wraps a self-regulatory envelope of Pedosphere (a vibrant soil layer), Hydrosphere (including ocean) and Atmosphere (Air). While the global temperature, atmospheric contents and circulation and ocean salinity are regulated by homeostasis to maintain environmental conditions, necessary for survival of life through a span of 3.8 billion years, the symbiotic relationship of biospheric components (interdependence of living organism) has developed and sustained a unique system of life through evolution, that is yet to be met anywhere in the universe.

Only a couple of centuries before, Leonardo da Vinci, the great Architect and Engineer described the soil layer on earth, as the skin of the planet.

Modern Scientists do not deny that this layer, like human skin continuously erodes, grows afresh from below, breathes, cools the body and subject to damage by contamination by pollution and addition of chemical fertilizers. Love Lock took over from da Vinci's "Soil Skin" and warned that with 60 to 70% of this skin damaged by deforestation and degradation, the health of our planet is in peril.

The role of the azoic layers like the Core, Mantel and Crust to sustain the cognizable life system in biosphere is little understood even by Life Scientists. But for the earth's magnetic field generated by relative movement of Core and Mantel, no Van Allen Magnetic Belt could have formed and cosmic particle raining over the earth would have made life impossible to survive. Similarly, formation of Mountains, Plains and Valleys which leads to classic Geochemical Cycle is consequent to Plate Tectonics and new Crust formation by Mantel circulation.. Even the Ozone shield that protects life from UV-Radiation is one of the regulatory processes. Similarly, the 5 extinction episodes have undoubtedly steered the evolution of life to the state what we observe on earth today, particularly, the cosmic bombardment that happened 65 million years before eliminating the Dinosaurs but for which Mammals could not have appeared and so do the offspring of Homo Sapiens.

Man the Prodigal Son or Privileged Guest ?

Making of Man on earth was neither a dictat of a creator, nor with Adam meeting the Eve in the garden of Eden, but through 3.8 billion years of persistent evolution and Natural Selection from the prokaryotic cell to the multicellular complex Hominids. There is no denial that humans carry the signature of the primitive organism and in odd with Genesis, is 90% Ape. Appearance of Man in the organic evolution too, is a mere flicker such that, if Earth is considered to be seven days old, Man appeared only in the last eleven seconds. But the last 2/3 rd. Second activities of modern Man has made him the privileged guest and the commander of this spaceship. Of late, he has become a powerful agent capable of bringing in large scale changes on earth. Modern Science and Technology has become a handy tool to produce the changes. Removal of mountains, creation of new sky-lines, diversion of river system, creation of lakes and reservoirs, clearance of Range forest ecosystem, reclamation of Bays and ocean etc. which Nature took million years to do, are made to happen in his own life time. Natural changes are slow, self-balancing and healed by recuperation. But Man made changes are sectoral and violent, therefore subject to Checks and Balances of Nature. Downstream and adverse impacts that commonly occur in case of such rapid changes are, water-logging, soil salinitization, floods and draught when hydrologic cycle of a region is interfered; land and soil degradation, water pollution in case of mining and industrial agriculture; soil and sheet erosion when forest cover is removed and coastal erosion when Bays and ocean are reclaimed. Thus, when Man takes the role of "Little God" to destroy, build or sustain an anthropocentric culture, Nature comes heavily to discipline the errand child. Since cultural changes are very fast, and evolutionary changes are extremely sluggish, almost negligible, conflict becomes a necessary byproduct. Thus terrorism has become a byproduct of modern civilization, making identical brothers on arms.

The anthropocentric changes have also cost heavily on other living species on earth. The great Mastodons vanished in the Pleistocene period in the hands of hunter Man. Scientists have noted an alarming rate of extinction of modern species of animals and plants since Man appeared in the scenario, more so after the Industrial Revolution. At least one million of the estimated three million species have succumbed during last quarter century, primarily by pollution, "Islandization of animals and plants", exploitation of habitats and resources and for vanity. Since some types of pollution are genotoxic, Man himself is exposed to the ill effects of his own achievements, which not only makes him a terror for other species on earth, but himself an endangered species.

Epilogue

It is seen that whenever the great Pontiff, the Pope Paul used to visit a country, climb down the aircraft and step onto the ground, his first action was to prostrate on the tarmac to kiss the Earth. For "Rest of us" rampant digging of earth for mining, constructional activities, communication lines etc. are acts of development and progress. The larger the bite of a shovel the more advanced we are considered. However, the "Rest of us" (the earth digger) long to reach the feet of the Pontiff (the earth kisser) with great reverence. It is of course true that plants shatter rocks to extract nutrients, animals burrow earth for shelter and Man has been ploughing land for agriculture, all for survival, like a baby growing on mother's breast. But the baby never "milks" the mother as Man does onto the earth for various developmental activities. Earth is not for digging but for living.

In short if Natural Selection has given rise to a unique intelligent species like humans to pioneer this planet, Man must show his worth and responsibility to husband the home by carrying over with him all the living beings. It is for this reason that the noting of a living earth is designed to inspire, respect and admire a planet carrying a coherent life system. "We are not alone, nor for ourselves alone "and the Earth is a Mother of all living things including Man.

25

Earth Day Enquiry

Who is Fiddling with the Earth ?

22nd April is observed as the Earth Day. The 2010 Earth Day assumes a greater significance because it is also the International Year of the Planet Earth (IYPE). Population pressure, increasing demand of earth resources, accumulation of wastes on land, sea and atmosphere, have brought in many global problems such as Ozone Holes, Global Warming, Energy Crunch, Resources Exhaustion and Pollution. It is "An Inconvenient Truth" to be told that all these earthly problems arise due to our "fiddling with the earth" to satisfy world hunger for energy, to meet our endless needs (also greed) and for vanity such as wars. We need an Earth Day, an IYPE or even catastrophe like cyclone, flood or draught to remember or cry for Mother Earth or Mother Nature.

The Planetary Age: (Scaling Father's age)

Our knowledge on the origin and age of the earth is fairly clear; the accepted age of the earth is 4.5 billion years. However, in 1654, the powerful Arch Bishop Usher proclaimed that the earth was created by God on a Monday, the 26th. October 4004 BC at 9.00 AM. Later on in 1897, Lord Kelvin, the powerful physicist of the day, calculated the age of the earth by considering the rate of its cooling from an original hot mass to the present solid earth and assigned earth's age as 20-40 million years. He did not bother that our planet has an internal mechanism of heat generation by natural radioactivity. In 1900, John Jolly took into account the total amount of salts of the ocean, divided it with the annual rate of delivery from all world rivers and arrived at the age of 90-100 million years for the earth. Similarly an annual rate of 0.3 mt. of sediment deposition in ocean, which has produced the presently known thickness of sedimentary rocks, gave an age of 1.6 billion years for the earth. Finally with techniques like radioactive dating the curtain of controversy was drawn and the age of the earth is resolved at 4.5 billion years.

While religious leaders and scientists have tussled for centuries to assign an age for the planet earth, a group of scientists met only a year before to decide the "fate" and "existence" of a planetary sibling Pluto, the most distant member of the solar family. "The planet was written off".

Life on Earth: (In Search of a Parentage)

The origin and evolution of life on earth has also been a long drawn debate: from the theory of Creationism where Adams and Eves are created from the body of the God to the theory of evolution where life started with synthesis of amino-acid in the primordial juice, followed by appearance of cynobacteria which slowly evolved into the tree of life and finally into Apes and Man. Credible experiments for primordial amino acid synthesis, signatures of stromatolites of cellular and algal impressions in rocks as old as 3 billion years old and a continuous spectrum of 500 million years of well preserved fossil records strongly support that life actually started on earth as early as 3 billion years before and through a process of "Natural Selection" produced the spectrum of life, culminating with the most intelligent species of man. However, the question that still remains unanswered is, whether the appearance of life was an accident, spontaneous or architected and if designed, who would be the designer or the architect? Not being satisfied with the state of art on origin of life on earth, some scientists, leading among whom are an Indian, a Singhalese and a British, have been strongly proposing for an extraterrestrial source for the life in our planet and that, life on earth came from extraterrestrial dust reaching on earth. Even a few months before some ISRO scientists in collaboration with TIFR-Bombay, demonstrated the existence of microbes in the outer atmosphere and supported the extraterrestrial lineage of earthly life. Scientists all over the world are active in search of extraterrestrial life while there is no dearth of media reports on flying saucers, space visitors and all sorts of scientific fiction based on life in outer space.

It is but an irony that while the modern man seeks out for the external life, little thought and concern is bestowed for the existing life on earth. No wonder, more than one third species of plants, animals and insects have got extinct since humans appeared on the history of earth and today almost a hundred species disappear every day due to human activities. Deforestation, biodiversity loss, monoculture practices, genetic manipulation and wars are nothing but fiddling of life on earth, where as terrorism is an extreme sign of intra-species degeneration.

Fiddling with the Atmosphere

The early atmosphere (proto-atmosphere) of earth was totally anoxic and could support only fermentational life. The present state of atmosphere with 21% oxygen could be made possible by addition of oxygen through millions of years of hydrolysis and photosynthesis. An atmosphere with 79% nitrogen, 21% oxygen and about 0.02% carbon dioxide sustained a comfortable and healthy life system of plants, animals and men. During last couple of centuries the atmospheric composition has been precariously perturbed by injection of ozone destroying elements which have generated gaping holes in the stratosphere and Greenhouse gases, which have produced Global Warming and climatic changes. Rupture of earth's ozone shield has exposed earth life to harmful UV radiation from sun and Global Warming has pushed modern civilization to the point of tripping. Locally, air over urban atmosphere have becomes a cocktail of many harmful gases.

Several curative measures have been suggested to engineer the atmosphere to combat Global Warming, prominent among them are: (a) To suspend millions of reflectors in the outer atmosphere to reflect back the solar radiation; (b) Spray sulphurous compounds to absorb solar heat (following volcanic clouds which have earlier produced global cooling) or (c) Spray iron powder on ocean surface to encourage plankton-bloom, which would in turn absorb carbon dioxide from atmosphere. Many however feel that such types of geoengineering projects are cures worse than the cause.

Man, the Little God in Action

Of late, man has become a powerful agent capable of bringing in large scale changes on earth. Modern science and technology has become a handy tool to produce the changes. Removal of a mountain, creation of a new skyline, diversion of a river system, creation of lakes and reservoirs, clearance of a range of forest ecosystem, reclamation of bays and ocean etc., which Nature takes millions of years to do, is made to happen in his own life time. Natural changes are slow, self-balancing and healed by recuperation, But man made changes are violent and subjected to Checks and Balances by Nature. Downstream adverse impacts that commonly occur in case of such changes are: water logging, soil salinization, floods and draughts when hydrological cycle of a region is interfered, land and soil degradation, water pollution incase of mining and industrial agriculture, soil and sheet erosion when forest cover is removed and coastal erosion when bays and ocean are reclaimed. Thus, when man takes the role of "Little God" to destroy, build and sustain an anthropogenic culture, Nature comes heavily to protect and restore the cosmic character. Besides, when cultural changes are very fast, ethical changes are slow and evolutionary changes are extremely sluggish, almost negligible, conflict becomes a necessary product and that is what one observes in the modern society. No wonder, terrorism is a byproduct and component of modern civilization where rapid changes have been brought in by fiddling with all sectors of the Earth.

26

Why Celebrate Earth Day ?

Equinox Earth Day: 21st March (When the sun crosses equator).
World Earth Day: 22nd April – A Teach-in Program of celebration scheduled after the end of Spring Semester - adopted world over including India.

Observe the protective instinct of a Mother, escorting her child on a busy urban road, a laborer woman in construction site or farm-yard carrying the baby tied onto her body with a loin cloth, even a monkey jumping from tree to tree with the baby tucked onto her breast, a mother dog breast feeding the puppies or a lioness strolling with the cubs. The basic instinct is same for all Mothers. If so, can we not expect the same with the "Mother Earth" for her myriads of siblings crawling over her body day and night, in cities, villages and countryside? Here are the arguments that the Earth, while wobbling around the Sun, like any mundane mother toiling with routine duties, is equally protective to her offspring (Earth-springs).

1. Imagine standing on an open vehicle running at a speed of 1375 km/hr. Even if you strongly believe in "Inertia of Motion" you will simply be thrown out onto the road. This does not happen to earth-residents in spite of the Earth rotating at that speed – we are neither thrown out into the abysmal space, nor even feel any such dispelling force. "She" holds us tightly with invisible arms of Gravity. That is why the legendary traditional name of the Earth is "*Dharitri*", that holds us safely.
2. The Earth is like an egg (*Anda* or *Brahma Anda*) with a hot metallic Core (resembles yolk), surrounded by a Mantel of molten rock (corresponds to albumen in the egg), over which a thin layer of solid Crust (shell of

the egg) floats. While the planet rotates with great speed, the Mantel and Core too rotate but at different speeds and generate an electro-magnetic field around the planet.

Hang a magnet, it orients along the earth's magnetic field. The magnetic field provides a protective umbrella of Magnetosphere around the Earth and prevents powerful cosmic particles and deadly solar wind to reach the Earth and at the same time protects the Ozone layer from destruction. In absence of this magnetic umbrella life could not have survived as we know today.

3. Earth's atmosphere has evolved through a long period of geological time, from zero Oxygen content to the present level of 21%, ideal for human metabolism. While the Nitrogen at 79% dilutes the burning capacity of Oxygen, traces of Carbon dioxide (<04%) absorbs infrared radiation of the Sun and keeps the atmosphere warm, but for which the Earth would be unhabitably cold like Mars. We continuously draw and consume the atmospheric Oxygen through inhalation and fossil-fuel burning, but the Earth replenishes the stock through photosynthesis and removes the excess Carbon dioxide into the Carbon-Sinks such as greeneries and oceanic dissolution. The Ozone Shield in the outer atmosphere is known to protect all forms of life from deadly UV-Radiation of Sun. While the gaseous constituents of atmosphere are kept balanced through homeostasis, the weight of the air column keeps our lungs functional without collapse or bursting. At higher altitude both the factors are changed making breathing difficult and life uncomfortable.

4. One of the great cosmic hazards to the planetary habitats is bombardment of meteorites from outer space. Meteorites hitting the Earth can wipe out large chunks of population and living beings. Some 60 million year before the great dinosaurs met their doom with such an astro-event. The earth's atmosphere provides a strong resistance to earth-bound meteorites, disintegrates and burns most of these astro-intruders before they reach the surface. Therefore, unlike the surface of moon and Mars, which are pockmarked with craters because of little or no atmosphere, craters on Earth are rare.

5. The shell of the "Egg-like" Earth, known as Crust, stands shattered due to external and internal forces and forms a mosaic set of plates which move imperceptibly as the Earth rotates. This causes Plate Tectonics and produces uneven terrain on the surface when the Plates collide and ride over one another. The uneven earth surface seen as Mountains, Valleys and Plains, makes water to flow or accumulate, disintegrates and weathers rocks, and transports sediments to form precious soil on the plains. Humanity survives with the productions from this aquatic and soil regimes. No wonder, the vernacular term of soil is *Matti* or *"Ma' ti"* (The Mother).

With all that stated above, who can deny that the Earth, if personified as Gaia, is not a protective mother to the "Earthsprings", specially the Homo sapien ? Whether we are aware of this "Planetary Protections" or not, observation of Earth Day is but a gratitude to our celestial parent, the Mother Earth. Celebration of Earth Day is akin to the celebration of Mothers' Day.

27 World Environment Day beyond Celebration

The UN General Assembly Stock Holm Conference on Human Environment was held on the 5th. Of June 1972 to ponder over the issue on Sustainable and Equitable Development. It led to the establishment of United Nation Environment Program (UNEP) and an annual celebration of the World Environment Day (WED). Every year on the 5th of June WED is celebrated world over on a specific theme relevant to contemporary environment issue, by way of street rallies, lectures, conferences, clean-up campaigns, tree plantation, poster competition etc. Some of the recent past themes have been:

1994: One Earth, One Family. (*Vasudeba Kutumbakam*).
1999: Our Earth, Our Future, Just save it.
2000: The Environment Millennium – time to act.
2001: Connect with the World Wide Web of life.
2002: Give Earth a chance.
2003: Water - 2 billion people are dying for it.
2004: Wanted Seas and Oceans – Dead or alive.
2005: Green Cities – Plan for the Planet.
2006: Desert and Desertification.
2007: Melt the Ice.
2008: Kick the Habit towards a low carbon economy.
2009: Your Planet needs you – Unite to combat Global Warming.
2010: Many Species, One Planet, One Future/Biodiversity – One Earth, One Future.

The list of the themes is an indicator of the concern for the fate of the earth in general and the fate of the living world that supports and serves the human society in particular. The concern for the earth's future can also be understood by two consecutive statements made by the Nobel Laureate Stephen Hawkins:

- In June 13th 2006, in a meeting in Hong Kong, Hawkins said " The survival of the human race depends on its ability to find a new home elsewhere in the universe, as there is an increasing risk of disaster."
- In July 10th,2006, in a New York conference he repeated " In a world, that is in chaos politically, socially and environmentally, how can the human race sustain another 100 years ?"

Not surprisingly, another reputed Australian Microbiologist, Prof. Frank Fennier, pioneer of small pox eradication, sent out a more pessimistic message in June, 2010 that " Humans to be extinct in 100 years".

Human knowledge and capability of space exploration could enable him "to find a new home" if earth becomes uninhabitable due to our own misdeeds such as pollution and political adventurism. But many feel that "A technologically maintained life in another planet or moon can not support the evolution of the earthly organism, more so the metabolic functions of man. Man's evolution has occurred on earth, is marked by the earth and cannot be exported from it."

The concern for the fate of the living world that supports us is understood by the Millennium Ecosystem Assessment Report, 2005 on biodiversity that, "Human activity alone has changed world's ecosystem, largely for the worse, more rapidly during last 50 years than during any period in record of human history." In the last few years, we have spread hundreds of chemicals – synthetic fertilizers and pesticides world wide which are harmful to all forms of life, appropriated 40% of the solar energy available for photosynthesis, converted all easily arable lands, dammed most rivers, raised planet's sea level, acidified it, poisoned large sections of surface and ground waters, all of which have led to ecosystem degradation, biodiversity reduction and species extinction. Fifty percent of the known species have become extinct since man appeared on earth's history. As such the present rate of extinction of species on earth is estimated at one specie in every 10 to 20 minutes, a rate 1000 times more than the normal natural extinction in geological history. The present species in danger are: 12.5% of the plants, 1 in 8 of the birds, 1 in 4 of the mammals, 1 in 3 of the amphibians, 4 in 10 turtles and 50% of the fishes. Even our fellow human tribes that are facing extinction due to pressure of modern civilization (external assault) are : the Amish and Red-Indians of America, the Polynesians of Hawaii and Indonesia, the natives of Australia and Andaman, the Sea-farers of Madagascar and several tribes of Africa. The geological history is punctuated by 5 known episodes of extinction caused by floods, transgression and regression of sea, volcanism, meteorite impacts and climate changes. According to some critics of modern civilization, "We" are the flood, volcanoes and meteors to this planet to usher the 6th extinction on earth, this time not by Nature but by man himself. Declaration of 2008-2009 as the Year of Planet Earth, 2010 as International Biodiversity Year and the latest theme of WED-2010, "Many Species, one Earth, one Future" are assertions that the basic causes are the nature of our unsustainable and inequitable development which has little regard to Nature and natural system.

The relationship between all living organisms is a co-operative one, characterized by co-existence and interdependence, well-known in the ecosystem as symbiosis at various degrees. The predator-prey relationship that appears destructive and exploitive to the immediate prey is generally beneficial for both the species. This is in contrast to Darwinianists who see life exclusively in terms of destruction and domination by the strongest (Survival of the fittest), a view modern science and modern man has accepted for legitimization of exploitation. Thus excessive aggression by exploitation is a part of the cultural evolution observed only in human behavior whose cultural evolution is pseudo-scientifically explained as God given power or "Man has been created to rule the planet".

When humans modify the ecosystem to gain something, it often has negative impact on other compartments of the ecosystem leading to trade off. For example, whether it is food production, industrialization or urbanization, it all leads to reduction of biodiversity. Reduction of biodiversity reduces the availability of ecosystem services. Like the services of a host of our fellow beings such as house-maids, delivery boys, transporters, traders, mechanics, plumbers, Bankers or Doctors in the society, the Eco-servers supply us market value goods such as healthy fruits, fish and flesh. They also supply natural medicines, filter our air and natural water, provide breeding grounds for fish, control erosion, buffer human community against storm and natural disasters, harbor insects that pollinate crops or attack crop-pests and weeds and even absorb carbon dioxides from atmosphere. With vanishing species, the servers cease to exist and our day to day living is inconvenienced or jeopardized.

The moment we destroy the natural world which takes care of the maintenance of the natural system, the more we have to take over responsibility and employ our ingenuity to maintain our surrounding environment. The servers gone, we look for substitutes. Left alone to maintain ourselves, some of us become mafia to exploit weaker, we turn cruel exploiter and violent- back to "uncivilization".

Loss of biodiversity is an effect of extinction of species, the process is irreversible and the loss is permanent to humans who are being served. This loss is also like emptying our tool box which time and again is used for repair the natural cycles op planetary food generation, air, water and nutrient movement and restoration of human health through recreation, entertainment and prophylactic relaxation. With population increase and new types of ailment looming on the horizon consequent to a synthetic life and gubernatorial habits, emptying of the natural medicinal kit box consequent to the extinction of ecoservers (such as the medicinal plants) is disastrous. Who knows what types of metabolic assaults, humanity will face in future in the natural feed – back loop. We need natural protectors around us, like the mangroves as coast guard and " green -friends" to generate oxygen and sequester carbon from the atmosphere. It will be a precarious voyage of " Ship of fools and rocks of short term economic planning" to exclusively rely on mere invention of substitutes which are invariably inadequate or produce negative impacts in one way or other.

The Ship of Fools and the Rocks of Short-term Economic Planning

For a baby, a nurse does not substitute a mother, nor do the parks and gardens in city substitute natural forest. Even a tractor is a poor substitute for a pair of cattle over a plough. The tractor consumes fossil fuel brought from outside, causes pollution, needs repairs and unlike the cattle, does not produce dung which ends up as fertilizer in land, fuels at home and in various use in Indian society. No wonder, since history began, this natural species of bovine animal has been a binding force and a stabilizing element (server) of Indian society in general and families in particular. Whereas, the tractor or any such mechanical equivalent of modern endeavors is found to breed a series of unrest in ecosensitive society.

We must realize that biodiversity gives resilience, usher safety, security and stability and is of great benefit to man. It is our sacred duty to preserve biodiversity handed over to us by the Mother Nature.

28 World Environment Day Celebration for Awakening

The UN General Assembly, in its Stockholm Conference on "Human Environment" held in 1972, proposed 5th June, to celebrate as World Environment Day (WED). The purpose of celebration was to arouse awareness among various levels, the alarming rate of environmental stress that earth is facing due to population explosion, resources depletion and industrialization. Each year a theme is selected and the celebration flagged off in the capital city of a country and carried on world over by way of seminars, meetings and projects. During the last 39 years of celebration, since it started in 1973, there has been a series of themes of global importance such as: Your Planet Needs You (2009), Kick that Habit - Towards a Low Carbon Economy (2008), Green Cities (2005), Water - 2 Billion People Dying for it (2003), One Earth - One Family (*Vasudeba Kutumbakam*) (1994), Poverty & Environment (1993), Global Warming & Global Warning (1989), A Tree for People (1986), Youth, Population & Environment (1985), Development Without Destruction (1978) and so on.

No doubt, the thematic celebrations have generated a tremendous volume of awareness among people at all levels, there has been little relief of environmental stress in the domain of any of the themes mentioned above. For examples, Berlin wall has been demolished, but States and Nations have been further fragmented and riddled with religious, social, economic conflicts and terrorism. "The earth has been flattened", leveled through Science and Technology, but the gap between rich and poor has widened. Forest cover has shrunk further, developmental projects like establishment of industries, power plants, SEZs and building of dams have encroached human habitats, violated human rights, produced millions of ecological refugees and urban migration has crippled city infrastructures in most developing countries - India is a living example. Carbon emission continues to increase, "Climatic change" remains a mere debate and lost in commercialized Carbon Trading in world Carbon Bazaar, water pollution in land and ocean (oil spill) have increased and water conflicts (water share/water wars) have spread over mountain glaciers, rivers, lakes, dams and trickled down to municipal districts and public taps. The celebration theme "Green Economy – Does it include you ?"- the 2012 Theme (when this write up was written), is pertinent and questions if Ecology and Economy are but *"Saut"* (two spouses of one man) in our developmental mechanism.

Increased environmental stress and global environmental deterioration, in spite of increased awareness is considered to be due to our (1) levels of environmental awakening; and (2) anthropocentric approach to environment which presupposes "Nature for service of man" and undermines Nature and natural elements.

Even if globally aware, our perception of Nature is determined by our experience to immediate surroundings. Environmental factors such as hot, cold, humid, smelly, acidic, dusty, noisy, bright, crowded, suffocating, even subjective feelings like violent, unethical (corruption) have variation in geographic space and time and when sensed, their perception depends on our levels of awakening (sensitivity, when instruments are used). Therefore, keeping our living room or factory floor clean, Powai green, demand of "Mumbai for Mumbaikars", *"Amar Sonar Bangla"*, "My country, My people, My nation", "Asia for Asiatic" - that was Hiro Hitto's slogan in 2nd. World war, "keep Australia white", *"Deutschland, Deutschland, Uber Ales"* – Hitler's sermon, are but various scales and levels of consciousness.

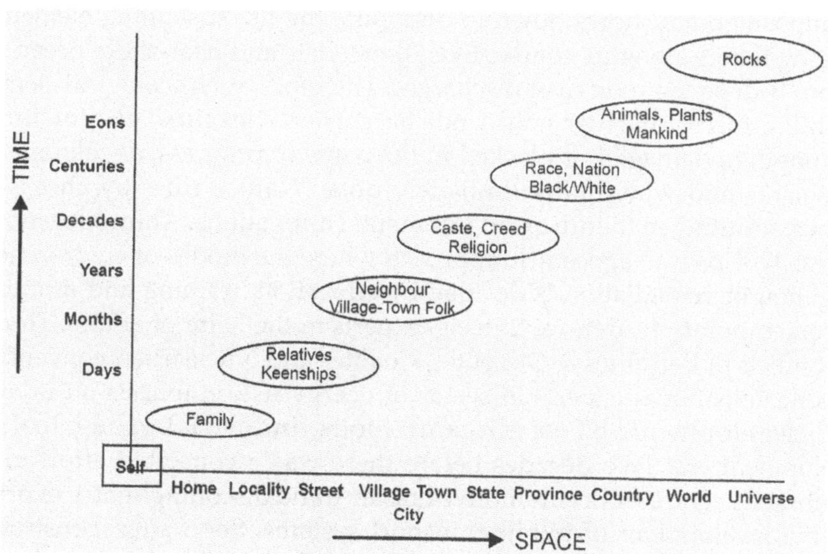

Sales and Dimensions of Environmental Awakening

Ego being the basic factor of human survival and existence, only a few noble souls have awakened to global level of awareness to feel the pain, pleasure and suffering of humanity as a whole irrespective of cast, creed, race, religion, State or Nation. Environment has no such "narrow domestic walls". While we are disturbed if a neighbor hammers a nail in his room at midnight for hanging a mosquito curtain, most of us do not hesitate to hold a midnight disco in our flat or favor for extension of loudspeaker use till midnight or beyond during various celebrations. In short, a good environmentalist is one who keeps his garden clean and green but throws the cuttings to neighbor's garden across the fence. In a more civilized way, gathers the cuttings in a plastic bag for municipal van to dispose in a dumping ground where the environment is further worsened. Air-conditioning increases the comfort of our living room by pumping the heat out but makes outside hotter. In the modern modes of environmental mitigations where economy rules over ecology, the "Marginals" are further marginalized, that is, "the rich get richer and the poor gets poorer", nay "the poor gets children".

Anthropocentric approach, that Nature and natural elements are meant only for humans, is the root cause of environmental deterioration and failure of remediation. Here "rocks or rivers may not have rights" but the future children of Mumbai have no opportunity to see the majestic hexagonal cliff of Gilbert Hill, cascading streams on green Chandivili Range or a clean Mithi river dissipating into the mangroves of Mahim. As much as a forest is an important source for our timber and cellulose needs, it is the only home, shelter and livelihood of a larger number of living species including tribals. Similarly, a river collects water in high-lands and nutrients from rock decomposition and flows down to distribute the life sustaining elements to all living things along its course. Even the deltaic and near-shore ocean lives are totally dependent on river discharges. Therefore, such ecological elements like hills, forest or river could not be cornered exclusively for human consumption, damaged or blocked in the name of progress, development or settlements and when indiscriminately done, Nature rules by checks and balance, resulting in failure of environmental mitigations. Anthropocentricity also easily slips into egocentric approach where the modes of environmental mitigation or remediation is decided by education, training and attitude of the contemporary leaders/architects/experts in the helm of affairs. Thus we see conflicts of Petrolites & Dieselites, Coalites and Nuclearites, conventional vs. nonconventional experts in sector of energy use, emphasis on urban or rural development, BT vs. Organic foods, industrial vs. agricultural development etc. Two decades before there was a concerted effort to free Mumbai city centre from automotive nuisance and discourage entry of private cars by development of public transport systems. Soon after, construction galore of flyovers and the Sea-Link reversed the scenario.

Intriguing observations of present day scenarios on environmental celebration with ecology pushed into the frame work of economy are, when "environmental disruptors" like coal and petroleum companies, mining industries, power plant sectors " go green" by mass indoctrination through media advertisements, fiscal supports for cosmetic remediation. Similarly, chemical and pharma industries do not hesitate to sponsor environmental events, automobile industries hold car and mobike rallies, produce "eco-

SUV" and mineral water/soft drink manufacturers soak thirst in *Greenathons*. CSR (Corporal Social Responsibility) is anthropocentric and cannot restore ecological damages as much as "*Daridra Narayana Bhojan* cannot eradicate world hunger, it perpetuates it".

Like celebration of many of our Indian festivals such as *Ganapati-puja, Dewali, Akshyaya Tritia* and *Holi*, which fail to revoke the essence and ethics of the festivals but lavishly commercialized, celebration of environmental events too, though increases public awareness, does not prevent ecological and environmental deterioration. It is therefore no surprise to find similarity of post-celebration scenarios of *Ganapati* immersion grounds, sites of rallies and alleys of greenathons.

29

World Environment Day 'Nature at our Service'

In our routine life we need a variety of services. Plumbers, Electricians, Carpenters, Sweepers, Venders & Delivery boys, Grocers, Drivers, Teachers, Doctors, Army & Police personnel, Priests and who not, all are Servers of the Society. Even IAS Officers belong to this class of server, although by contrast some pose to be the Master. In any ecosphere degradation begins when servers turn predator (*Rakshyaka* turns *Vakshyaka*). In UK the powerful Scotland Yard Cops address the man on street as "Sir". A strike in any section of the Servers brings great inconvenience to the society and individuals. Similar to these Societal Servers, Nature too provides critical services to humans. Forest ecosystem in general and Trees & Plants in particular are Nature's ecoservers, which sustain human habitats and maintain health and happiness. Many of the ecoservices of the plant kingdom are highlighted below:

Trees for Fuel & Fibers: The only visible value of a tree lies in its fuel and fibers (Timber). 99% of the kitchen and hearth in rural India is lit by biomass like wood, twigs, dry leaves and charcoal made from wood. Even funeral pyres in India are heavily wood dependent. Coal, which runs Power Plants, industrial furnaces and smelters, are but fossilized Jurassic forest. Gasohol from sugarcane, biodiesel from *Jatropah* and petroleum from algae are ready to substitute fossil oil when situation arises. The most visible value of tree is in the quality of the timber. Use of timber in homes, buildings and Railways are well known. Scaffolding in construction industries, production of paper depends on bamboo forests. Similarly, jute and cotton provide natural fibers and Malbury tree harbors silk worms. Latex from rubber trees keeps automobiles on wheels.

Food Bank for all: Besides a variety of fruits like apple, orange, mango, *banana* and *jamun*, the plant kingdom virtually supplies all food requirements – cereals, tubers, oil seeds, sugar and green vegetables. Even animal products like milk and meat are generated by feeding the animals with vegetative fodders. Plants and trees supply spices, vitamins, cosmetics, colors, medicines and medicinal products that Man needs. A single plant like *Neem* is known to provide remedy for a dozen ailments, besides a herbicide called Neemicide. The delicious red wine and the sparkling beer are but plant products. Progressive deforestation in many countries have been found to decrease honey production because all honeys come from flowers.

Our Oxygen Factory: We need Oxygen for survival. The latest fascination for *Pranayam* is basically for optimum inhalation of Oxygen for a healthy living. The early atmosphere of earth had little Oxygen, hence none or poor forms of life. It is only when photosynthesis appeared, Oxygen evolved and life flourished. A mature tree like *Neem*, mango or cedar produces enough Oxygen in a season, sufficient for inhalation of 1o people for a full year. Mumbai has only one tree for every 6 persons. An American calculation shows that a cedar tree with a leaf canopy of 7 sq.mt. if survives for 50 years, will generate 6 million dollar worth of Oxygen during its life time, when its timber value in market is mere 5000 $. (A 9 kg. or 7.9 Liters Oxygen cylinder costs 54 $). An Indian estimate puts this figure to 5.3 lakh rupees for a 55 years old tree.

Great Carbon Sink: Forests are effective carbon absorber from atmosphere. The very process of growth means intake of Carbon dioxide from air. Therefore in the present Carbon Bazaar, aforestation is a lucrative Carbon Credit in most developing countries.

Nature's Air Conditioner: Carbon in atmosphere may produce global worming, but the same in tree produces global deeming. Transpiration from leaf surface absorbs latent heat which in turn produces cooling of the space surrounding the canopy. The American Forestry Association estimates a minimum air conditioning capacity of a tree at 73 $ compared to an Indian estimate of Rs. 90,000 a year. Urban plantation is strongly recommended to prevent "Heat Island" over cities.

The Rain Maker: Large canopy forest attracts cloud and increases precipitation by cooling of overhead air and by seeding of micro-droplets of water from the transpirated moisture. While the overhead canopy of trees increases rain fall, the root system in the ground produces soil by disintegration of hard rock and holds it firmly to prevent erosion, siltation and flooding downstream. Intricate net-work of root prevents free flow of rain water, reduces runoff, increases percolation, there by raising the water table of the region.

Air Purifier: Industrial and urban sectors have produced unacceptable levels of air and noise pollution respectively. Whereas trees are effective sound breaker and reduce noise pollution along highways, around mines and factories, their large foliation arrests fine particles from air and cuticle absorbs gaseous pollutants like Carbon monoxides and oxides of Sulfur and Nitrogen.

Cultural Synergy: The green color of plants is soothing to eyes while the colorful flowers and "Autumn colors" of leaves are aesthetics. Religious, social and commercial (market) gathering under large trees or group of trees are rituals of rural folks. Urban environment where people are isolated and atomized, Gardens and Parks promote connectivity. Greeneries have a soothing effect on human psyche. Many plants and trees like *Tulsi*, Banyan and *Pippal* are objects of worship in India. Lord Buddha attained enlightenment under a *Pippal* (*Aswastha*) tree whose long stalked leaves easily flutter and generate a comfortable breeze under its canopy.

One can not have a more friendly Ecoserver than the plants and trees of the forest, without which life will be at stake. Next time when you pass by a tree remember its contribution for all the comforts it has provided us.

Living in a City without Trees will be a Nightmare

30

World Environment Day Theme 1913

Food - Eat, Think and Save

Thought for Food is Food for thought on World Environment Day – 2013
(TheWED-2013 Theme flanked by two pictures of BT-Brinjol, the popular Indian vegetable – the trio with confused looks and the other with growth aberration, depict the complex issues on Global Food)

–Sahu

5th of June is World Environment Day. Every year WED is celebrated with a theme relevant to contemporary issues. Looking into the food wastages in affluent societies when one in eight people in the world are chronically hungry, 850 million go hungry every day and when hunger kills five million children every year – one in every five seconds, the 2013 WED theme "Think, Eat and Save", could not be less appropriate.

1.3 billion tons of food, one-third of total produce, worth one trillion Dollars, are wasted or lost every year, more than four times what is needed to feed the world hungry. Even in India 58000 crore rupees worth of agricultural food items get wasted every year due to lack of storage facilities and poor purchasing capacity of people.

Obviously people in rich countries are over-fed, obese and indulge in large wastage of food. In USA, obesity accounts for 65% of its population. The quality of food they eat also raises many health and environmental problems. Many "modern foods" carry human carcinogens, obviously because of introduction and use of thousands of chemicals in our daily life, many of whom are known biodisruptors. Even the simple microven pop-corn bag is found to carry PFOA (perfluorooctanoic Acid), a chemical which produces cardio-vascular ailments. Diseases like obesity, diabetes, BP, cancer, renal failure, heart disease including genetic disorders are related to food habits. Whereas carbohydrate rich diet has resulted in high incidence of diabetes in South Asia, and India is known as "World's Diabetic Capital", meat rich diet leads to increased cholesterol and heart disease.

The modern method of food production in industrial and commercial scales has led to monoculture agriculture and loss of biodiversity. Use of synthetic fertilizers and chemicals has boosted production but degraded top soil and polluted both inland and coastal waters; genetic manipulation and introduction of synthetics and substitutes have increased the quality of products but has raised eyebrows.

Chemical fertilizers used for growing corn for animal feed entered run-off water into Gulf of Mexico creating a "Dead Zone" of fishery and algal boom that robbed off Oxygen for ocean life, effecting the fishing industry. There are 200 such Dead Zones in world ocean. In India, run-off from lands that heralded Green Revolution is glaringly visible in Yamuna pollution and the integrated run-offs of east flowing rivers increased the Nitrate level of coastal waters of Bay of Bengal. The Oxygen robbing of the Nitrates results in "Blue Baby Syndrome" when Nitrite, a reduced form of Nitrate, finds way into human blood. Endosulphan spray in *Kaju* plantation is now confirmed to have produced wide spread child paralysis in Kasarogard District of Kerala. Not only industrial agricultural productions have degraded the environment, industries not directly related to food production have contaminated the food chain. The Minamata disease of Japan arose due to power plant discharges into Minamata Bay contaminating the coastal fish with Mercury, and the "Itai Itai" disease of Cadmium poisoning in Jintsu Valley was due to Cadmium contamination of paddy plants due to mine water discharge from a Zinc mine upstream.

Industrial fishing techniques using sonar technology, satellite navigation system, depth scanner and enormous net made out of synthetic fiber, has eliminated 90% of the larger fishes, deprived small fisher folks of their vocation. Inland fisheries need massive inputs of feeds, energy and biocides and known to interfere with local Water Table.

World meat consumption is on increase due to increased production of pork and poultry. Adding antibiotics to their feed causes chicken and farm animals to gain weight faster. Animals raised outdoors rarely suffer from respiratory ailments and other illness. But caged chicken accumulates stress hormones in the body. Industrial agriculture and animal husbandry gives pathogen greater opportunity to inject every layers of food chain and ultimately effects human health. Spread of Avian and Swine Flu has jumped species barrier from animals to humans, killing many. Antibiotics used in animals too leak to humans making either of them resistant to it. The scepter of Mad Cow Disease that appeared in Europe on the fag end of the last century still haunts beef-eating nations. It was a misadventure for increase beef production to enjoy "Double-decker Beef Burger" by interfering with herbivorous bovine animals by feeding them with animal protein.

For eating of meat or fish, the ones lower in the food chain generally reduce the harm done by the product. In case of fish, smaller herbivorous are healthier to eat than the larger carnivorous species like Tuna, sword-fish or sharks.

Many consumers are giving up meat altogether as health and environmental benefits of doing so become clearer. Even McDonald is asking suppliers to stop using antibiotic growth promoters in animal foods. Consumers are demanding more grass-fed meat, milk or eggs for health reason. Grass-fed products are higher in Omega-3 fatty acid which lowers cholesterol and obesity. Ethical non-veg. foods, economically and socially management practices in food production, and organic farming are now common *Mantras* in many Nations.

A basic meal of local productions reduces Green House Gas emission at least 4 times compared to the same meal imported from outside. Today an "American dinner plate" travels at least 2000 Km, before it reaches the palate of the eater, "virtually marinated with Crude" because of the long distance transport. Cod fish caught in North Sea is sent to China for threading and exported to America for consumption. Chinese and Australian apples dominate Indian market, pushing out Kashmiri product. Global transport of food has brought relief to mitigate food scarcity in poor countries, but has destroyed local trades and control poor nations by the rich. Gandhi used to say, if the need of people is met by local productions, many of the present day problems would not arise.

Over and above the socio-environmental issues of the world food and food-industries, India is beset with rampant adulteration and contamination of food and food products. Festival sweets made from "Spurious *Mawa*", colorful *Jilebbis* and metal (silver?) coated *Barfis,* Chromian green peas and adulterated Turmeric/Chili powders add large amount of toxic Heavy Metals to Indian food-basket. Author's report on Heavy Metals in *Palak* grown along Rly. tracks of Mumbai and Mercury contamination of fish are but tips of the Iceberg.

31

Our Carbon Foot Print

Human activities annually adds several billion tons of carbon dioxides to earth's atmosphere and this has led to a sharp rise in average global temperature, because carbon dioxide absorbs solar heat radiation. Global Warming has become a popular term, not merely for hot summers, shrunken winters and melting glaciers, it also means climatic change that disturbs pattern of rainfall (monsoon vagaries), ushers stronger and more frequent coastal hurricanes and cyclones, sea level rise and land submersion, species extinction and appearance of tropical diseases. These have been widely discussed in media, scientific conferences, trade and business circles and in international conventions. The only way to avoid these global disasters is by giving a brake to carbon emission go "Carbon Neutral" or simply turn to a Carbon Offset technique like tree plantation. Trees sequester carbon dioxide from atmosphere and offset impacts of Global Warming.

Of the total Greenhouse Gases (GHG) annually added to atmosphere, US accounts 30%, European countries 28%, China and India combined only 12%. The actual per capita carbon dioxide emission of US is 28 Tons, when China and India have 5 and 1.5 Tons respectively. The principal sectors of GHG emission, carbon dioxide being the main gas, are: Electrical and Heating (24.5%), Transport (13.5%), Agriculture (13.5%), Deforestation (18.2%), Industries (13.8%) and Waste (3.6%).

Our Carbon Foot Print (CFP)

Carbon Foot Print is the amount of carbon dioxide we emit annually in our day-to-day activities for survival, progress and even when we go to war. We breath-out carbon dioxide which adds to atmosphere, so also cattles, who, beside breathing out, also belch out a large amount of methane, a Greenhouse Gas 20 times stronger than carbon dioxide. The electrical power we consume at home, office, streets, industries and places of entertainment, comes from power-plants burning coal; the automobiles we drive around, the trains and aero planes that take us to far up places consume fossil fuels, all emit carbon dioxide. The food and drink that comes to our dinner table, even the waste we produce and dispose add carbon dioxide to atmosphere. For examples:

Every unit of electrical energy in our monthly bill means 750 Gms of carbon emission. The larger the bill, larger our CFP in this sector.

A Hyundai (Sonata) car on traveling 5000 km/yr. emits 1000 kg. carbon dioxide and a Fiat (Panda) emits 750 kg.

A Mumbai-Delhi return trip accounts for 180 kg. emission by train but 330 kg. by flight (With normal load of passengers).

A bottle of wine on the table has emitted 200 Gms. of carbon dioxide and eating of a cheese-beef burger leaves a footprint of 3 kg of carbon dioxide.

The annual carbon budget in all the sectors of life style when added together gives the size of Carbon Foot Print. The larger the home and number of gadgets and appliances in it, the longer the list of consumer goods, the more frequently one travels and an extravagant life style, the larger is the CFP of the individual. Give up the habit of consumerism and lavish life style, the CFP size is reduced and you will be a global patron in the crusade against Global Warming. An average American has a CFP of 28 T/yr. whereas an average Indian has only 1.5 T/yr. Therefore USA with only 4% of world population contributes 25% of GHG emission and India with 16% of world population contributes 4% of GHG to atmosphere. "Reduce, Recycle and Reuse" helps in decrease of Carbon Foot Print.

Estimation of CFP in electrical energy consumption or in transportation is simple but calculation of CFP in food front is more complex because it involves not only the method of production but also the distance it travels before consumption. In a globalized world where lambs are brought up in New Zealand and their meat consumed 11000 miles away in England, cod fish caught in Norway, filleted in China and eaten in Europe, and Italian cheese travels to California to make pizza-top, carbon values for an identical food product varies widely. Modern foods generate more carbon for its transport than in its actual production. An American meal travels an average 1800 km by ship, plane and truck before reaching the dinner table, virtually marinated in crude oil. A Kashmiri apple or *Bhusawal* banana eaten in Mumbai will account for a smaller CFP than an Australian or Chinese apple and South-African banana respectively. To make consumers carbon conscious, some multinational stores like Tesco and Wal-Mart have started printing "Carbon Tag" on food items as much as the calorie contents for the health conscious customers.

Go Green; Offset your Carbon Foot Print:

You can decrease Carbon Foot Print by thinking "renewables"- go for Green Energy such as, wind power, solar heater and even by patronizing nuclear power, none of which emit carbon. However use of biofuel like gasohol, ostentatiously called the green fuel of the future, is a poor off-setter because its generation is land intensive and Jatropha or palm plantation eats away into forest lands, which are carbon sink. In actual practice, one can decrease annual carbon emission by an order of:

- 25 kg. by replacing a 75-watt incandescent lamp with a 20- watt CFL
- 500 kg. by recycling glass, plastics and papers,
- 400 kg. by taking a bus or train to work instead of driving.
- 350 kg. by line drying of laundry instead of in a dryer,
- 350 kg. by switching off electronic appliances from stand-by mode, refrigerator door sealed and AC-coils clean.
- A vegan meal gives a smaller CFP than meat but supplies equal calories.

Be proud to be Carbon Neutral

If your annual CFP is 1 Ton, you can offset the carbon debit and proudly declare Carbon Neutral by plantation of tree, which should sequester 1 Ton of carbon dioxide from air during its life time (40 yrs.). An average tree sequesters 22 kg. of carbon dioxide annually. In all practical purposes, to keep one tree alive for a full lifetime of 40 years, about 5 trees need to be planted, 4 of which may die immature, but 5 of them combined would sequester 1 Ton of carbon dioxide. Then, why not start tree plantation, become a tree protector and offload the carbon burden accumulating on your head? In other words, every tree we cut increases our CFP or Carbon debt and we owe an explanation to our children for ushering the misery of Global Warming.

Offset your Carbon Foot Print by Planting a Tree

Advisories

Scientists, intellectuals, industrialists and politicians acknowledge that Global Warming or Climatic Change is disastrous for global community and the basic cause is consumerism and our vanity for material wealth, technological capability, and a feeling of supremacy over Nature. Here comes the famous *Mantra* of M.K.Gandhi: "Need vs. Greed", the adverse impacts of which are now being realized in the science of Global Warming.

Reference has been made above that GHG emission in transportation and global movement of people, goods and foods weigh heavily on atmospheric carbon. Global Warming is the price we have to pay for going globalization in trade and transport. Here again, the Gandhian principle that "If man can live satisfied with what his surrounding (earth) gives, many of today's problems would not arise" has now been realized through Global Warming. The meaning of "*Swaraya*" or "Self-dependence" might have been lost in modern India, but now is recognized at the highest level of modern science.

Glaringly, the recent two successive Nobel prizes have gone to the crusaders against Global Warming, one to Wangiri Mathai of Africa for aforestation – the sole technique which offsets human CFP by sequestration of carbon dioxide, and the other to Al Gore and IPCC for world awakening on Global Warming. Mr. Al Gore was in India a few years ago in course of his crusade against Global Warming.

Equally noteworthy is the voice of a living legend, the Nobel Laureate Dr. Stephen Hawking, giving a call to humanity to "think of leaving this planet because we have made a trash of it". It is not only the land and ocean that have been trashed by dumping of modern wastes, more importantly, the atmosphere is now trashed by pumping into it a host of Greenhouse Gases, carbon dioxide, methane, CFC, nitrogen-oxides and what not, all due to our modern life style. Unfortunately, even if a section of the privileged Homo Sapiens migrate to another planet, survival will be next to impossible because all our metabolic parameters are earth bound.

32

Ozone Hole

A Hole on our Roof

16th September is observed as World Ozone Day. On this day of 1987, the Montreal Protocol was signed under an UN convention to restrict production and use of Ozone depleting chemicals such as CFCs (Chloro Fluoro Carbon). CFC, otherwise known as Freon is used as principal refrigerant in fridges, air-conditioners, aerosol propellants, fire hydrants and foam industries. In the lower atmosphere, where we live, CFC is stable and nontoxic, but as it rises up to the higher atmosphere on to the zone known as Stratosphere, the intense UV-radiation of the Sun breaks the CFC molecules and sets its Chlorine atom free. The liberated Chlorine atom from CFC attacks and decomposes the Ozone molecules back to Oxygen. A single Chlorine atom can break 100,000 Chlorine molecules in a chain reaction and can remain active for a century. The lower Stratosphere between 20 to 40 km. above earth surface has accumulated a significant amount of Ozone, to the extent of 300 to 500 DU (Dobson Unit) in course of last hundreds of millions years. The Ozone content of the near surface atmosphere, where we live, is merely a meager 0.3 parts per million (ppm), that is, three molecule of Ozone for every ten million molecules of air. The depletion of the Ozone has been recorded to the extent of 100-150 DU (minimum record: 85 DU) over the South Pole where it is known as the "Great Ozone Hole". The size of the Hole (the area of depletion) over the Antarctica has been recorded to be as large as the size of United States of America, making animal and human lives in Australia and New Zealand, closer to South Pole, to face the danger of exposure to

Ultraviolet radiation from the sun. The Ozone rich belt of the Stratosphere absorbs the harmful UV-rays coming from the Sun and provides a protective shield for all forms of life on earth. Among the harmful effects of UV-radiation, skin carcinoma and ocular damage in humans, destruction of chlorophyll in plants and phytoplanktons are well known.

CFC was discovered in 1930s and its early use was in the order of 20,000 T/yr. But by 1970-80s its use has gone up by 270,000 T/yr., thereby its large accumulation in upper atmosphere and effect on Ozone layer was noticed by 1980. It is felt that, in spite of complete phasing out of production of CFCs, the already accumulated gas would continue to damage the Ozone layer for another 75 years before the "Hole" is repaired by natural process of Ozone formation. The years between 1980, when the Ozone Hole was discovered and 2080,by which the great hole is expected to be repaired as a result of Montreal Protocol, is known as *Ultraviolet Century* by many Scientists. Consequent to the phasing out of CFCs, under the Montreal Protocol, new substitute of Hydro Fluoro Carbons (HFC) have been developed for the refrigeration industries. However, the HFCs are strong Green House Gases (GHG) and add to Global Warming.

One of the dubious problems of formation of Ozone Hole above the South Pole is that, while most of the CFC production and use are in the industrialized countries of North-hemisphere, the "Ozone Hole" is observed over the South Pole. Stratospheric wind circulation around a spinning spherical body like Earth produces "Polar Vortex" over either Poles, but the extreme low temperature over Antarctica generates a Polar Stratospheric Cloud, which set up ideal condition of Ozone depletion. Scientists also feel that (and also noticed), similar holes in a smaller scale may slowly appear over the Arctic region and in the lower latitudes over industrially rich lands where CFC use and emissions are maximum.

Since the Chlorine atom in the CFC molecule is the "villain" element that breaks up the Ozone molecules, Scientists have looked for other natural sources of Chlorine, such as, the aerosol derived from sea-spray (the ocean water is a mild solution of Sodium Chloride) and volcanic eruptions which add Chlorine gas to the atmosphere and cause Ozone depletion. The Southern Hemisphere has more oceanic mass and may account for the large Ozone Hole over the South Pole. Although the contribution of Chlorine from ocean-spray and volcanoes are significant in amounts, the sea-spray Chlorine is washed down by rain and unlike CFC, the emissions from volcanoes are unstable compounds and can not reach the Stratosphere where the actual reaction of Ozone decomposition takes place in presence of UV-radiation from the Sun. The essence of the argument is that, the present Ozone Hole over South Pole is basically anthropogenic, an outcome of use of CFCs and once the production and use of CFC is stopped the hole will slowly heal back and humanity will be spared from the deadly UV-radiation from the Sun.

Indeed, the Montreal Protocol of United Nation is a great step (and probably first of its kind) of international co-operation of world nations to face a common environmental threat arising out of our stampede for progress and modern civilization. It is also hoped that similar understanding to combat Global Warming under the Kyoto Protocol will be translated into practice in the interest of a sustainable Earth.

33

World Water Day

Earth is otherwise known as the water planet. Observed from the space, it is a blue wobbling sphere, three fourth covered with water. 97.2% of the global water is saline, 2.14% frozen as icecaps on poles and mountaintops. Only a miniscule of 0.6% is fresh and potable. Even this portion is extensively polluted.

Water is essential to life, 75% of the body weight is only water. It enables us to eat, excrete, digest, absorb nutrients across the diaphragm of food tract, circulates blood in arteries and veins. One can survive few days without food, not few hours without water. Therefore, the search for extraterrestrial life begins with finding water only. As a matter of fact, life on earth originated in water some 3000 million years before and continued to be there till 600 million year Before Present, only after which the amphibian appeared with evolution.

In the long history of our planet, the total water content of the earth including oceanic, terrestrial, juvenile, magmatic together with lithospheric water, that is, water of crystallization and hydroxyl ions in minerals, has remained constant, except perhaps, in early history of the earth, some water molecules could have broken down (dissociated) to their element constituents of oxygen and hydrogen. The hydrogen has escaped thereafter leaving the oxygen in the primordial atmosphere. There is a continuous movement and transfer of water molecules among lithosphere, hydrosphere, biosphere and atmosphere. The global hydrological cycle is the visible part of this great transfer. In other words, the water molecules once in the body of Cleopatra, Caesar or *Ravana* could be now in any one of us.

The great hydrological cycle represented by oceanic evaporation → atmospheric circulation → precipitation → evapotranspiration → terrestrial flows → return to ocean, is primed by sun's energy and maintains a dynamic equilibrium of diverse life systems on earth. But for this, the earth surface would be monotonous, no hills, valleys or snow peaked mountains, no rivers or lakes, no greeneries or flowers, no sea or beaches and perhaps no life.

Water is a universal solution, has a great dissolving power of ionic salts and being amphoteric can behave both like acid (H) and alkali (OH). The most peculiar property of its expansion below 4 degree Centigrade makes ice float and thereby preserves aquatic life below ice sheets in arctic lakes and ocean.

It dissolves away harmful salts, dilutes pollutants, washes out and cleans earth's surface of debris and wastes, redistributes sands, silts and clays and on accumulation, acts as a great sink. But for the holding of a large amount of salts in ocean, the topsoil would have been extensively salinitised and barren.

Man uses water for three principal purposes:

1. For domestic uses including drinking, washing and bathing – 10%
2. For industries and power generation – 10%
3. For agriculture and animal husbandry – 80%

Accordingly, water is classified into 5 different types:

1. Class A. For drinking;
2. Class B. For bathing;
3. Class C. For entertainment and fishing;
4. Class D. For transport and shipping; and
5. Class E. Sewerage.

Human interferences in water have been basically to generate added benefits. Extended exploitation such as below, has led to adverse impacts and damage to this vital life supporting system.

1. Artificial rain produces maldistribution of rainfall.
2. Deforestation and soil loss decrease ground infiltration and deplete groundwater reserves.
3. Damming of rivers interferes with natural flow and process of distribution of land fluxes (nutrients and particulates) and produces water logging.
4. Over-pumping of groundwater depletes water table, wilts away deep-rooted trees with consequent loss of green canopy.
5. Application of fertilizers and pesticides pollutes water and salinitizes soil.
6. Urbanization and transport networks interfere with natural drainage system resulting in flooding.
7. Industrial effluents and sewerage discharges pollute rivers, lakes and groundwater.
8. Pollution of water results in water borne diseases such as gastroenteritis, hepatitis and malaria.
9. Ports and harbors pollute near-shore water, kill aquatic animals and destroy mangroves.
10. Ocean mining and Oil Spill pollute ocean water and endanger marine life.

In order to supply hygienic water for drinking purposes water purification by chlorination has long been practiced. Though an effective bacteria killer, chlorine, even in ppb (parts per billion) level in water, is now considered carcinogenic. An alternative technique has been to subject the water to UV-radiation, which basically destroys the proliferation capacity of the bacteria by targeting the DNA and damaging the reproductive mechanism of the microbes. Most Scientists feel that unlike the chlorination technique, UV-radiation of water is totally safe, although at still higher energy dosage of shorter wavelengths, food irradiation is looked upon with suspicion. A minor dose of UV-energy can temporarily distort the symmetry and leave residual stress on water molecules. The residual stress can easily change the dipolar moment of the molecule and consequently the basic properties in molecular level, albeit in negligible magnitude. Scientists are yet to question the possibilities of intake of such water molecules, stressed by UV-radiation along with a set of DNA-aberrated bacteria for generations. Present trend indicates that like any other new scientific discoveries "bottled water" is a sign of progress.

34 The Island City of Mumbai

A Typical Wetland

World Wetland Day is celebrated every year on 2nd of February to keep us aware that Wetlands play crucial role on our environment. Wetland is a stretch of land (actually an environment) between water and land, more often than not, soaked in water arising out of rain, surface and subsurface flows, rise and fall of ground water and temporary or permanent ingression of sea. River banks, lake shores, ponds and reservoirs, marsh, bogs, swamps, mudflats, saltpans, mangroves and creeks in coastal zones are wetlands of one type or other. Being in the interphase of landmass and water body, wetlands display a dynamic environment characteristic of aquatic and terrestrial ecosystems and hold a rich variety of flora and fauna. Wetlands are great sources of economic and environmental benefits.

The island city of Mumbai is surrounded by sea, actually arose by filling up of shallow sea and draining out of wetlands and continues to have a variety of wetlands such as mangroves, mud-bank or mud-flats, marshes, salt pans, creeks, beaches etc. While mangroves are in perpetual threat of destruction, the vast stretches of saltpans around are poised for development and settlement. The importance of mangroves in protection from ocean incursion like tsunami and cyclone is well known. The mud-banks (mud-flats) are made up of organic ooze and soft sorptive clay (something similar to *Multana Matti,* known as *Montmorillonite* in scientific term) which absorbs all the toxic substances discharged from the city by way of sewage, storm water runoff and leaching from the dumping yards at Govendi, Kanjur, Malad and Gorai. The saltpans and mud flats around rarely rise more than a meter above sea level. When sea level rise due to global warming is a forgone conclusion, development of settlements on the low lying salt pans around Mumbai is a hypocrisy and can only be considered to be a conspiracy of builders and opportunist political planners. No amount of sea wall to protect the "developed salt pan" is considered sustainable in long run.

The Island City of Mumbai – Surrounded by Sea and Powai Lake in Right

Powai is a neosettlement around Powai Lake and technically, the watershed of an inland Wetland. That the inland water bodies often serve in flood protection by regulating water flows was realized during the Bombay rain deluge of 2005 when the over silted Powai Lake failed to hold the heavy discharge into Mithi river, which on older days was a dynamic wetland but presently choked by human encroachments. The benefit of Powai Lake has been summarized as follow:

The ambient temperature of Powai is (was) 3 to 4 degree centigrade lower than the surrounding region. Equivalent cooling of a space of 2 km × 2 km to a height of 10 mt. over Powai would need 200,000 tons of AC units and cost Rs. 10 billions (@ Rs. 5000/- per ton). The electricity bill @ Rs. 5/- per day per ton will alone amount to rupees one million per day.

35 Mumbai Rain Deluge, 2005

Lest we Forget

On the 26th of July, 2005, when a continuous downpour fell 990 mm. of rain in 24 hrs. over Mumbai, the city life was paralyzed and came to a grinding halt. About 1000 people died (more than 500 in the city alone), 52 local trains damaged, all Main line trains cancelled following 10 days till 6th. Of August, 900 BEST buses, 4000 Taxis and 37,000 Autos were damaged and 10,000 Trucks were grounded. For the first time, Mumbai Air Port was closed for 30 hrs and 700 flights cancelled or diverted and Mumbai – Pune Express Highway too was closed because of land slides on the *Ghat*. Banks stopped transactions from 26th and on the following 27th due to loss of connectivity. The city got totally disconnected from the rest of the world.

Fig. 35.1: Lest we Forget the Rain Deluge of July 26, 2005 (*Source:* media)

Fig. 35.2: The Ones which ruled the Road Lie Buried in the Deluge of July 26, 2005 (*Source:* flickr)

Mumbai gets an annual rain fall of about 2500 mm. and heavy downpours are not uncommon. Most of the rain water is drained out westward into the Arabian Sea through a few streams and rivulets like Poisar, Dahisar, Oshiwara and Mithi rivers. Mithi, also known as Mahim river, originates from the tail-water discharges of Vihar and Powai lakes and after flowing 18 km. through Powai, Sakinaka, Kurla, Kalina, Vakola, Bandra-Kurla Complex (BKC), Dharavi and Mahim meets the sea at Mahim Bay. The river drains an area of more than 8,000 hectare in the west-central region of the Island City. Upstream in the catchment area of Powai and Vihar, the river is narrow (average of 5 m. wide), slopes high and during monsoon, its cascade flows and falls attract sight seers but downstream after BKC, it widens to 50-60 meters when the slope becomes flat and sustains a niche of thick mangrove. The lower end of the river is tidal.

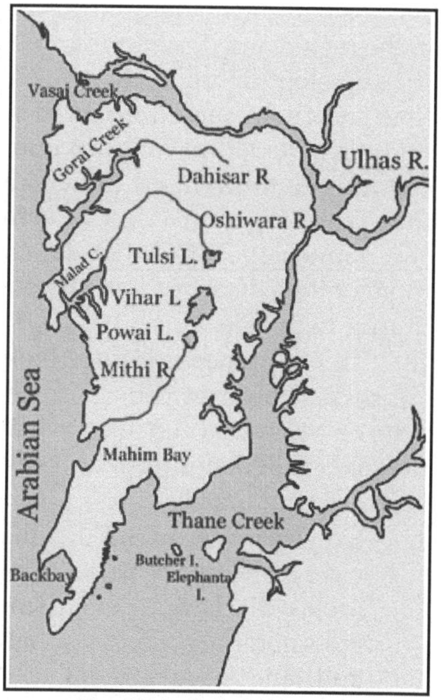

Fig. 35.3: Quietly Flows the Mithi River (*Source:* Google)

Cascading streams in natural environment like those in Khandala attract visitors and Mithi in the upstream section at Powai or Vihar is not an exception. A rivulet flowing in the backyard of a residence increases the value of the house and quality of life of the residents. A river passing through a colony or township considerably enhances the beauty of the township. Most importantly, the water course also provides a channel for clean communication, a venue of hobby and entertainment like boating and angling and finally, it also flushes out and removes dirt and rubbish from the settlement and promotes a streak of greeneries along its bank. No wonder, great cities and civilizations have sprung along water channels, large or small, such as on Euphrates & Tigris, Nile, Indus, Ganges or Godavari. However, misuse and violation of a natural course turns out to be the very cause of catastrophe to settlements which once flourished along the course. The 26/7 rain deluge in Mumbai, arising out of overflow of Mithi river is a clear case of violation of a natural water course. When natural water runs off pavements and into drains and sewers, the river at the end of the pipe floods more often and more severely than would be the case if plants, soils and wetlands soaked up some of the deluge. Blind urban developments overlook natural elements, interferes natural drainage system and precipitates or perpetuates flood disaster upon future citizens of the region. Thus the sprawling slum and urbanization, combined, have interfered free flow of Mithi river. The river which could have been a beauty line and blessing to the west-central region of Mumbai (one would have described it as the bracelet on Mumbai Devi) turned out to be a curse and dreaded serpent (in her groin).

Soon after the 26/7 deluge, which was apparently a backlash of Nature, the Government of Maharashtra created a Mithi River Development and Conservation Authority, under the command of MMRDA and Municipal Corporation, for remediation of urban flooding. The remediation measures were carried out in two phases during last two years and included de-silting and restoration of the width at critical sections of the river, evacuation and resettlement of unauthorized settlements encroaching into the river and closure or notification to close a large number of polluting industries operating in the region and discharging solid and liquid effluents into the river. Reports of "slip-slop" work by the executing parties have been reported by media time and again, including unscrupulous contractor de-silting at one end and dumping the silt at another end of the river. Many citizens and residents continue to apprehend the efficacy of the remediation measures and feel that the danger of bank overflow of Mithi river is not over. Reputed environmentalists feel that the river, even after de-siltation will not be able to smoothly discharge all the run off water if rainfall reaches 25 mm./hr during high tide.

The apprehensions are legitimate, because the "Authority" have not addressed the root causes of flooding of Mithi river and appear to have gone on a easy and conciliatory path of appeasement, a classic style of "neither the snake killed, nor the stick broken, but the relief is, the serpent has escaped (at least temporarily)".

1. Experts of CPWRS, Pune, have opined that decreasing the slope of the river in the upstream section may decrease denudation and flow velocity (delay discharge). Even small check dams across the river will serve the same purpose. As a matter of fact, rampant quarrying, excavations and land development in the catchment head has exposed top soil, decreased ground water percolation and increased surface run off and which the "Authority" has not addressed.
2. The very act of creation of the two reservoirs – Vihar and Powai lakes at the head of Mithi river, a century before, dwindled down the flow in Mithi and deprived annual flushing and cleaning downstream. Normally, the two reservoirs ought to hold back excess rain water during cloud burst, but failed to do so because the storage capacity of the lakes (especially of Powai lake) has been drastically reduced by heavy siltation due to quarrying, deforestation and land development in the catchment.
3. Clearance of the passage of Mithi river by removal of the hutments only, is merely a cosmetic step, because the major diversions and obstructions of the river flow, caused by "giant" organizations have gone unnoticed. For examples:

(a) Of the two run-ways of Mumbai Air Port, one runs straight over the river and the other diverts the river course.

(b) Reclamation and constructions of Bandra-Kurla-Complex directly come under way of Mithi discharge. MMRDA, the architect of the Complex and main Commander of Mithi River Authority Project has its Head Office in the Complex. When *Rakshyka* (protector) becomes *Bhakshyaka* (swallower), where is the place of ethics,- why blame Nature ?

(c) Destruction of mangrove, establishment of Mahim Nature Park and various reclamations at Mahim Bay (not to mention of the Sea-Link project) prevent free movement of water mass in the critical junction of Mithi and Arabian Sea. The mouth of the river at the Bay is considerably narrowed.

(d) A large number of housing societies and established major and minor industrial complexes with a net-work of roads and communication channel, have sprung up in the catchment area with due permission of the Municipal Corporation but with little regard to the regional drainage.

When the major "offenders" of the river course have gone unquestioned, bulldozing of weak and meek (slum dwellers) is a "tell tale", like the lion drinking water upstream, tells the lamb, "why are you making the water muddy".

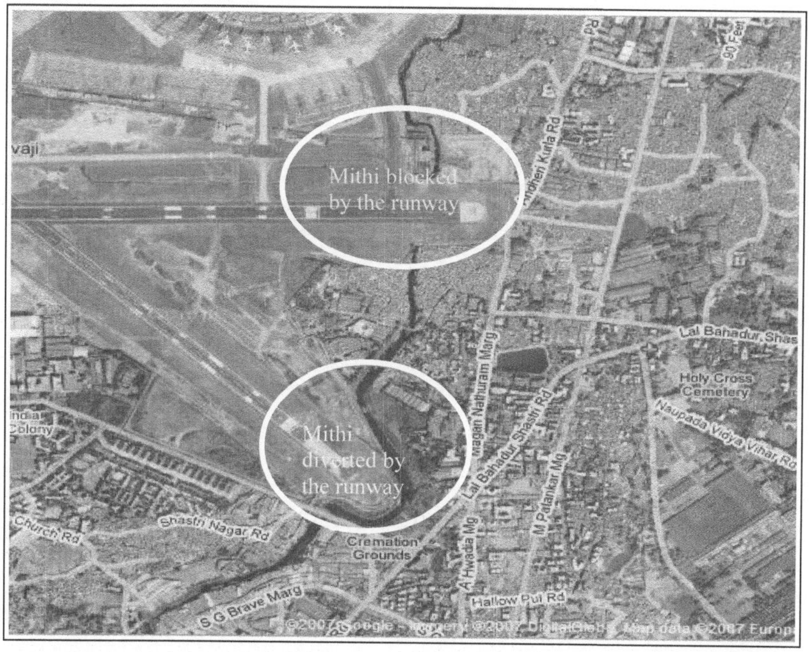

Fig. 35.4: The Runways of the Airport have run-over Mithi River (Google.)

If the Government really means business the "Authority" must have biting power to take remedial measures over all sections of the obstructers of Mithi river flow, continue to function as an independent regulatory body and have a say on all developmental works in the catchment region.

A significant remediation measure, but apparently not been carried out is, opening up the Mithi river mouth (outfall at Mahim Bay) for increased and smooth discharge of flood water. The measure involves dredging and clearance of the river mouth, which also means free back flow and ingression of tidal bore during high tide unless a suitable barrier is constructed. Dredging activity may further damage the already stressed mangrove niche, which again is a natural tidal barrier.

A similar situation but in a grand scale has been successfully attended in "Thames Barrier" which also is designed to take care of the sea level rise expected to produce by global warming but primarily to protect flooding of the lower section of London city.

Fig. 35.5: The Thames Barrier Protects City of London from Tidal flooding. (Google images)

In the mean time let us hope that "mother Nature", who we remember only when a back lash is administered, will be kind to Mumbai by not bringing heavy down pour similar to the one we got on the 26/7 of '05.

36

Aviral and *Nirmal* Ganga
Is it Possible?

Introduction

Water is the elixir of life and the central actor in all environmental drama. Like the Water-Holes in forest where all animals converge, most river courses in world have had settlements, ancient civilization and culture. Ganga is no exception.

Ganga arises from Gomukh of Gangotri glacier, flows some 2525 km. through Himalayan mountain terrain, Gangetic plains, Peninsular Uplands and through a long deltaic environment before reaching the Bay of Bengal. The Ganga basin is about one million sq.km., covers 11 States and provides water to 40% of India's population. Major tributaries like Yamuna, Sone, Ghagra, Gomti, Gandak, Kosi and Damodar add 60 % of its water wealth. About 400 million people live on the river and some one hundred large, medium and small cities and towns have grown along its bank. With increased growth of settlements and modern needs, Ganga is very much exploited, stressed and polluted beyond recuperation and has lost its *Aviral* and *Nirmal* status. Action by Government through GAP and NGRBA has not produced results and recent entry of the IIT Consortium in the race of remediation of the river provides a ray of hope.

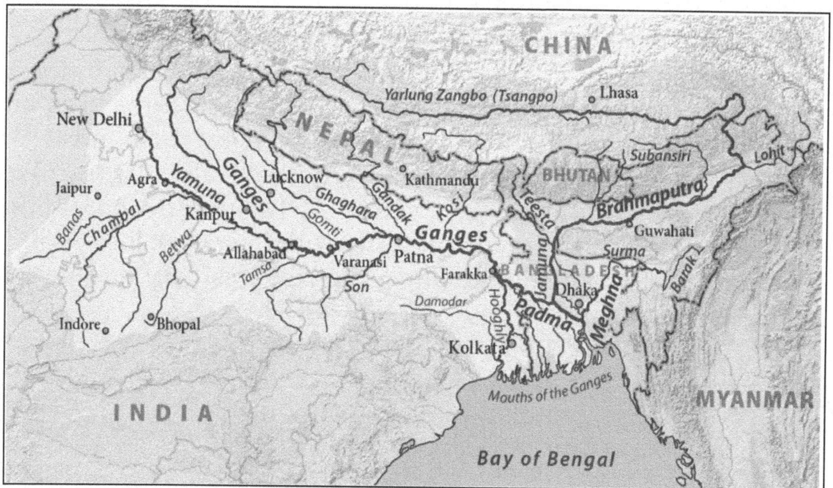

Ganga Basin and Tributaries of Ganga

Basic Functions of River (Ganga)

When a rain drop falls on earth surface, a twin process begins: (a) Physical pulverization of rocks to produce finer particles and (b) Chemical reaction with the pulverized particles to release soluble nutrients and form clay minerals. The function of a river like Ganga is to collect the threesomes in bulk and flow down to distribute the water, soil and nutrients to all who need and live near its course and near shore region. Like any other rivers, Ganga has been doing it since it originated after the Himalayan upheaval some 40 million years ago. Man appeared on the scenario only a few thousand years ago in the fertile Indo-Gangetic plain and like any other living species reaped the benefit from the river for centuries. Modernity set in an anthropocentric culture and the baby (The Man), instead of surviving on mother's breast, started milking the mother Ganga by "Using and Abusing" and appropriation of her water wealth through Dams and diversions of flow.

Ganga water, considered holy, sacred and therapeutic, not because of a blind belief imbibed by religious dogma, but because of the presence of antibacterial constituents like highly electropositive copper cations and colloidal sulphur derived from stray copper-sulphide mineral deposits in the Himalayan rocks. The traditional habit of rural folk drinking water as the first act in the morning, from a copper pot kept overnight serves the same purpose. Today this Nature given therapeutic properties of Ganga has been erased by over-pollution of the river.

Ganga Water Appropriated

The Dam density in Ganga basin is highest in the world, 1/18 km of channel flow. Some 300 of them are planned in Himalayan terrain alone, are in ecofragile and highly earthquake prone zone. Opposition to the Himalayan hydroelectric projects across Ganga and its tributaries continues in every sections of Indian societies, from Activists, legal, religious and scientific Institutions, Media and Publics. But the energy craze, professional, business and political opportunism seem to have overpowered the protests.

Large scale diversion of water from Ganga takes place in the upper reaches at Haridwar, Binjor and Narora for agricultural uses and by Industries and Municipalities at various locations on its course and at Farakka for "Hooghly Flushing." In return of the abstracted water, the river receives back wastewaters of sewerage, factory effluents and contaminated agricultural runoff. The victims of this water withdrawal are the people living downstream and the aquatic life along the river, estuary and near shore region in Bay of Bengal.

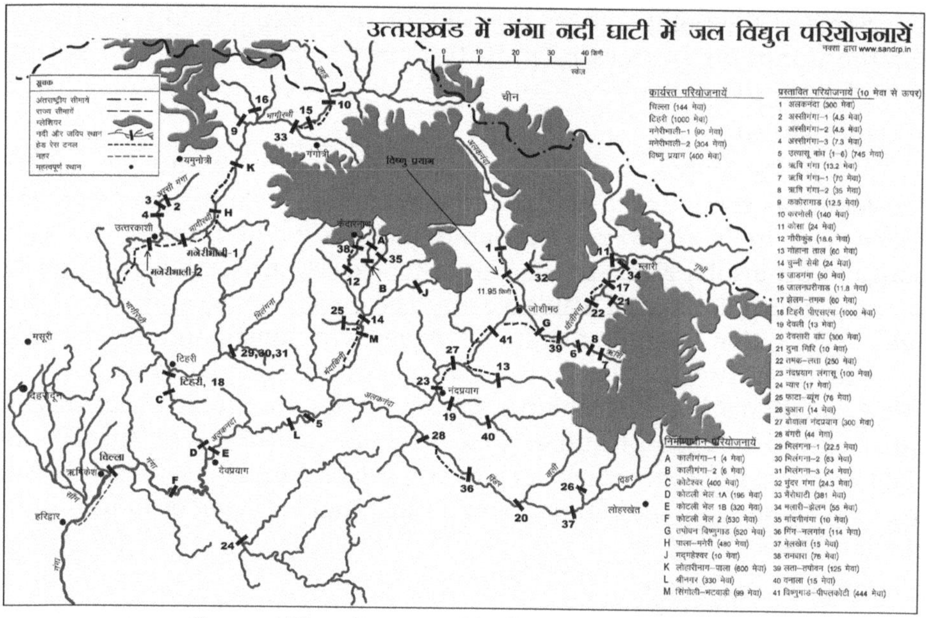

Ganges' Flow interrupted by Dams in Uttarakhand

Ganga Abused

The "Abuse" of Ganga does not end by robbing her flow through Dams and Diversions, apparently for human use. But many other commissions degrade the river throughout its course. These are:

1. Settlements all along its Flood Plain and associated human activities like bathing, cattle washing, open defecation and gubernatorial social and religious rites. Frequent changes of stream course due to erratic sedimentation and excavation has taught little lesson to the Flood Plain Settlers.
2. Discharge of untreated sewerage from large settlements of cities and towns, some 100 of them are situated on its bank.
3. Discharge of solid and liquid effluents from Industrial units like Tannery, Textile, Chemical, Petro-chemical, Fertilizer, Distilleries, Power Plants, Slaughter Houses and Hospitals.
4. Agricultural runoff from land undergoing extensive "Chemical treatment of Green Revolution". 60% of the chemical fertilizer and probably the total residue of pesticides, herbicide and insecticides applied in the industrial agricultural practices in the entire Ganga basin enter runoff water and ends up in the Gangetic flow.
5. Discharges from Mineral and Mining Industries including river bed and Flood Plain mining of sands and gravels disturbs natural flow, but difficult to stop if construction and housing practices are to be supported.

Some of the point sources of pollution are amenable to remediation, but the nonpoint sources of pollution and sociocultural habits defy technological solution.

A Larger Threat

While the above "Uses and Abuses" of Ganga for anthropocentric developments continues to agitate the minds of sensible Indians, there is a larger threat to the river from a group of modernist who propose linking of Ganga to Peninsular rivers by a series of canals (The Garland Canal Project) to transfer surplus asset of water wealth. The project however does not take into consideration the future shift and vagaries of rainfall and likelihood of reduction of melt water supply from the vanishing Himalayan glaciers due to Global Warming and change in tilt of the Gangetic Plain due to anticlockwise rotation of Indian Plate while in collusion with the Tibetan Plate. Besides, the numerous water conflicts between Indian States for sharing river waters discourages undertaking of the grand scheme of India's River Linking Project.

Thoughts on Solution:

1. Brake and discipline in Power consumption (Any way 60% of the Power now stands abused). This will reduce Dams and Power Plant Emission in Ganga basin.
2. Shift from Chemical to Organic fertilizer (At least change to Bentofert, where fertilizer grains are coated with Bentonite Clay mineral).
3. Mandatory ETP or FGD for Municipalities, Industries and Power Plants for Zero Pollutant Discharge (Problem: where to throw the Residues?).
4. Control Flood Plain mining of Sands and Gravels.
5. Control Pilgrim's Picnics and Transgressive Tourism on Himalayas and misadventures like Himalayan Car Rallies.
6. Put Garland Canal Scheme in Abeyance.

37

A thought on Mineral Water

Till today the standard technique of water purification for public supply has been by chlorination of water to kill the harmful germs and bacteria. But when residual chlorine in purified water was found to be a major cause of cancer, many developed countries stopped chlorination of drinking water and instead adopted the new technique of Ultra Violet radiation to deliver microbe free drinking water off the tap through commercial machines like Aquaguards. As much as no doubt was raised when chlorination was introduced to supply pure drinking water, no voice has been raised against UV-radiation of our daily drinking water mainly because of absence of any other alternatives and the "Inconvenient Truth" that modern man has not left any source of natural water unpolluted in any corner of the earth. Today, Bottled Water or Mineral Water as it is called is the only water available for drinking and commercial organizations are vying to exploit the situation in enchanting brand names.

Like chlorination episode, UV-radiation of water has also its downstream effect but little understood or cared for even by learned Scientists. Unlike chlorination, which kills the harmful bacteria in water, UV-radiation does not kill the bacteria but impairs their reproduction capacity by targeting their DNA, so that the bacteria can not proliferate. Thus, when one drinks the radiated water, the sterile but DNA-aberrated bacteria pass into human alimentary canal with every possibility of at least a few getting attached to our body cells by the simple process of symbiosis. Gradually the attached bacteria are "swallowed" by the "swallower" body cell by a process known as endosymbiogenesis. According to Linn Mrgulis the distinguished professor of Geosciences in Univ. of Massachusetts "serial endosymbiogenesis" leads to development of new forms of life, which also carries with it the DNA signature of the "swallowed" bacteria, in this case that of the DNA-aberrated ones in the UV-radiated water. That means, intake of UV-radiated water is likely to result in appearance of DNA-aberrated offspring in future generation to come. In other words, while going for a solution to provide safe drinking water we are perpetuating a curse on our future offspring — *"living on a borrowed safety"* indeed.

38

Gandhian Environment

2nd October is celebrated as the birthday of Mahatma Gandhi. Today, when the world is reeling with violence, pollution and environmental degradation, Gandhian philosophy and policy of economic development is considered by many thinkers as the only straw for sustainable development. Although, during the days of Gandhi ji, the type and magnitude of present day environmental problems were practically nonexistent, many of Gandhian principles are considered to be pillars of environmental protection and holistic living. A few such principles are mentioned and discussed below:

1. A well-known statement of Mahatma Gandhi is: *"The Earth has enough for everybody's need but not for even a single person's greed."* Modernists argue that the area between need and greed is amorphous and yesterday's greed (luxury) is today's need. However, transformation of greed to need has given rise to resources crunch and consumerism. To meet the modern needs and aspirations of the current generation

including those in developing countries we require five times the present activities continuously for fifty years. Obviously a finite Earth can neither sustain the demands and supplies for the newfound comforts, nor can it assimilate the "Exhausts" of increased production and usage. Even today we are living on a borrowed future.

2. Gandhi emphasized: *"Man must learn to live and depend on what his immediate surrounding earth gives and not depend on things from distant sources."* This vital principle has been brushed aside in the name of globalization. Results: Trade control and exploitation and increased transport and communication. The Inconvenient Truth of Global Warming is merely one of the downstream impacts of fossil fuel burning in Transport and Communication extravaganza. For example, in America, before a dinner plate reaches the palate of the eater it has travelled at least 2000 Km., practically marinated in crude. Cod fish caught in North Sea, shredded in China is consumed in Sweden. In India Californian and S.African orange dominates over Nagpur orange.
3. In the field of industrial production, for example in Iron & Steel industry, in a populous countries like China or India, Gandhi vouched: *"Let there be one million cupolas of one ton capacity each to produce iron and steel in places where steel is required, instead of a single giant one million ton steel plant which needs large inputs to be brought in and outputs to be dispatched to places of requirement."*
4. The highest concept of *"Holism"* or holistic spirit in a living system is propounded by Gandhi Ji in a section of his famous prayer *"Vaisnaba jana to tene kahie ... "which takes the dimension of consciousness beyond the limits of sensory organs of human beings.* It identifies and equalizes others with the self for feeling the pain and pleasure in the living society.

The above *mantras* of Gandhi Ji, may at once appear archaic, nonviable and uneconomic but need serious consideration in the context of sustainable development, and socio-economic and environmental crisis the present world is undergoing.

Index

D

E

F

G